Robert Louis Stevenson and Joseph Conrad

Robert Louis Stevenson and Joseph Conrad

Writers of Transition

Edited by

Linda Dryden, Stephen Arata,
and Eric Massie

TEXAS TECH UNIVERSITY PRESS

This book is typeset in Adobe Caslon. The paper used in this book meets the minimum requirements of ANSI/NISO Z39.48-1992 (R1997).

Book design by Mark McGarry, Texas Type & Book Works

LIBRARY OF CONGRESS CATALOGING-IN-PUBLICATION DATA
Robert Louis Stevenson and Joseph Conrad : writers of transition / edited by Linda Dryden, Stephen Arata, and Eric Massie.
p. cm.
Includes bibliographical references and index.
Summary: "Assesses points of convergence between Robert Louis Stevenson and Joseph Conrad. Extends arguments about the authors' South Seas literature, offering new critiques on the writers' literary histories, writing styles, romance and adventure modes, fictions of duality, experience in Victorian London, explorations of the human psyche, and fame"—Provided by publisher.
ISBN 978-0-89672-653-6 (hardcover : alk. paper) 1. Stevenson, Robert Louis, 1850–1894—Criticism and interpretation. 2. Conrad, Joseph, 1857–1924—Criticism and interpretation. 3. Stevenson, Robert Louis, 1850–1894—Literary style. 4. Conrad, Joseph, 1857–1924—Literary style. 5. Dualism in literature. 6. Liminality in literature. 7. Self in literature. I. Dryden, Linda, 1954– II. Arata, Stephen. III. Massie, Eric.
PR5496.R58 2009
823'.809—dc22   2009001840

Printed in the United States of America
09 10 11 12 13 14 15 16 17 / 9 8 7 6 5 4 3 2 1

Texas Tech University Press
Box 41037
Lubbock, Texas 79409-1037 USA
800.832.4042
ttup@ttu.edu
www.ttup.ttu.edu

Contents

Preface

This volume of essays was proposed as a result of the conference convened in Edinburgh in 2004 titled "Stevenson and Conrad: Writers of Land and Sea." The event attracted contributors from Italy to Hong Kong, from Germany to Australia, and from New Zealand to the UK. More than fifty delegates delivered papers in the St. Trinnean's Centre at Pollock Halls in Edinburgh, just at the foot of Arthur's Seat. It was a full and enjoyable three days: the delegates went on tours of Stevenson's Edinburgh, visited the Writers' Museum, and had guest talks from the latest biographer of Stevenson, Claire Harman, and from the veteran Scottish actor John Cairney.

Stevenson was more thoroughly represented than Conrad among the papers because this was the third biennial RLS conference. Nevertheless, the delegates embraced the dual-author spirit of the event, and there were thus some excellent meditations on how we can begin to think about Conrad in the context of Stevenson and vice versa. Even before the conference it was clear from the abstracts that a volume of essays on Stevenson and Conrad was needed in order to capitalize on and disseminate some of the excellent work that had been done in this area. Stevenson has been mentioned in connection with Conrad in the past, but there is no sustained study that brings the two together: the papers submitted to the conference were clearly breaking new ground, focusing as they did on the legacy left by Stevenson and on how Conrad was necessarily influenced by the earlier writer.

There is no doubt that Conrad, currently, has a much more solid reputation than Stevenson in terms of being a serious, indeed, for some, difficult, writer. However, during the 1990s interest in Stevenson began to blossom, and serious monographs began to appear that acknowledged how some of his later work anticipated modernism. One thinks of Alan Sandison's *Robert Louis Stevenson and the Appearance of Modernism* and Hirsch and Veeder's *Jekyll and Hyde after One Hundred Years* and, of course, the work of Barry Menikoff, Jenni Calder, and others. Some of the most obvious connections between the two involve their historical proximity: the fact that Stevenson died one year before Conrad began publishing and the fact that they both published stories set in exotic locations. These connections are well known, but others being considered are a shared heritage, a will to modernism, imperial skepticism, and even Stevenson's influence on Conrad. Conrad was aware of how his contemporaries drew comparisons, even while he deliberately distanced himself from Stevenson. In fact, they shared many acquaintances in the literary world, and it is hard to conceive that because of these acquaintances the name of Stevenson did not crop up at regular intervals.

But another reason for considering the two together is to continue the rehabilitation of Stevenson's reputation as an artist begun in the 1990s. With Edinburgh now a UNESCO City of Literature, it is inevitable that much attention will focus on Stevenson as one of the city's most famous literary sons. It is therefore important to guard against being carried away by the more stereotypical cultural inheritance in which Stevenson becomes part of a Scottish "Occidentalism" (to steal an idea from others, responding to Said). Rather than allow Stevenson to represent a sort of post-Kailyard Scottishness, we need to consider him in the wider context of his contribution to our Western literary inheritance. Within that context the essays contained here reposition Stevenson as one of Conrad's immediate precursors, and thus *Robert Louis Stevenson and Joseph Conrad: Writers of Transition* addresses a significant gap in our understanding of the connection between these two influential authors.

LINDA DRYDEN
STEPHEN ARATA
ERIC MASSIE

Abbreviations

Abbreviations of Conrad's Works

C	Chance
CL	Collected Letters of Joseph Conrad
HD	Heart of Darkness *(Armstrong edition unless otherwise stated)*
LE	Last Essays
LJ	Lord Jim
NNL	Notes on Life and Letters
NNTFF	The Nigger of the "Narcissus," Typhoon, Amy Foster, Falk, and other stories
NNTOS	The Nigger of the "Narcissus" and Typhoon and Other Stories
OI	An Outcast of the Islands
SA	The Secret Agent
TLS	'Twixt Land and Sea
TU	Tales of Unrest
UWE	Under Western Eyes
V	Victory
WT	Within the Tides
Y	Youth

Abbreviations of Stevenson's Works

ET	The Ebb-Tide
JH	Strange Case of Dr. Jekyll and Mr. Hyde *(Dury edition unless otherwise stated)*

MP   Memories and Portraits

SL   Stevenson Letters

SS   In the South Seas

TI   Treasure Island

WRLS   The Works of Robert Louis Stevenson *(Vailima edition)*

Robert Louis Stevenson and Joseph Conrad

Introduction

LINDA DRYDEN

It is often argued that Joseph Conrad inaugurated literary modernism with his chilling tale of Belgian imperialism in Africa, *Heart of Darkness*, first published in *Blackwood's Edinburgh Magazine* in 1899. Yet no genre or new literary tradition has a unique starting point: modernism grew out of a variety of literary genres, cultural changes, and social and political movements. Our literary traditions, like our culture, are contingent upon literary history and the history of ideas as well as cultural shifts and historical events. Consequently, we cannot dismiss the debt that Conrad owed to writers like Robert Louis Stevenson even as we recognize Conrad's contribution to the development of literary traditions. Had Stevenson and Conrad ever met, they would not have had a good gossip about romance, but they may well have chatted about the sea, the Far East, and mutual friends. Such a conversation never happened: Stevenson died in Samoa in 1894, aged forty-four; Conrad was a merchant seaman until the publication of his first novel, *Almayer's Folly*, in 1895. Yet in Stevenson's tales of human duality, dark passions, and colonial skepticism there is a crossover between high Victorian literature and the birth of modernism. This transition deserves exploration.

The life experiences of both writers reveal similarities. As a young man, Stevenson was exiled from his native Edinburgh by ill health and sought congenial climates in France, Switzerland, and, in pursuit of Fanny Osbourne, America. Conrad went to sea at seventeen and experienced Europe's far-flung empire. He never returned to live in his native Poland. Both became writers in exile, adopting a new country and a new culture. After years of wandering, Stevenson settled in Samoa and never saw Scotland again; Conrad established himself in England and chose to write in English, his third language.[1]

As itinerants and exiles Stevenson and Conrad had much in common, although they were very different kinds of exiles. Stevenson was forced abroad for his health, while Conrad had pressing political reasons for leaving Ukraine. They were both friends with Henry James, though Stevenson regarded James as an equal, while Conrad was more deferential, referring to James as *"cher maitre"* in their correspondence. After all, when Conrad arrived on the literary scene James was a more powerful figure than he had been in Stevenson's day. Stevenson was a close friend of W. E. Henley, who published *The Nigger of the "Narcissus"* (1897), marking a breakthrough in Conrad's writing career. Both were acquainted with J. M. Barrie, Sidney Colvin was a mutual friend, and S. S. McClure published both authors and visited Stevenson at Saranac.

The literary connections do not end there. In 1892 John Galsworthy and Ted Sanderson set out to visit Stevenson at Vailima; on their return journey in March 1893, having failed to reach Stevenson, they boarded the *Torrens* at Port Adelaide and encountered Conrad as first mate (Karl 321–23). Galsworthy and Sanderson became lifelong friends of Conrad's, again linking him with Stevenson. The connection is tenuous but tantalizing in suggesting the proximity of the two writers. During a previous voyage to Australia in 1892 Conrad sealed his literary career by showing an early draft of *Almayer's Folly* to a young Cantabrigian on board the *Torrens*. W. H. Jacques was probably the first person to read any of the story, and his positive response, according to Frederick Karl, inspired Conrad to persevere (Karl 319–21). That Conrad met Galsworthy and Sanderson is noteworthy, because at that point Stevenson was engaged in just the type of subversive imperial fiction that would inaugurate Conrad's literary career.

A more sober personality than Stevenson, Conrad sought the status of an English gentleman. Stevenson was, by nature, flamboyant: his distinctive style of dress, lanky frame, and peripatetic lifestyle signaled a bohemian and artist. Compared with Conrad's conservatism, Stevenson cut a striking figure: pictures from Samoa reveal an exotic, often unkempt, Stevenson surrounded by the assorted relatives of Fanny whom he supported, along with his widowed mother. Their adopted countries reflected a radically different direction in later life, Stevenson opting for tropical Samoa and Conrad, the temperate climes of rural southern

England. Yet Stevenson and Conrad shared an experience of the exotic and the tropical that resonates through their work. It was this, and the Eastern locations featuring so vividly in Stevenson's late works and Conrad's earliest, that united them in the popular imagination.

While Conrad conversed with Galsworthy and Sanderson on the *Torrens*, Stevenson was finalizing *The Ebb-Tide* (1894). Writing to James in June 1893, Stevenson acknowledges its bleak atmosphere: "My dear man, the grimness of that story is not to be depicted in words. There are only four characters, to be sure, but they are such a troop of swine!" (*CL* 4:261). Much the same applies to Conrad's early Malay tales and later novels such as *Victory* (1915) and *The Rescue* (1920). Subverting the myth of the rectitude of the imperial adventurer, with Davis, Herrick, and Huish, Stevenson creates the type of degenerate self-seeking outcast that Conrad imagines in Almayer and Willems. As early as *Treasure Island* (1883) Stevenson's notion of adventure is far more circumspect than that of R. M. Ballantyne, G. A. Henty, or H. Rider Haggard. Far from being the celebrated writer of boys' adventure tales, Stevenson infused his stories with the subversive themes and compromised "heroes" that is Conrad's familiar territory. On the eastern edge of the southern hemisphere in 1892–93 Stevenson and Conrad were inspired to write fiction that heralded a break with the bluff confidence of Victorian imperialism and anticipated the dawn of literary modernism.

Early readers of Conrad drew comparisons with Stevenson. The anonymous reviewer of *An Outcast of the Islands* (1896) in the *Spectator* famously suggested that Conrad could become "the Kipling of the Malay Archipelago," comparing the novel to a Stevenson story "grown miraculously long and miraculously tedious" (Sherry 61). Despite deploring such comparisons, when Conrad collaborated with Ford Madox Ford on *Romance* (1903), they aimed to write an adventure novel to "tap the audience for Stevenson, Anthony Hope, and Rider Haggard" (Karl 438). Conrad wanted to emulate Stevenson's financial success, even while deprecating his reputation. Upset with Ford's comments about *Romance*, Conrad later complained: "Sneers at collaboration—sneers at those two men who took six years to write 'this very ordinary tale'—whereas R.L.S. single handed produced his masterpieces etc etc." (*CL* 3:59). He is nettled by implications that Stevenson wrote a better romance in a much shorter period, but the comparisons were hard to ignore, especially given *Romance*'s poor reception compared with the runaway success of *Treasure Island*.

Conrad struggled against Stevenson's reputation, writing to J. B. Pinker on January 8, 1902: "I am no sort of airy R. L. Stevenson who considered his art a prostitute and the artist no better than one" (*CL* 2:371). Yet an unsigned review of *Typhoon* (1903) in the *Speaker* hails Conrad as Stevenson's successor: "There are times in reading his work when we think that Stevenson with new experiences has taken up his work when it broke off in his noble fragment *Weir of Hermiston*" (reprinted in Karl 546). Conrad was angered by such comparisons. His comment to Alfred Knopf in 1913 suggests qualified admiration but ultimately an attempt to supersede rather than emulate Stevenson: "When it comes to popularity I stand much nearer the public mind than Stevenson who was superliterary, a conscious virtuoso of style; whereas the average mind does not care much for virtuosity" (*CL* 5:257). If Conrad means that Stevenson was a dilettante, he would have said so.[2] He probably means that Stevenson saw himself as a connoisseur of style who pitched his art beyond the commonplace. The statement is odd, though. Stevenson enjoyed more popularity with the reading public as a writer of children's verses and boys' adventure fiction. The literary public (or the literary and educational establishment) valued Stevenson above all as an essayist, and it is perhaps this that Conrad alludes to. We can understand Conrad's statement better in context. In 1913 he was poised finally to break into the popular market with *Chance*, but success was yet to come. Conrad responds at length, over three pages, to Knopf, his enthusiastic advocate at Doubleday, trying to press his case over *Chance* with Doubleday, which Knopf duly did. Conrad advocates for himself at Stevenson's expense, for self-publicity, envious of Stevenson's reputation but resistant to attempts at artistic comparisons.

This issue of style is critical. While denigrating Stevenson, Conrad was himself conscious of how he wrote, despite his own style being quite different, even experimental. Conrad was himself a "virtuoso," if not of style then at least of method, as H. G. Wells later explained in his *Experiment in Autobiography* (1934):

[I]t was all against Conrad's over-sensitized receptivity that a boat could ever be just a boat. He wanted to see it and to see it only in relation to something else—a story, a thesis. And I suppose if I had been pressed about it I would have betrayed a disposition to link that story or thesis to something still more extensive and that to something still more extensive and so ultimately to link it up to my philosophy and my world outlook. (Wells 619)

As Wells's comments reveal, Conrad was trying to position himself within a new breed of writers as distinct from the "Victorian" writers, among whom Stevenson was then a leading light. Stevenson suffers in Conrad's estimation by the very fact of his historical proximity both to the nineteenth-century literary scene and to Conrad's modern world, not to mention in relation to the literary marketplace. The benefit of hindsight allows these proximities to be seen, as contemporary critics had noticed, as linking rather than sundering them. He may have resented comparisons, but that Conrad was always looking over his shoulder at Stevenson reminds us of the need to consider them as near contemporaries. It is thus the intention of this collection of essays to probe the Stevenson/Conrad nexus to produce new understandings about two of the most famous writers of the late nineteenth century.

Writing twixt Land and Sea

Colonial scepticism in "The Beach of Falesá" (1892), pessimistic reflection on the Englishman in *The Ebb-Tide*, and the startling representation of duality in *Strange Case of Dr. Jekyll and Mr. Hyde* (1886) signal Stevenson as a writer of transition. Stevenson remained unconvinced by the certainties of much of the literature of the Victorian tradition, favouring darker themes and approaches that anticipate Conrad. Fredric Jameson recognizes a tentative connection, arguing that Conrad's work spills "out of high literature into light reading and romance." Although he fails to register Stevenson's more serious tone, perpetuating the misreading of his vocation as a writer of light literature, Jameson locates Conrad as "floating uncertainly somewhere in between Proust and Robert Louis Stevenson" (Jameson, *Political Unconscious*, 206). This is perhaps a problematic statement and one that some of the authors in this volume seek to address by way of positioning Stevenson as a modernist.

Aware of Stevenson's post-Victorian sensibilities, in 1931 J. B. Priestly said there was "nothing Victorian about the way in which Robert Louis Stevenson . . . tells a story" (Priestly 117). Interest in influences on Conrad's imperial fiction has done much to enhance Stevenson's reputation for subversive imperial tales. However, we need to look beyond his exotic tales to realize the full impact of Stevenson's vision on subsequent writers. The dark atmosphere and troubled dualism of Stevenson's novels counter the positive outlook of the high Victorian novel, in which closure generally means retribution for the villain and reconciliation and a positive future for those who struggled in adversity. The psychological preoccupations of *Jekyll and Hyde* and *The Master of Ballantrae* (1889), and the subversive messages of his adventure fiction, including *Treasure Island*, indicate a writer struggling with competing impulses and problematizing the confident voice of late-nineteenth-century imperial ideology. Recognizing Stevenson's vision as symptomatic of fin de siècle disillusionment and uncertainty challenges the traditional reception of his fiction as "light literature," plunging us into the murkier sensibility of emergent modernism. It is here that Stevenson and Conrad interconnect.

Stevenson's tales of fatally flawed, divided human beings struggling to reconcile savage instincts with civilized values anticipate the appalling career of Kurtz in *Heart of Darkness*.[3] Like Jekyll/Hyde, Kurtz is a man of conflicting impulses, ultimately succumbing to an innate savagery, his "Hyde." Jekyll's dilemma defines a fin de siècle realization that the integrity of the self is in doubt. After the 1885 W. T. Stead exposé of child prostitution and the 1889 "Cleveland Street affair" involving the aristocracy and "rent boys," Victorian belief in the "gentleman" was severely shaken. A decade later, the fictional horrors committed by Jekyll/Hyde and the actual horrors perpetrated by late Victorian "toffs" are amplified in Kurtz, an imperial adventurer-gone-wrong. Kurtz is no "toff," but like Jekyll he uses (and abuses) the language of philanthropy. Like Stevenson's doppelgänger, Kurtz demonstrates that the most upright citizen is prone to the basest of actions. Such realizations strike at the heart of Victorian confidence, exposing fault lines in the imperial project and suggesting that the European imperialist is no better than the "native" he seeks to subjugate. Just as Jekyll unleashed a primitive, savage self that was as much a part of his identity as the urbane doctor, Kurtz succumbs to the repressed savage in his own psyche.

Identity is critical for both Stevenson and Conrad. Kurtz is thought to be a journalist or a painter, but his true identity is elusive: "even the cousin . . . could not tell [Marlow] what he had been—exactly" (*HD* 71). This uncertainty signals Kurtz's kinship with Jekyll, the good citizen "gone bad," though we might differentiate by suggesting that Kurtz's identity was always slippery, whereas the enjoyment of immoral pleasures by respectable gentleman such as Jekyll was widely recognized, if not publicly acknowledged. Conrad, like Stevenson, recognized the multifaceted nature of human identity, the possibility that the most apparently respectable, upright citizen could succumb to the most primitive urges. Kurtz's eloquence and high imperial project—"he could perform a power for good practically unbounded"—contrasts starkly with his postscript: "Exterminate all the brutes!" (*HD* 50–51). This inner contradiction suggests a literary inheritance from Jekyll: dwelling within Kurtz are the twin impulses that drive Jekyll's weird experiment. Kurtz's inability to reconcile these leads to a psychological "horror," but Jekyll devises his own means:

> If each, I told myself, could but be housed in separate identities, life would be relieved of all that was unbearable; the unjust might go his way, delivered from the aspirations and remorse of his more upright twin; and the just could walk steadfastly and securely on his upward path, doing the good things in which he found his pleasure, and no longer exposed to disgrace and penitence by the hands of this extraneous evil. (*JH* 59)

Realizing that "man is not truly one, but truly two," and that it "was the curse of mankind that these incongruous faggots were thus bound together," Jekyll anticipates Kurtz's dilemma (*JH* 59). Hyde murders Carew reveling "in the same divided ecstasy of mind, gloating on [his] crime, light-headedly devising others in the future" (*JH* 67). With similar remorselessness Kurtz rejects Marlow's efforts to save him and crawls like an animal back into the jungle. Within the gothic tradition,

Stevenson imagines the physical manifestation of an inherent evil;
Conrad, the modernist, imagines the self-destructive struggle when contained within the bodily frame and a psyche with no recourse to the pre-
ternatural, but the results are equally catastrophic.

Stevenson's novel is rooted in the doppelgänger tradition of gothic literature, such as that of Hoffmann, Melville, and Poe, and in the Scottish
romance tradition, notably Hogg's *Private Memoirs and Confessions of a
Justified Sinner* (1824), but it is a distinctly modern novel.[4] It builds on the
lighthearted gothic of *The Dynamiter* (1885) through metropolitan locations and preoccupations with shifting identities. While *The Dynamiter* is
a satiric romp through London, its theme of urban terrorism anticipates
Conrad's chilling tale of murder, espionage, and heartless political expe-
diency, *The Secret Agent* (1907). The anxieties of the fin de siècle, the
recognition that the foundations of Victorian self-belief and self-
justification were exhibiting a dangerous fragility, are detectable symp-
toms of modernity in Stevenson. They are ominously present in his
metropolitan fiction, but also in colonial tales like *The Ebb-Tide* and "The
Beach of Falesá." Breaking from the constraints of Victorian realism,
Stevenson prepares the way for Conrad's modernism through his tales of
urban terror and imperial misadventure.

The ne'er-do-wells of *The Ebb-Tide* anticipate Conrad's self-regarding
failed adventurers trapped in an outpost on the Malay Archipelago or
Kayerts and Carlier in their forsaken corner of Africa. Attwater possesses
the sadistic tendencies and will to power that make Kurtz so notorious.
This story of a recluse on a Pacific retreat invaded by three degenerate
Europeans provides a template for Conrad's *Victory* (1915) and prefigures
Wells's sordid parable of human animalism, *The Island of Dr. Moreau*
(1896).[5] *Treasure Island* registers a subversive message about the nature of
heroism and gentlemanly conduct. Inverting the romance and adventure
formula, the villain Long John Silver has a charisma usually reserved for
heroes and evades retribution to live an exotic life of exile.

This human duality resonates through some of Conrad's short stories,
notably "The Secret Sharer" (1912), in which Leggatt, a man who inadver-
tently commits murder, is a reminder to the tale's captain/narrator of his
own complex self. Like Silver, Leggatt is a criminal who escapes retribution by setting out to sea to seek permanent exile. Both stories chart a

journey of self-discovery for protagonists confronted with evidence of the appeal of the darker self, an appeal that Jekyll understood only too well. Psychological exploration is complemented by instances of the supernatural in both authors. The Scottish romantic tradition finds expression in the gothic tones of *The Master of Ballantrae*, a story of obsession, paranoia, and revenge tinged with suggestions of demonic possession; in "Markheim" (1884) and "Thrawn Janet" (1881); and most obviously in *Jekyll and Hyde*. Conrad treats these themes with a lighter touch in "Karain" (1898), but in *The Nigger of the "Narcissus"* there is a sense of possible darker forces at work. Conrad rarely employed the psychological horror of the supernatural as overtly as Stevenson, but his explorations of superstition, obsessive personalities, and doppelgängers signals his debt to those who used the romance and the gothic as vehicles into the psyche.

Like Conrad, Stevenson was never shackled to the demands of the Victorian novel. As Priestly suggested, Stevenson was more of a modernist than a Victorian: he inscribed in his fiction a troubled response to the metropolis long before the doubts and fears of Conrad's metropolitan fiction emerged. Stevenson explored the darkness and disorder in the heart of humanity, sometimes playfully but often in the ominous tones of a post-Victorian sensibility. For this reason it is vital to contest the reductive categories within which Stevenson has been confined. This collection of essays is testimony to the fact that, despite Conrad's reservations, and despite the fact that Stevenson died before he could have read a word written by Conrad, they share an inheritance and an artistic vision that merits substantial investigation. It is the object of this collection to investigate them and thus to breach the barriers that have for so long separated the work of Stevenson and Conrad.

Stevenson and Conrad: Writers of Transition

The essays that follow explore the shared traditions out of which Stevenson and Conrad emerged. In some cases thematic similarities are highlighted; in others, differing approaches to subject matter; and some essays deal with the writers' treatment and use of historical events. Those that take a historicist approach attempt to recuperate the cultural climate of late-nineteenth-century England, refracting the narratives through the lens of a recovered history. In other places we find stories and novels linked through theoretical argument in stimulating new juxtapositions of narratives. Each essay displays a keen awareness of the value of undertaking a project that links these two authors.

Part One deals with Stevenson and Conrad as writers of transition. It opens with Richard Ambrosini's foregrounding of Stevenson within the late Victorian canon and demonstrating Stevenson's proximity to Conrad both historically and in terms of his aspirations for his fiction. In questioning the validity of the modernist canon, this essay argues that both authors cross artificially imposed literary boundaries. Eric Massie agrees with Ambrosini's arguments, applying them specifically to *The Ebb-Tide* and *Victory*. By providing a detailed examination of the premises on which this volume is based, Ambrosini and Massie deftly set the tone for many of the critical appraisals that follow.

Liminality and the sea provide the starting point for Nathalie Jaëck's exploration of the formal and stylistic innovations that mark Stevenson and Conrad as transitional writers. In Jaëck's reading, the sea becomes a metaphor for the openness and indeterminacy that characterize texts such as *Treasure Island* and *Lord Jim*. Showing both the fragility and the ingenuity of their textual "paper boats," Jaëck provides a model for rethinking the movement from Victorian realism to High Modernism. Laurence Davies's essay is "a contribution toward a history of social doubling and the social double." Davies charts how the doppelgänger motif highlights social and political concerns in the novel. Exploring possibilities of doubling in Stevenson and Conrad, Davies says: "The history of reading works such as the *Strange Case* and 'The Secret Sharer' is as much a narrative of the One and the Many as it is of the One and the Dual."

Part Two focuses on Stevenson and Conrad's imperial fiction. Andrea White's opening essay for this section takes the unusual angle of comparing "A Smile of Fortune" with *Jekyll and Hyde*. White uses the Derridean notion that acts of exclusion illuminate our understanding of the organizing structures of our experience. She demonstrates how even in an imperial outpost the metropolis insinuates itself into the individual psyche and compromises the desire for a unified self. Monica Bungaro examines *Heart of Darkness* and *In the South Seas*, emphasizing the imperial encounter with the Other and showing how in both texts the relationship between cultures becomes one of exchange and will to comprehend and assimilate the culture of the Other. Bungaro's conclusion is that both writers recognize the innate humanity of the Other rather than his/her difference. Ann C. Colley employs a historicist approach to critique the allusions to cannibalism in the same two texts. Colley's premise is that Stevenson relied on his own experience and research on Samoa for his accounts of cannibalism, whereas Conrad used anthropophagy to infuse his narrative with gothic horror. Echoing Jaëck, Robbie B. H. Goh draws our attention to the various, and variously signifying, liminal spaces that so fascinated these writers and that seem to proliferate especially in their South Seas tales. Robert Hampson's concerns in *Treasure Island* and *Victory* involve place and space, maps and topography. Taking the notion of reading in its widest sense, reading maps, signs, and imagery is for Hampson an integral part of the creation of *Treasure Island*. On the other hand, he decodes the homosocial world that Jim Hawkins inhabits as part of its credentials as a bildungsroman.

The final part of the volume deals with social and psychological contexts for Stevenson and Conrad. Thus, Deaglán Ó'Donghaile's essay places *The Dynamiter* and *The Secret Agent* within the cultural context of nineteenth-century Irish political terrorism and unrest. Offering fascinating insights into the historical events on which the novels are based, Ó'Donghaile provides compelling reasons for regarding them as illuminating in terms of the effects of and responses to terrorism. Martin Danahay revisits the topos of the doppelgänger to reveal significant differences in Conrad's and Stevenson's respective attitudes toward the self, the city, and the possibilities of community and human connection. It is perhaps, Danahay implies, a mark of the generational gap between the two writers that Stevenson's stories display a residual attachment to traditional "bonds of obligation" between human beings, while Conrad's tales stress the inevitability of human isolation in the search for authenticity. Jane V. Rago links *Heart of Darkness* with *The Suicide Club* through theories of evolution and degeneration as used in the language and assumptions of the homosocial worlds of both texts. Rago reveals that male opinions and behaviors in these texts are informed by the scientific and evolutionary theories of the nineteenth century.

Nancy Bunge puts Conrad and Stevenson in exhilarating dialogue with two twentieth-century figures whose theoretical paradigms did much to shape modern understanding of the artistic imagination, Sigmund Freud and Carl Jung. Using *Jekyll and Hyde* and *Heart of Darkness* as test cases, Bunge aligns Conrad with Freud in their shared understanding of the nature of human evil, while Stevenson's views on evil are shown to parallel those of Jung. In the final essay in the volume, questions of psychology and of liminality combine in Stephen Donovan's investigation of spiritualism in relation to the works and lives (and even, perhaps, the afterlives) of our two authors. Like Danahay, Donovan provides evidence of a generational rift between the two writers. Stevenson remained open, in a way seemingly unavailable to his modernist successors, to the possibilities—aesthetic as well as social—suggested by spiritualist endeavors. Conrad, bound by what Donovan calls a "patrician view" of his literary calling, shied away from the vulgarities and crankeries associated with much paranormal research in the period.

NOTES

1. Conrad's choice of English for his writing caused some accusations of betrayal of his native country and its language. See Karl, 9–15, for the history of these accusations.

2. "Dilettante" is one of the definitions of *virtuoso*, but that hardly applies to Stevenson, and it would not seem to be what Conrad had in mind.

3. Much of the discussion of *Heart of Darkness* and *Jekyll and Hyde* that follows is a revised version of material in D. C. R. A. Goonetilleke's edited collection *Joseph Conrad's Heart of Darkness* (Routledge, 2007).

4. For more discussion on the modern gothic and urban settings, see Linda Dryden, *The Modern Gothic and Literary Doubles*, in particular, "City of Dreadful Night: Stevenson's Gothic London," pp. 74–109.

5. For a fuller discussion of the similarities between these two stories, see Cedric Watts, "*The Ebb-Tide* and *Victory*," *Conradiana* 28, no. 2 (1996): 133–37.

PART ONE

Stevenson and Conrad: Writers of Transition

History, Criticism, Theory, and the Strange Case of Joseph Conrad and R. L. Stevenson

RICHARD AMBROSINI

ONCE UPON A TIME, literary historians applied supposedly ideology-free value judgments formulated by literary critics to confer only on certain works a monumental status. Those days are long gone, and unlamented. Today's theoretically aware disciplinary discourse takes for granted that the past is an intertextuality of "documents" reflecting the ideology of their times. Oddly, however, when it comes to the transition from late Victorian to modernist literature, the old orthodoxies about periodization and aesthetics that have hegemonized English Studies since their foundation do not appear to be all that questionable, and, as a result, a greater documental significance is granted to certain monumental texts than to others previously excluded from the old modernist canon.

It is a time-honored practice for every critical theory to privilege the literature that its principles are best suited to describe. A new theory cannot but be the result of a set of prejudgments evolved from the reading of particular texts: the tenets of New Criticism found confirmation in well-wrought urns, just as Roland Barthes's distinction between *readable* and *writable* texts was based on complex and obscure novels and short stories (Compagnon 245). This is why, however innovative, a theory is fated to become in its turn another orthodoxy, complete with its own canon. Fair enough. But finding old and new canons unthinkingly superimposed, and literary history, criticism, and theory concurring in conflating otherwise irreducible approaches, is strange. Yet this is what happens when, for example, two writers born seven years apart from each other are forced into different historical epochs only because a succession of value judgments have created a distorted retroactive perspective on their opuses;[1] if it is done with Robert Louis Stevenson and Joseph Conrad it means that their case is very strange indeed.

What distinguishes the current Anglo-American variant of "theory" from its predecessors is its practitioners' business savvy: having made all literary histories unmarketable, they have pragmatically (and lucratively) replaced them with anthologies. One of these, enjoying great subliminal authority because it has the same name as the most famous antivirus on the market, reserves a special treatment to our two authors: its editors simply pretended Stevenson never existed, while Conrad's 1899 *Heart of Darkness* is paired off with a 1977 essay by the Nigerian author Chinua Achebe. Stevenson's exclusion is not based on any contemporary theoretical prejudgment but on a perpetuation of earlier ones by critics otherwise viewed today as "fools in old-style hats and coats" (Larkin, "This Be the Verse," l. 6).[2] The sanitization of Conrad's text, instead, is only the latest of the many selections operated within his corpus, all aimed at forcing him into a modernist mold.

Luckily, the current discredit of the modernist canon has made the issue of Stevenson's exclusion/inclusion irrelevant. The problem is Conrad, because his monumental status, bestowed on the assumption that he is a modernist, has obscured the documental significance of his colonial fiction, which could emerge only when read in its late Victorian context, since it was all written in the 1890s. It was then, at the outset of his writing career, that he envisioned a horizon of expectations for his works, as he sought ways to reach out to the British public by combining literary ambitions and the adoption of the popular narrative forms available in the literary market. In this fundamentally dialogic attempt he found models and inspiration in the corpus of writing created by the supreme late Victorian manipulator and creator of subgenres, Robert Louis Stevenson, his "secret sharer."

Conrad was the first to keep this relationship hidden, as witnessed by the sparse references to Stevenson in his correspondence. The picture emerging from his letters is puzzling, because Conrad appears to ignore Stevenson the novelist, referring only to the celebrated essayist—the "Virtuoso Cymballist [*sic*]" (*CL* 4:47). At times he disparaged what he could never become, as here to J. B. Pinker: "I have no literary tradition even which will help to spin phrases—the chewed up silly phrases. I am not a 'Sedulous Ape.' I wish sometimes I were" (*CL* 4:21).[3] Luckily, the tastes of the reading public had changed from when Stevenson was the standard-bearer of the "new cult of prose stylism" initiated by Walter Pater (Merritt 27; Fowler 213–34) and while he was proofreading *Chance*, his first commercial success, Conrad could confidently claim: "When it comes to popularity I stand much nearer the public mind than Stevenson who was super-literary, a conscious virtuoso of style; whereas the average mind does not care much for virtuosity" (*CL* 5:257).

Struggling to be established, and while reviewers kept comparing him unfavorably with Stevenson, Conrad could not afford to be so graceful.[4] When Pinker dared complain about his lack of professionalism, compared to his predecessor, Conrad lashed back: "I am no sort of airy R. L. Stevenson who considered his art a prostitute and the artist as no better than one" (*CL* 2:371).[5] He had reasons to be touchy about such comparisons: neither publishers nor magazine editors showed any interest in *Seraphina*, a collaboration with Ford Madox Ford, and a few weeks later they were forced to change its title to *Romance*, thus publicly admitting their debt to Stevenson. Such a change was inevitable, since this story of a young Englishman who escapes to the Caribbean, where he is kidnapped but finally succeeds in defeating a band of pasteboard pirates, is indeed an unsuccessful mix of *Kidnapped* and *Treasure Island*, even though sexed up with a romantic love story. It was a brazen attempt to exploit Stevenson's fame, and Conrad imagined how reviewers would have sneered "at those two men who took six years to write 'this very ordinary tale'—whereas R.L.S. single handed produced his masterpieces etc etc" (*CL* 3:59).

Conrad's choice of settings and subgenres, as well as the names of several of his characters, belie his feigned ignorance of Stevenson the novelist.[6] Perhaps his most revealing tribute is *Victory* (1915) in which, having secured with *Chance* the popular recognition he had sought in vain for almost twenty years, he returned to Stevenson's last novel, *The Ebb-Tide*. At that point he could afford to engage with the Scotsman's shadow without feeling any anxiety of influence (Epstein 189–216; Watts, "The Ebb-Tide and Victory," 133–37). The Stevenson who was Conrad's "secret sharer" was the writers' writer who had intentionally chosen to occupy in the British literary establishment a liminal position similar to the one into which Conrad, as a Polish expatriate, had been forced by historical events. It might have been because they were both moving from the fringe of contemporary European culture, but the moral imperative shaping their aesthetic programs impelled them to reach out to an ideal universal audience when addressing the novel-reading public.

Secure in his artistic identity as a master stylist of the essay, Stevenson approached fiction with the detachment of a writer oblivious of the genre hierarchies upheld by his contemporaries. Having witnessed in France and the United States the rising power of the media years before other British authors, he chose to contaminate his pure prose by engaging with a variety of popular narrative forms. His openness toward the challenges posed by the new mass readership was ethically motivated, and he responded to changes in the literary market by adapting for "his" bourgeois public the pleasure-creating mechanisms at work in commercial subgenres (Ambrosini, "Ethical Value," 31). If he chose adventurous tales, it was because he believed that the truly creative writer is able "to show us the realisation and the apotheosis of the day-dreams of common men" (*Thistle* 18:332).[7]

Conrad voiced similarly universalistic aspirations in his 1897 artistic manifesto, the preface to *The Nigger of the "Narcissus."* The artist, he claims, must appeal to the "subtle but invincible conviction of solidarity . . . which binds men to each other, which binds together all humanity." In the novelist's case, voicing this appeal requires an "unremitting never-discouraged care for the shape and ring of sentences," since only in this way "the light of magic suggestiveness may be brought to play . . . over the commonplace surface of words" (*NNTFF* xxiv–xxv). This model for a poetically resonant fictional language was carried out and tested in *Heart of Darkness* and *Lord Jim*, the two texts in the

Conrad canon with the highest incidence of metaphors (Yelton 111). However, he eventually redefined this aesthetic project while writing *Lord Jim*, the last of those early fictions that in a later essay he called his "paper boats, freighted with a grown-up child's dreams" (*LE* 143). On completing *Lord Jim* he embarked on an engagement with the tastes and reading habits of the British public, combining a manipulation of his readers' expectations with an ironically mimetic use of the English language. In so doing, he reformulated his "conviction of solidarity" as a refusal of an elitist conception of literature. The 1920 author's note to *Chance* echoes the 1897 preface wherein Conrad explains that this novel's success mattered so much to him because until then he had feared he might become "a writer for a limited coterie," a condition odious to him because it would throw a doubt "on the soundness of my belief in the solidarity of all mankind in simple ideas and in sincere emotions" (*C* [Methuen] viii–x). Conrad's poetic prose and his experiments with subgenres, then, were both motivated by ethical principles. He became a modernist icon while aiming at commercial success to fulfill the moral basis of his writing.

Conrad the artist and Conrad the pursuer of a mass readership were two halves of the same person. He cannot be impaled on only one horn of the opposition between avant-garde "artistic" literature and popular fiction on which the modernist canon is based. His literary ambitions were never in conflict with his desire to win a wider readership: having to address an audience that until the end of his life remained culturally and linguistically foreign to him, he never overcame an insecurity that could be allayed only by mass recognition. Ironically, his posthumous canonization as a modernist icon ended up obscuring his repeated crossings of linguistic, cultural, and class boundaries.

The creative use of a plurality of narrative forms allowed twentieth-century writers to reinvent for postmodernists a wider conception of literature, bearing testimony to the seminal importance of Stevenson's and Conrad's extended experimentation with subgenres derived from popular culture. From *Treasure Island* in 1881 to Conrad's death in 1924 this experimentation spans the entire spectrum of late Victorianism and

High Modernism. Awareness of it could, potentially, lead us to rethink old literary taxonomies as well as new critical prejudgments.

The first to recognize Conrad's position on the boundary between "high" and "low" literature was Fredric Jameson, who wrote that Conrad "marks, indeed, a strategic fault line in the emergence . . . not merely of what will be contemporary modernism . . . but also, still tangibly juxtaposed with it, of what will be variously called popular culture or mass culture, the commercialized cultural discourse of what, in late capitalism, is often described as a media society." He locates this "fault line" in the break at the center of *Lord Jim* between Marlow's psychological investigation into the *Patna* case and Jim's adventure in the Borneo village of Patusan. This second part represents for Jameson a "shift between two distinct cultural spaces, that of 'high' culture and that of mass culture," Patusan being "a virtual paradigm of romance as such, . . . the prototype of the various 'degraded' sub-genres into which mass culture will be articulated (adventure story, gothic, science fiction, bestseller, detective story, and the like)." Having reached this invaluable insight into Conrad's strategic position, however, Jameson is puzzled by his own literary-historical reconstruction: "[E]ven after eighty years, his place is still unstable, undecidable, and his work unclassifiable, . . . floating uncertainly in between Proust and Robert Louis Stevenson" (Jameson 206–7).

Jameson's unthinking application of two critical commonplaces of twentieth-century criticism distorts the significance of this watershed moment in British literary history. Marcel Proust himself would have differed if he had heard someone suggest that he was Stevenson's irreducible other; in *Le Temps retrouvé*, when a fashionable lady makes a similarly slighting remark about Stevenson, Charles Swann breaks out with an "affirmation péremptoire: 'Mais c'est tout à fait un grand écrivain, Stevenson, je vous assure, M. de Goncourt, un très grand, l'égal des plus grands'" (Proust 716). More important still, Stevenson intentionally crossed the "strategic fault line" between elegant essayist and purveyor of adventure yarns, and when friends urged him to stick to the essays and travelogues so appreciated at Eton and Oxford, he refused, declaring that he was tired of floating in the air like a "literary cherub—a head and a pair of wings, with nothing to sit down upon," longing instead "to be something more than the darling of a literary set" (*SL* 3:278n11).[8] The problem is that Jameson, compiling as he does the Marxists' and modernists' contempt for "commercialized" cultural forms, is only interested in the "tangible juxtaposition" between the modernist conception of high art and "degraded" fiction writing and therefore utterly disregards the possibility that Conrad may have consciously engaged in such practice— let alone the possibility that in doing so he was developing prototypes created by Stevenson.

That Stevenson thus pioneered an experimentation that was continued by Conrad of course does not necessarily make his texts "better"—as posited by philological models obsessed with assigning primacies. The reverse is often the case. With *The Secret Agent* (1907) Conrad tried to exploit the vogue for spy stories initiated by Erskine Childers's *The Riddle of the Sands* (1904). Instead of replicating Childers's successful formula, he chose as a model an obscure story, "Zero's Tale of the Explosive Bomb" (1884), which Stevenson had written twenty-two years earlier. This unassuming divertissement had initiated a minor subgenre, the so-called peccant engine story (Arnett Melchiori 69), in which continental anarchists and Irish nationalists were portrayed as comic bumbling figures incapable of carrying out bombing outrages. Stevenson's humor noir was far more amenable to Conrad's ironic treatment of the anarchist threat than Henry James's *The Princess Casamassima*, a response to the same bomb campaign that inspired Stevenson's story. But Conrad superimposed on this model a domestic tragedy, thus radically changing its nature. In general, this is true of most of his genre experiments, and this is why it was Conrad's exploitation of the tragic potential of sensational plots, instead of Stevenson's intellectual playing with formulaic fiction, that inspired so many twentieth-century writers who chose to contaminate themselves with popular literature. (The first name that comes to mind is Graham Greene—Stevenson's cousin's grandson, by the way.)

Conrad expected *The Secret Agent* "to produce some sensation" (*CL* 3:459), but his attempt to titillate the British reading public resulted in a disaster. As on no previous occasion, reviewers zeroed in on the "Slavonic . . . note" in his fiction (Sherry 195), and he commented bitterly: "I've been so cried up of late as a sort of freak, an amazing bloody foreigner writing in English" (*CL* 3:488). This fiasco, however, impelled him to explain to the French translator of *The Secret Agent*, Henri-Durand

Davray, why an awareness of his alienness from his audience's cultural and linguistic associations was a crucial element in any interpretation of his texts, writing on January 26, 1908:

> Don't forget that the thing is written for the English—having in mind the effect it ought to produce on an English reader. This is always my aim. And this is why as an English writer I lend myself so little to being translated. It is easy to translate, for example, a *national* writer like Kipling. His interest lies in the *subject*, while the interest of my work lies in the *effect* it produces. He talks about *his compatriots*. I write *for them*. (*CL* 4:28, emphasis in the original, my translation)[9]

Unable to count on a referential system based on unconsciously absorbed physical and mental sensations, Conrad was forced to resort to a variety of means to produce his intended "*effect*" by alerting his readers and startling them out of their familiar way of perceiving and reading. Having failed with his early exotic fiction, he changed tactics by attempting to create the suggestively impressionistic language envisaged in the 1897 preface. However, neither his choice of words, sentence patterns, and rhythms nor his later, repeated revisitations of contemporary formulaic fiction, subversive as they were of readers' expectations, succeeded in producing the right "*effect*" (Ambrosini, *Conrad's Fiction*, 50–52).

Only once did he manage to pass himself off as a "*national* writer," when he used an English first-person narrator to voice a series of questionings on what happens, out there, to "one of us." Ironically, he was to pay dearly for this success. Recent critics have discounted his rhetorical ruses, reading his colonial fiction as if, like Kipling, he were talking about the English, not writing "*for them*." If so, it is largely because an unholy mix of literary history, criticism, and theory obfuscates the correlation between Conrad's manipulations of genres—in the 1890s, exotic tales were as popular as spy stories were in the 1900s—and the dialogic nature of his texts. Luckily, Stevenson can help clarify that context, thus enabling us to put into focus the documentary value of Conrad's colonial works.

*

John Richetti praises Stevenson's "The Beach of Falesà" and *The Ebb-Tide* as "versions of *Heart of Darkness* transposed in Polynesia" (Richetti 576), even though they were written respectively seven and six years before Conrad's novella. Such an absurd distortion reflects a literary-historical perspective on the two writers' colonial fiction based on an evolving set of theoretical prejudgments. Albert Guerard, examining Conrad's early Malay stories, notes in parentheses that "[a] glance at the South Sea Yarns of Stevenson . . . indicates in what sense Conrad 'brought serious-ness' to the exotic novel of adventure" (Guerard 88).[10] Later, less fastidi-ous critics who focused on the two authors' "romanticism" were ready to acknowledge a continuity between Stevenson's last and Conrad's earliest novels (Eigner 239–43; Thorburn 54–60 et passim); lacking, however, an awareness of how closely romance was linked with imperial ideology, they were unable to recognize, as Andrea White does, that both writers "challenged the possibility of . . . longed-for, dispassionate adventure," and, having "recorded the dissolution of the dream of pure adventure," became the first to question "the basic tenets of the literary genre that had traditionally promoted European expansionism." In this new critical context, an apodictic granting of "seriousness"—one would expect—would be out of place. Surprisingly, instead White claims that "Conrad's criticism extends beyond Stevenson's" because, while both "see the native as the victim of imperial intrusions," Stevenson depicts "an innocent, romanticized native whose paradise has been lost by unscrupulous European intruders, a subversive but somewhat simplified view that Conrad's fiction does not permit." And why so? Because "imperial intru-sions in Conrad's modernist texts enact a complex reality."[11] Not only, then, does White reformulate Guerard's supremacy trope, albeit in politi-cal rather than aesthetic terms, but in doing so she also spells out what her predecessor took for granted: that Conrad, being a modernist, cannot but endow his texts with a greater "seriousness," however qualified. White's untroubled use of literary-historical categories makes her con-clusion almost too predictable: "Conrad's early novels . . . more openly spearheaded the generic subversion and more significantly demanded a new view of the imperial subject" (White 196–98).

In fact, Conrad's "subversion" would have been impossible if Stevenson had not opened a space critical of adventure by making the rejection of the glamour associated with this idea a constant theme in both his fiction and his nonfiction. This theme has been overshadowed by what his first serious critic, William Archer, called the "athletico-aesthetic point of view" recurrent in his early essays (Maixner 168). His first two travel books, *An Inland Voyage* (1878) and *Travels with a Donkey in the Cévennes* (1879), construct first-person narratives in which a young man is made to discover the vacuity of dreams of adventures induced by his inability to face the challenges of domesticity. With his third and last travelogue, *The Amateur Emigrant*, his disillusionment with adventure acquires definite political overtones. Stevenson's protagonists' adventures invariably end with a trauma, leaving Jim Hawkins cursing the stage of his exploits and David Balfour in tears at the thought of Alan Breck condemned to flee to France while he enjoys his newly found inheritance. In the Pacific, Stevenson's critique of adventure went beyond rejecting the literary tradition originating with *Robinson Crusoe* and came to include his own past work. If there was a primacy in the subversion of adventure, it is to be found entirely within Stevenson's oeuvre. By writing the first realist colonial novels, he created for Conrad, as Edwin Eigner notes, "a British and an American audience interested in the South Seas and more than willing to accept the phenomenon of a serious, psychological writer of highly pitched adventure stories" (Eigner 242).[12]

Before arriving in the Pacific, Stevenson shared the common British view of empire, but—and this is why he is invaluable to us—his writing changed once he found his own island and discovered the reality of colonialism. In December 1890, a few weeks after he had settled in Samoa, he wrote to Henry James about the difficulties in representing the South Seas. Imagine, he confided, "writing a book of travels on the spot; when I am continually extending my information, revising my opinions, and seeing *the most finely finished portions of my work* come part by part in pieces. Very soon I shall have no opinions left. And without an opinion, how to string artistically vast accumulations of fact?" (*SL* 7:65–66; emphasis added). The political and cultural clash taking place before his eyes required new interpretive and representational tools. Interestingly, as his world view changed it was precisely the "most finely finished portions" of his work—the fine stylistic prose he was famous for—that turned out to be an obstacle. His South Seas nonfictional and fictional works provide us then with an insight into how a European intellectual came to terms with his new environment by radically questioning his previous identity as an artist. No wonder, then, if at the time he wrote this letter he had stopped writing fiction and concentrated instead on creating an ad hoc impersonal, scientific language for his ethnographic treatise *In the South Seas* (1896).

In Samoa, then a German colony, Stevenson sided openly with the islanders. When they rebelled, he gave shelter to insurgents and acted as a messenger among the chiefs hiding in the bush. The letters he sent to the *London Times* protesting against the German colonial authorities proved such a nuisance that the Foreign Office tried to have him deported (McLynn 434–35). Indeed, it speaks volumes of how muddled certain strained and mechanistic translations of political categories into literary assessments can be when one thinks that the only European writer who put his life on the line to defend a colonized people may be considered today a "guileless innocent" (Fernando 301) incapable of transcending an exotic vision of the colonized (Gilmour 192).

Aside from the change in Stevenson's identity as a writer and his active militancy, what further makes his colonial fiction a precious historical document is that it can be precisely located within the context of late Victorian culture. An essayist before he became a novelist, he was an intellectual, a polygraphic writer, a restless experimenter with literary forms, and an amateur historian.[13] Among his friends and admirers were some of the most representative figures of his times: writers, poets, painters (John Singer Sargent), art historians (Sidney Colvin), drama and literary critics (William Archer), anthropologists (Andrew Lang), and psychologists (F. W. H. Myers). Particularly relevant was how his point of view was informed by the tradition of anthropological studies pioneered by Scottish philosophers, economists, and novelists (Stocking, *After Tylor*, 50; Crawford 170). Stevenson was uniquely positioned to bring to bear on his colonial encounters a wide range of ideas derived from his contemporary culture. This is why, rather than using, as Alan Sandison suggests, the "Conradian prism" to refract the "Stevensonian ray" (Sandison 317), it is far more revealing to use the dense intertextual web in Stevenson's biography, letters, and fiction to cast light on Conrad's colonial texts.

First witnessing the reality of colonialism, Conrad did not have at his disposal interpretive tools equal to Stevenson's—as is evident if we compare his "Congo Diary" with *In the South Seas*. Unlike Stevenson, who registered his impressions on the spot, by the time Conrad started writing, the experiences he re-created were already settled in the past. (In his first Marlow tale, "Youth," an autobiographical story based on a sea journey that had occurred sixteen years earlier, the narrator admits that "for me all the East is contained in that vision of my youth" [*Y* 42].) Stevenson, arriving in the South Seas at the peak of his fame, could afford to disappoint those readers who expected him to churn out Melvillian South Seas idylls.[14] Conrad, as an outsider trying to carve out for himself a space in the editorial market, could not afford to do so.

This does not make him less significant in a study of late-nineteenth-century intellectual history—provided his colonial texts are viewed as the end product of a cultural mediation their author engaged in with what he assumed was his British readers' outlook both on their representatives in the colonies and on their imperial subjects. His Marlow tales, in particular, are eminently rhetorical constructs aimed at creating figures of white men viewed by an English sea captain, one of the "us" Conrad—or at least, the public persona he created in his autobiographical writings *The Mirror of the Sea* and *A Personal Record*—so desperately wanted to be himself.

Herein lies the key to the dialogic nature of the colonial fictions in which Conrad thematized truths he at the same time hid from and disclosed to a readership he was trying both to ingratiate and provoke. He succeeded so well in rendering the "process of negotiating the tenuous personal and cultural identities so often described in anthropological works" that not only have his texts become a privileged terrain for literary studies on imperial ideology, but also James Clifford has lamented how "[a]nthropology is still waiting for its Conrad" (Hunter 20; Clifford 96).[15] They have proved to be a mirror in which succeeding generations of Western readers have seen reflected their fears and their ignorance. If to Andrea White they appear to have "significantly demanded a new view of the imperial subject," it is because so many twentieth-century literary theories have perpetuated this mirror effect (White 198).

No wonder, then, that Conrad's treatment of the colonized has proved capable of transcending the culture of his times better than Stevenson's. "The Beach of Falesá" and *The Ebb-Tide* are a gold mine for a study of "the close articulation . . . between the domestic and colonial spheres of otherness" and are particularly rewarding for readings interested in how issues central to Western realist fiction such as class, religion, and sexuality could be dramatized also in a colonial setting (Stocking, *Victorian Anthropology*, 234). Nonetheless, one cannot but accept the fact that his eventual questioning of late Victorian adventure yarns has been clouded by later readers' responses, and therefore, however invaluable as historical documents, they do not provide a fit subject for today's theoretical prejudgments. Conrad's self-distancing from the same genre, instead, has remained visible for later generations of readers, even when the critical horizon of expectations shifted from the aesthetic to the political. Largely, the disappearance from that horizon of a novelist-anthropologist such as Stevenson has led to numerous distortions in the reception of Conrad's colonial literature, because, partly as a consequence of this gap in literary history, the effort to historicize British late-nineteenth-century literary representations of the empire ended up blowing out of all proportion the perceived documental value of his texts. And this is another reason why the strange case of Joseph Conrad and R. L. Stevenson is so important to us today.

NOTES

1. Stevenson died when he was forty-four, the day of Conrad's thirty-seventh birthday and a few days after Conrad's first novel, *Almayer's Folly*, was accepted by a publisher. Ahead of him Conrad had a thirty-year-long career.

2. Stevenson had been a model writer for the holders of the first chairs in English literature at Oxford and Cambridge, Sir Walter Raleigh (Merton Chair, Oxford, 1904), the author of one of the first major studies on Stevenson's style (1895), and Sir Arthur Quiller-Couch (King Edward VII Professor, Cambridge, 1912), who wrote the posthumous chapters of *St. Ives* (see Gross 194, 200). Quiller-Couch claimed that on hearing of RLS's death his first thought had been: "Put away books and paper and pen. Stevenson is dead. Stevenson is dead, and now there is nobody left to write about" (Quiller-Couch 96).

3. In "A College Magazine" (1887), an autobiographical essay in which Stevenson recalled his self-training as a writer, he famously wrote: "I have thus played the sedulous ape to Hazlitt, to Lamb, to Wordsworth, to Sir Thomas Browne, to Defoe, to Hawthorne, to Montaigne, to Baudelaire and to Oberman" (*Thistle* 13:212).

4. Even after Conrad turned to his sea experiences, the comparisons kept dogging him. When *The Nigger of the "Narcissus"* appeared, a critic remarked that "if 'The Ebb-Tide' had never been written, it is conceivable that Donkin might have established himself as the type [of the vicious cockney] instead [of Stevenson's Huish]. As it is, he only reminds us of someone else" (Watts, *Joseph Conrad*, 80).

5. Conrad may be referring to the controversies raised by an essay, "A Letter to a Young Gentleman Who Proposes to Embrace the Career of Art," in which Stevenson urges young aspiring authors to weed their "mind at the outset of all desire to money" without forgetting, however, that the ultimate test of what he calls "idealism in honesty" is to bear in mind that "the end of all art [is] to please" (*Thistle* 20:284–85). The essay appeared in November 1888, when Conrad was the proud captain of the *Otago*; perhaps he heard about the controversy from W. H. Henley, who after quarreling with Stevenson in late 1887 became one of his fiercest critics.

6. Among the Stevenson characters whose names recur in Conrad we find "Singleton" (*The Nigger of the "Narcissus"*) from *The Wrecker*; "O'Brien" and "Selkirk" (*Romance*) from, respectively, *Treasure Island* and *The Wrecker*; "Jones" (*Victory*) from "Zero's Tale of the Explosive Bomb"; and "Ransome" (*The Shadow-Line*) from *Kidnapped*.

7. All references to Stevenson's works in this chapter are to *The Thistle Edition of the Works of Robert Louis Stevenson*, 25 vols. (New York: Charles Scribner's Sons, 1924).

8. His first travel book, *An Inland Voyage* (1878), was adopted at Eton for translations from English into Latin, and a society at Oxford chose the same slim volume as the "best specimen of the writing of English of this century" (Maixner 8).

9. "Mais n'oubliez pas que la chose est écrite pour les Anglais—au point de vue de l'effet a produire sur un lecteur anglais. C'est toujours mon but. Voilà pourquoi je suis tellement un ecrivain Anglais se prétant peu a la traduction. Un ecrivain *national* comme Kipling p. example se traduit facilement. Son interêt est *dans le sujet* l'interêt de mon oeuvre est *dans l'effet* qu'elle produit. Il parle de *ses compatriotes*. Moi j'écris *pour eux*."

10. The comparison, one would think, is in itself slighting enough, but Guerard uses all the typographical resources at his disposal to explain why his having even only cast a "glance" on Stevenson should not be read as a suggestion that Stevenson is in any way a precursor of Conrad. Not only is the remark insulated from the text within a two-page-long parenthesis in which he discusses Stevenson's colonial fiction, but in an endnote, then, he thanks a colleague for drawing his attention to these similarities.

11. In response to Guerard, Linda Dryden suggests instead "how far from the adventure tale Stevenson had moved. The shift continued with Conrad." While recognizing that "Conrad went further by questioning the essential values espoused by the romance and adventure genre itself," she demonstrates that it is possible to view the two authors' colonial fictions without being drawn into any kind of supremacy game (Dryden, *Joseph Conrad*, 50, 53).

12. In *The Ebb-Tide* the schooner's approach to Attwater's island marks the moment in literary history in which hyperliterary language and symbolically impressionistic settings were introduced for the first time in an adventure novel. It is no coincidence, therefore, that Jacques Rivière used this description in his essay "Le

roman d'aventure" as an example of the kind of fiction required to revitalize the French novel (Price 35–82).

13. In 1881 Stevenson applied for the chair in history and constitutional law at the University of Edinburgh but did not make it by only a few votes—even though he had more pertinent publications than the successful candidate (Menikoff 22–26).

14. Sidney Colvin, who years later became a close friend of Conrad's, could not contain his distaste for how Stevenson in the South Seas kept writing about his "beloved blacks—or chocolates . . . ; to us detested, . . . and oh so much less interesting than any dog, cat, mouse" (*SL* 8:279n1).

15. The most illuminating case of how relevant the questions raised in Conrad's colonial texts would remain for Europeans confronting other cultures is, of course, that of another anglicized Pole, Bronislaw Malinowski, who claimed he was the Conrad of anthropology, as opposed to W. H. R. Rivers, whom he portrayed as the Rider Haggard of the discipline (Ginzburg 113). Unfortunately, as John W. Griffith reminds us, in the most notorious passage in his diaries Malinowski, "that most culturally relativistic of early field anthropologists," echoes "the most brutal racist cant of a Kurtz: 'At moments I was furious at them. . . . On the whole my feelings toward the natives are definitely tending to, 'exterminate the brutes'" (Malinowski 69, quoted in Griffith, 55n19). Interestingly, Malinowski, who discovered Stevenson only while he was conducting his research in the South Seas, ended up identifying with the Scottish writer. Furthermore, it has been suggested that Stevenson's *Vailima Letters* (and perhaps his short story "The Bottle Imp") provided Malinowski with the initial inspiration for his most seminal ethnological theory, based on the *kula*, a gift-exchanging practice common throughout the South Seas (Ginzburg 112–16).

Stevenson and Conrad:
The Ebb-Tide and *Victory* Revisited

ERIC MASSIE

*I*N AN IMPORTANT discussion of Joseph Conrad's significance as an early modernist writer, Fredric Jameson states:

> Conrad marks, indeed, a strategic fault line in the emergence of contemporary narrative, a place from which the structure of twentieth-century literary and cultural institutions becomes visible as it could not be in the heterogeneity of Balzacian registers, nor even in the discontinuities of the paradigms which furnish materials for what is an increasingly unified narrative apparatus in Gissing. In Conrad we can sense the emergence not merely of what will be contemporary modernism (itself now become a literary institution), but also, still tangibly juxtaposed with it, of what will variously be called popular culture or mass culture, the commercialized cultural discourse of what, in late capitalism, is often described as a media society. (Jameson 203)

Conrad's position on the fault line described by Jameson has resulted in his work's being much admired and much studied in the wider context of literary modernism, and justly so. In this essay I will argue that Stevenson deserves to be considered alongside Conrad on that strategic fault line. The text that places him there is *The Ebb-Tide*. Later, I want to consider the extent to which Conrad's *Victory* and *The Ebb-Tide* may be viewed as parallel texts.

The core elements of *The Ebb-Tide* allow comparisons to be drawn with Conrad. It can be argued that this text builds on the critique of empire Stevenson had begun in "The Beach of Falesá," which itself, I would suggest, marks a turning point in Stevenson's fiction. Stevenson and Conrad, in the focal texts under discussion here, mount a challenge to the grand narrative of British imperialism in the late nineteenth and early twentieth centuries. Both cross Jameson's notional "fault line," carrying with them elements of the discourse of adventure fiction that had characterized their earlier work. Both are also located within a historical frame of reference. In an 1892 letter to Adelaide Boodle, Stevenson writes:

> Well, there are a lot of poor people who are brought here from dis-
> tant lands to labour as slaves for the Germans. They are not at all
> like the King or his people, who are brown and very pretty; but
> these are black as negroes and as ugly as sin, poor souls, and in
> their own lands they live all the time at war and cook and eat men's
> flesh. . . . Some times they are bad and wild and come down on the
> villages and steal and kill; and people whisper to each other that
> some of them have gone back to their horrid old habits, and catch
> men and women in order to eat them. But it is very likely not true;
> and most of them are only poor, stupid, trembling, half-starved,
> pitiful creatures like frightened dogs. (*SL* 7:227)

Stevenson writes, of course, as a contemporary witness in the discourse of his class and race. He cannot be viewed as a twenty-first-
century egalitarian but is a product of his age. He describes Pacific islanders in a manner similar to that of Conrad in *Heart of Darkness*, using terms similar to those that prompted Chinua Achebe to label

Conrad a "bloody racist." The basic rhetorical elements of this discourse are located in a historical frame of reference, and it is significant that they link Stevenson and Conrad as they describe Pacific and African peoples, respectively. They both offer a new and radical critique of imperial attitudes and policies, but both are limited in the range of their attacks because they share many of the attitudes of the time. Both writers are concerned with the role of Europeans in the colonies, but both Stevenson and Conrad marginalize the subaltern subject, which is, perhaps, the main thrust of Achebe's objection to *Heart of Darkness*. Neither writer *can* write from the point of view of the colonized subject: both are bound up in the colonial process. Their colocation on the fault line relates in no small measure to their association with late-nineteenth-century assumptions about race and their growing need, born of personal experience, to question these assumptions.

There has been, perhaps, a tendency to see Stevenson and Conrad as very different writers. John McClure, in a discussion of colonial writing, states:

> Conrad's whole perspective on imperialism differed fundamentally from that of other English authors of his time and provided him with a uniquely broad view of the issues. Alone among writers like Kipling, Haggard, Henley, and Stevenson, Conrad lived both as a native of a colonized country and as a member of a colonizing community. Thus he achieved what they never could, although some, like Kipling, tried: a view from the other side of the compound wall. Having stood among the colonized, he could never accept the most basic issues of empire as resolved. As a result, while Kipling writes mostly about the conflicts involved in perfecting the techniques of imperial domination, Conrad's works explore the issue of domination itself. (McClure 92)

The suggestion is that Stevenson, an *English* author according to McClure, is to be regarded as holding similar views to Kipling's in relation to the assumptions and workings of empire. Of course, Stevenson is not an English writer but a Scot, and as such had an ambivalent view of empire, being himself a member of a culturally subaltern nation.

Similarly, Conrad, a Polish national who experienced two imperial influences, Russian and British, is also placed in an ambiguous relationship to the imperial project. In view of the points of similarity that exist between Stevenson and Conrad, it is odd, perhaps, that they have been viewed as very different writers.

Obviously, the perception of Stevenson as a writer of children's adventure fiction has been revised in academic circles as a result in no small part of the efforts of the Stevenson academic community. The perception has been revised, but it has not been demolished. A body of critical opinion still tends to want to create first- and second-division status. Writing in 1996 about the critical perception of Conrad and Stevenson in an essay titled "*The Ebb-Tide* and *Victory*," Cedric Watts states:

> During Joseph Conrad's lifetime, reviewers of his work frequently compared him to Robert Louis Stevenson. In view of the subsequent decline in Stevenson's fortunes and the rise in Conrad's, those reviewers later seemed, in retrospect, rather naïve. Generally, they noticed superficial resemblances but overlooked important differences. The superficial resemblances are easy to discern. Both Stevenson and Conrad deal with seafarers, with adventurers in exotic locations, with ambiguous characters and with outcasts of various kinds. The differences include the following: Conrad is usually more sophisticated and intelligent, with a wider range of moral, philosophical and particularly political awareness; and he was richer in technical and linguistic resources, greater imaginative panache, and, as a realist, is more persuasively and astutely observant. Nevertheless, though Conrad has grounds for regarding Stevenson as an inferior writer, there is evidence that he was sometimes indebted to Stevenson's work—or at least to a novel in which that author was a collaborator. (Watts, "*The Ebb-Tide* and *Victory*," 133)

Watts's article appears to look for points of departure rather than points of intersection and to acknowledge superficial likenesses without ever conceding fundamentally connective tropes. The assumptions in Watts's argument require some examination. He presents an argument in an apparently objective manner while using terms that rely on value judgments themselves problematic in relation to substantiation. He looks at his subject from a viewpoint that is restricted by his feeling for his subject, a danger to which we are all exposed. However, references to superior intelligence and sophistication are partisan and lead to the conclusion that Watts relies on personal preference instead of any set of observable criteria when evaluating these two writers. Watts focuses on possible *resemblances* between the two texts, confining himself in the process to particularities and avoiding any discussion of the underlying ideological premises. In consequence, he misses an important opportunity to examine the similarities between the two writers. The effect is to simultaneously acknowledge, while actually disregarding, the significance of the common ground that exists in both texts. On one level the trio of beachcombers Jones, Ricardo, and Pedro parallels the trio of *The Ebb-Tide*, but there are also embedded, symbolic elements that connect the texts on a thematic level. I will return to these later.

The defensiveness that characterizes Watts's essay is peculiar, because Conrad's fortunes *did* rise following the end of the First World War. However, Conrad's reputation is securely established and does not need to be defended by an attack on Stevenson; Watts's attack does seem to be unfair to Stevenson. Stevenson, ahead of most of his contemporaries, realized that the intrusion into indigenous cultures by Western capitalism was a blight. He stated that view at a time when it was neither acceptable nor, indeed, widely acknowledged. Stevenson's subsequent decline in popularity, in the final stages of his career, is directly related to the production of texts that openly challenge the assumptions of late-nineteenth-century racial theories and the superiority of one culture over another. Of course, the relative fortunes, or reputations, of Stevenson and Conrad are also linked to the simple expedient of survival. Conrad was still alive when the mood changed regarding anti-imperialist literature following the First World War, by which time Stevenson's "The Beach of Falesá" and *The Ebb-Tide* had dropped from view and had been pigeonholed elsewhere.

The dangers of adopting a partisan approach towards one's author should be apparent to every critic: the insistence on superiority over another may limit the extent to which we can trace commonality of purpose and method. Stevenson need not be denigrated in order to advance Conrad, nor vice-versa. Instead, a more productive line of inquiry may be to attempt to evaluate the connection between *The Ebb-Tide* and *Victory* as an example of the cross-fertilization of ideas that flow between writers engaged on a similar project. In his important book *Robert Louis Stevenson and the Appearance of Modernism*, Alan Sandison emphasizes the significance of *The Ebb-Tide* as a modernist text. While concurring with that view unreservedly, I would further suggest that it is, perhaps, *the* text that entitles Stevenson to be regarded as a coworker alongside Conrad. The critical response to empire begun in "The Beach of Falesá" is developed in the later text so that it offers a condemnation of the working of imperialism that stands comparison with *Heart of Darkness*. Indeed, Attwater is, arguably, an even more terrible figure than Kurtz: Attwater is not an emblematic, atavistic figure but a dangerous, self-justifying precursor of the twentieth-century dictator figure.

Conrad follows the Stevenson text assiduously enough to suggest that he did not consider Stevenson as "inferior" a writer as Watts contends. Conrad incorporates several of the structural and thematic elements of *The Ebb-Tide* into *Victory*. The adoption of the remote island as a symbol of empire; the trio of villains; the obsessive insistence on gentlemanly behavior; and the trio's plans to kill the island's "ruler" as a prelude to stealing his riches suggest something more substantial than Watts's perception of "merely intermittent resemblances." The representation of the trio in *Victory* along lines corresponding to those used by Stevenson in *The Ebb-Tide* indicates a rather more comprehensive indebtedness than Watts concedes to be the case.

The parallels between the texts may demonstrate thematic connections of importance. Conrad shares an outlook on imperialism with Stevenson. This may be related, as I have suggested, to the insider-outsider relationship each had to the British imperial project: Stevenson the Scot and Conrad the Pole engaged with, yet were set apart from, the center of imperial power embodied by the upper-middle-class Attwater figure. The political outlooks of Stevenson and Conrad are not so fundamentally different, especially as they inform their writings on empire and exploitation, and so the thematic links in the two texts are, perhaps, to be expected. The reworking of the central tropes of an earlier work in a later one is not uncommon, as, for example, Jean Rhys's refiguring of *Jane Eyre* in *Wide Sargasso Sea* illustrates. The difference is, of course, that Rhys tells the tale from a different narrative standpoint: from the point of view of the Other. Conrad's adoption of the key elements of *The Ebb-Tide* is framed within the same set of cultural assumptions that inform Stevenson's writing. The concern for indigenous cultures demonstrated by Stevenson in both "The Beach of Falesá" and *The Ebb-Tide* is shared by Conrad in *Victory*, and Conrad's suspicion of unregulated European commerce parallels Stevenson's own anxieties regarding the corrosive influence of Western capitalism.

In order to examine in more detail how these links are established, several specific points require elaboration. In terms of the character parallels, Heyst enjoys a similar status to Attwater as the lone figure in control of the remote island, but he also shares Herrick's sense of the absurdity of life. Heyst is, like Herrick, detached from and disenchanted with humankind. A direct parallel with Attwater's evangelical fervor is absent. It is refigured in Heyst's skepticism, but the effect is the same: it desensitizes the character to the plight of those around him. In Heyst's case this becomes apparent in his relationship with Lena. Heyst arrives at the conclusion that appearances above everything else are what count, so he projects a hollowness and preoccupation with externals that prefigures the "modern" existential hero. In this sense Heyst resembles Herrick in his inability to commit himself to anything or to anybody: he is suspended in his own inactivity. Conrad seems, then, to refigure the "island ruler" Heyst as a composite of characteristics drawn from both Herrick and Attwater.

Heyst experiences the same sense of emasculation as that experienced by Herrick in the opening chapters of *The Ebb-Tide*, as the beachcombers face up to the realities of their failure. Like Herrick, Heyst is only able to ruminate on his unhappy condition: he can do nothing to improve his and, by extension, Lena's situation. An important link is forged here, and it connects Stevenson and Conrad to early modernist writing. The inability of Herrick in *The Ebb-Tide* and Heyst in *Victory* to make sense of the "modern" world is significant. Herrick's succession of failures is central to the "Trio" section of *The Ebb-Tide*. He has attempted much and attained little. To that extent *The Ebb-Tide* may be read as a novel of predicament.

Similarly, Axel Heyst, in the words of the critic Daphna Erdinast-Vulcan, is "the *fin-de-siècle* protagonist who realizes that appearances are all that one can ask for or have in this world; who scorns life—or rather 'what people call by that name'—for the 'fatal imperfection' of its gifts which, he believes, 'makes of them a delusion and a snare'; who has managed to 'refine everything away' by turning the earth to 'a shadow,' who has 'lost all belief in realities'" (Erdinast-Vulcan 256–57).

Heyst's dislocation from the increasingly threatening short-term future is a near mirror image of Herrick's dysfunctional response in the calaboose when he is occupied in scratching the opening phrase of Beethoven's Fifth Symphony on the wall rather than seeking a means of survival. In colonial literature of the late nineteenth century this is unusual. More commonly, Europeans are portrayed, for example by Kipling, as efficient and brave *and in control.*

As symbols of a declining empire, both Heyst and Herrick stand diametrically opposed to Second Lieutenant Bobby Wick, Kipling's hero of the short story "Only a Subaltern." Kipling's character, committed to service of queen and country in India, is brought down by cholera as he attempts to raise morale among his sick troops. The sickness in the Kipling tale, a cholera epidemic in an English regiment in the Indian army, is real and functions as the stimulus to personal gallantry. In *The Ebb-Tide,* sickness is the presence of a *malaise,* either physical or moral or both, that is linked to the corrosive effects of imperialism.

Both *The Ebb-Tide* and *Victory* emphasize imperialist exploitation: Attwater accumulates wealth through pearl fishing; Heyst is engaged in coal production. The exploitation of indigenous resources by white Europeans is fundamentally important to an appraisal of both texts. Attwater's pearl fishery is hugely wasteful and destructive, and, as a metaphor for European exploitation, it is persuasive—the detritus that accumulates on Attwater's island as a result of his economic endeavors and the consequent pollution of the environment parallel the destruction of the island population as suggested by Stevenson in the opening line of *The Ebb-Tide:* "Throughout the island world of the Pacific, scattered men of many European races and from almost every grade of society carry activity *and disseminate disease*" (*WRLS* 18:3, emphasis added). Here, then, the ailing empire is connected to both the actual and metaphorical spreading of disease by the European traders. But both Herrick and Heyst suffer from a metaphorical "dis-ease" also, having been exposed to the realities of life in the empire, and neither, unlike the other members of their oppositional trios, is capable of ignoring the excesses.

The irony that underpins Heyst's rescue of Lena from Schomberg only to land in an even more dangerous predicament neatly parallels the experience of Herrick as he escapes the calaboose to become subject to the regime on Attwater's island. Perhaps the most striking connection to *The Ebb-Tide* is the appearance of the trio on Samburan. They are driven by greed to relieve Heyst of the riches attributed to him by Schomberg. As composite types they correspond to the patterning of the trio in the Stevenson text. The self-styled Mr. Jones resembles Herrick as the fin-de-siècle *flâneur*, given to lounging and generally disporting himself as a gentleman of leisure. Ricardo has characteristics that link him to Davis, for example his desire, if not the resolve, to carry through a dangerous project. Pedro resembles the simian aspect of Huish: a primordial force held uneasily in check. The structural method by which Stevenson divides the action of *The Ebb-Tide* is paralleled in the Conrad text as an emphasis on symbolic significance in the second half of the narrative becomes apparent. The difficulties arising from the mixing of fictional modes are important in establishing that Conrad, following Stevenson, experiments with a blend of realism and symbolic representation to create something new that characterizes these early modernist texts.

Last, Stevenson and Conrad are concerned with the collapse of certainties as they become conscious of the human cost of the imperial project, and the inability to rationalize appropriate responses evidenced by Herrick and Heyst is, perhaps, symptomatic of the crisis of empire. The early modernist response to empire is not constrained within the shaping discourse of adventure romance but is rather characterized by an experimental blend of symbolic and metaphorical devices that often substitute for overt references to taboo subjects. Both Stevenson and Conrad attempt to make sense of a world in which judgment is removed from the traditional loci—the standards of consensus, societal authority, and textual authority—to individualized, phenomenological responses in which certainty is removed and meaning is located in individual experience.

Conrad's and Stevenson's Logbooks and "Paper Boats": Attempts in Textual Wreckage

NATHALIE JAËCK

$\mathcal{T}$HE SEA is evidently a privileged literary setting for both Conrad and Stevenson: it is indeed, more widely, a topos of the contemporary adventure novel from Kipling to Verne, from Defoe to Dumas, away from domestic spheres and naturalist cities, a distinctive element of exoticism and deterritorialization. Yet, in *Lord Jim* or *Treasure Island* the sea is much more than a picturesque background or even a major ingredient of adventure. Conrad and Stevenson use it above all as a formal model, as a literary horizon; the sea arouses in them a major formal inspiration and explicitly presents them both with a literary challenge, that of importing into their novels the formal characteristics of the sea. More than a subject matter then, the sea becomes literary material. It becomes, to reword a key sentence by Jacques Rivière, "the form of fiction, rather than its matter" (Rivière 69), and it does it in two major ways.[1]

The sea is first an intermediate space that adequately materializes the transitional literary position they find themselves in, in between two literary continents, realism on the port side and modernism on the starboard side; in between two closely referenced literary axiomatic systems; in a kind of neutral space that is often analyzed as the slack waters of literature. The sea thus provides them with a positive, intense natural twin for their literature. It powerfully highlights the formal possibilities of transit and demonstrates that the middle is a valid and fertile methodological space that both writers decide to explore and to settle their literature in, in between, "out of sight of land—all in the blue" (Sandison 36).

So the transitional quality of the sea legitimates to some extent Stevenson's and Conrad's literary position, but it is also explored by them as a formal ideal, as the perfect surface they would like their literature to become. Characterized by infinity, multiplicity, indeterminacy, horizontality, "neutrality," as Barthes defines the notion, the sea materializes a closely related space in which progression is essentially random, in which identities are blurred, in which what is at stake is not the static result but the dynamic course. The sea offers the methodological model of an open, blank space ordered by no paradigm, organized along no overhanging structure, a model in which topology replaces typology, a working metaphor for their "paper boats," as Conrad adequately put it.[2]

Consistently, Conrad and Stevenson stage what we could call the "becoming-sea" of their texts, a kind of textual effusion that enacts the wreckage of the realist text. I would like to argue here that, lying in ambush within the novels, apparently harmless literary stowaways eventually board the main text and totally scupper it, opening serious leaks in its integrity. The most efficient of these literary pirates are Captain Flint's logbook in *Treasure Island* and Kurtz's journal in *Heart of Darkness*, but Jim's abortive final letter or Jekyll's long-repressed manuscript play exactly the same dissolving role. These literary "Hydes" constitute the real loot of the texts more than ivory or doubloons, and are their actual literary treasures; bearing the physical mark of the sea, these sweeping subversions radicalize the principles of the main texts. They are uncompromising drafts of Conrad's and Stevenson's literary ideal: unfinished, with no beginning and no ending, neutral opaque blank surfaces to be explored in a random variety of ways.

*

It is thus first as an inspiring natural metaphor for their literary position that I would like to consider the sea. Conrad and Stevenson consciously settle in a valid space of their own between realism and modernism. They explore and exploit the literary possibilities of the transitional, undefined liminal space they historically occupy. Far from being insufficient precursors to modernism, they created a very reflexive type of literature, which actively, knowingly, and joyfully occupies "the middle," a literature that *chooses* to be transitional, that explicitly makes the choice of transit and refuses crystallization in any system.[3] Conrad and Stevenson find their literary legitimacy and originality in such exploration of neutrality, in their claim that literature should be unreferenced, contingent ground. Stevenson is explicit in a letter to Henley: "O the height and depth of novelty and worth in any art! And O that I am privileged to swim and shoulder through such Oceans! Could one get out of sight of land—all in the blue? Alas not, being anchored here in the flesh and the bonds of logic being still about us. But what a great space and a great air there is, in these small shallows where alone we venture!" (*SL* 4:252). "Out of sight of land," in transit—this is where Conrad and Stevenson elect to work, in between two tidal literary waves, in the slack, and the sea provides them with the ideal metaphor. "*Infini carrefour*" (Deleuze, *Foucault*, 104), "infinite crossroads," the sea materializes indeed the ideal in between space, the constant course, the absence of any fixed point at which to settle, the idea that the bearings are always temporary, contingent.

Both writers constantly build the sense that what the reader gets is not a final result but a transitory text in progress, a contingent version, or even a diversion from the major text. Such is indeed the narrative starting-point in *Heart of Darkness*. The *Nellie* is waiting for the turn of the tide; her story is thus suspended and will remain a blank in the text, a virtual story, while Marlow engages in a textual deviation, in a seemingly improvised, transitory alternative text. Explicitly, the text of *Heart of Darkness* is thus there to fill in a blank before the actual text begins: a literary appetizer that eventually becomes all there is. The end of the novel replays and radicalizes the same process. Kurtz's journals that Marlow protects so jealously from the literary scavengers who want to share the remainders might be the wrong journals: "I was not even sure whether he had given me the right bundle. I rather suspect he wanted me to take care of another batch of his papers which, after his death, I saw the manager examining under the lamp" (*HD* 75). The novel thus constantly challenges its own stable status. It toys with the idea that the text is a random version that might be a decoy, and that there is always a textual remainder, another pending text.

In *Lord Jim* the transitory nature of the narration is a structuring leitmotif. First, Marlow is repeatedly explicit about the fact that both the structure and the contents of the story depend on his own random meetings as well as on his own unreliable, selective memory. Had his course been different, had his memory worked in a different way, the story would have developed along other lines (*LJ* 137).[4] Marlow's narrative method is a perfect illustration of Deleuze's ideal writing, of his plea "for geography against history" (Deleuze, *Mille Plateaux*, 243), of his idea that writing is not imposing a definite form on life but exploring it randomly, opening divagating lines: "Ecrire n'a rien à voir avec signifier, mais avec arpenter, cartographier, même des contrées à venir" (Deleuze, *Mille Plateaux*, 11). Second, the frame narrator also explains that Marlow's "yarn" has been told over and over again in several circumstances ("Many times, in distant parts of the world, Marlow showed himself willing to remember Jim, to remember him at length, in detail, and audibly. Perhaps it would be after dinner. . . . 'Oh yes. I attended the enquiry,' he would say" [*LJ* 33–34]), and the reader is thus aware that the final product he is given to read is essentially contingent and transitory, that the text is only one virtual occurrence, only an accidental composition, only a temporary, unstable solution.

In *Lord Jim* Conrad achieves the transitory ideal. The text is an instance of constant variation; it is not articulated toward a final, definite meaning; it is essentially oscillating; it never reaches any fixed, steady point. Even the most solid leitmotif, "he was one of us," the most regular call of the text (*LJ* 32, 78, 93, 224), fails to anchor it. Each occurrence is a mutation from the preceding one. The repetition of the signifier becomes intensified by the difference in the signified, and even when it is the same, the text is different, its meaning is transitory. Marlow's narration constantly winks at the other directions it could have taken; it opens innumerable lines of escape. As Marlow tells Jim's story, his memory very often diverts him to a side-track, triggering a random digression, bringing the reader to the brink of a text to be: "One voyage, I recollect, I tipped him a live sheep out of the remnants of my sea-stock: not that I wanted him to do anything for me—he couldn't, you know—but because his childlike belief in the sacred right to perquisites quite touched my heart. It was so strong as to be almost beautiful. The race—the two races rather—and the climate . . . However, never mind" (*LJ* 37–38). The many dashes, the suspension marks, that even within this divagation inscribe further possibilities of escape for the text, make it essentially unstable, ready to break loose and change courses, a "free and wandering tale" (*LJ* viii) that is constantly tempted to stray, that refuses stabilization.

The bridge to *Strange Case of Dr. Jekyll and Mr. Hyde* is obvious: there as well, the final text, Jekyll's manuscript, despite Utterson's barricading efforts, is as unstable a solution as Hyde himself is. Running the constant risk of being destroyed, it is written as an urgent, incomplete, hesitating text in which the first-person narration is merely transitory, essentially oscillating: an empty shell with no stable referent. Jekyll's manuscript is another frail paper boat, and the adjective "full" in the title of the final chapter, "Henry Jekyll's Full Statement of the Case," is only an ironic decoy. The text ends in transit, in imminence; it ends on the threshold of its own ending, awaiting the final mutation from Jekyll to Hyde but awaiting also a tentative manuscript to an ever-evading authoritative version. It is thus suspended in indeterminacy.

We reach here the essential formal characteristic Conrad and Stevenson borrow from the transitory sea, namely, its indeterminacy, its neutral quality according to Roland Barthes's definition: "J'appelle Neutre tout ce qui déjoue le paradigme" (Barthes 31), "all that eludes paradigms." Barthes is clear about the fact that the neutral is in no way a lack of anything; it is on the contrary an intense activity, a divagation (Barthes 39) the aim of which is to prevent meaning from setting: "Déjouer le paradigme est une activité ardente, brûlante" (Barthes 31). As an illustration, Gilles Deleuze argues that the sea is "the ultimate smooth space," "l'espace lisse par excellence" (Deleuze, *Mille Plateaux*, 598), a natural incarnation of the ideal nomadic surface in which points are subordinated to lines, in which the interval, the course, matters more than the fixed point, in which the final destination is nothing more than a transient halt. Such a definition of the sea becomes an active working metaphor for Conrad and Stevenson, a concrete and explicit source of literary inspiration, as Conrad explains to Anièla Zagorska: writing is "cette galère—where we are navigating whilst using pens by way of oars—on an ocean of ink— pour n'arriver nulle part, hélas!" (Ambrosini, *Conrad's Fiction*, 32). Yet Conrad's expression of regret is clearly ironic here: none of his novels arrive anywhere, no more so than Stevenson's. The parallel endings of *Strange Case* and *Lord Jim* testify that there is no final destination but indeed a continuous present of the course. Jekyll's manuscript ends on a question mark: "Will Hyde die upon the scaffold? or will he find the courage to release himself at the last moment? God knows; I am careless" (*JH* 73). Compare Marlow's final paragraph: "Who knows? He is gone, inscrutable at heart" (*LJ* 416). As *Treasure Island* makes clear, what matters is thus not where the text is bound for, but "the voyage out" (*WRLS* 5:309).

In these sealike texts, then, a striking characteristic is that topology replaces typology: "la topologie des énoncés s'oppose à la typologie des propositions comme à la dialectique des phrases" (Deleuze, *Foucault*, 16). The notion of topology was developed in contemporary mathematics. The term was coined in 1883 to define a type of analysis that wanted to get away from the logic of sets and that developed the concept of adjacent, closely related spaces, the idea of neighboring progress. Indeed, Conrad and Stevenson explicitly rebelled against naturalist typification and pleaded for texts that could create neighboring zones of indifferentiation, that would constitute opaque surfaces, "all in the blue." Stevenson's famous outcry, "My two aims may be described as—1st: War to the adjective. 2nd: Death to the optic nerve" (*SL* 8:193), echoes one of Conrad's maritime definitions of literature in *Lord Jim*: "The sheet of paper portraying the depths of the sea presented a shiny surface under the light of a bull's-eye lamp lashed to a stanchion, a surface as level and smooth as the glimmering surface of the water" (*LJ* 20). Their literary manifesto unfolds in these two quotations. Conrad's sentence, saturated with the three occurrences of the word *surface* in a pleonastic formulation ("a surface as level"), highlights the fact that for him a text is literally a topology, a map in which the reader can progress by connection, horizontally. Stevenson's declaration of war against the adjective drives in the nail and anachronically reminds the reader of Barthes's analysis: "[L'adjectif] est un contre-Neutre puissant, l'anti-Neutre même, comme s'il y avait une antipathie de droit entre le neutre et l'adjectif. . . . Il colle à un nom, à un être, il 'poisse" à l'être' (Barthes 85). The enemy is the naturalist apical, irrefutable vision, the morbid, typifying adjectives that fix meaning. On Conrad's sheet of paper, even under the peering scrutiny of the overhanging lamp, the surface of the text remains "shiny" or "glimmering." It reflects only itself; just as the surface of the sea, it allows no vertical intrusion in the subject, no penetration of its secret, no assessment of its depth.

Likewise, in *Lord Jim* Marlow's disordered, achronological collection of viewpoints can only be read horizontally, with effects of reverberations, echoes, but it cannot solve the ontological opacity of the character, who remains "inscrutable at heart." In the same way, Stevenson's texts are hodological, nomadic; they do not lead to a resolution but instead to a dissolution of meaning. In *The Master of Ballantrae*, at the end of the textual course, after collecting many random and partial testimonies, Mackellar's epitaph, far from putting the text at rest, dissolves Mackellar's narrative position and constitutes a blank space of interpretation. Jekyll's manuscript ends on a succession of topological utterances with no identifiable first-person narration, while *Treasure Island* decides to leave the final word, or rather the final undialectical fragments, to the parrot, this "two-hundred-year-old deconstructionist" (Sandison 48).

The topological preference of these two authors is a dissolving influence on the key notion of the speaking subject. As Stevenson's flippant radical resort to the parrot demonstrates, there can be no final word, no ultimate truth, no destination for a text, and there can be no autonomous narrator, either. The parrot is a kind of narrative sponge, an undifferentiated origin of speech. It is a neutral subject of enunciation. To some extent "it speaks" in him. Once more, of course, the notion of indifferentiation is directly borrowed from the sea, which contests the notions of identities, of separate bodies. It seems as if the texts were experiencing a kind of "oceanic feeling," a sense of limitlessness, of formlessness and exchange, of general effusion.[5] As the limited example of the parrot shows, the subject in Conrad's and Stevenson's texts very often becomes essentially mobile, a random variable whose voice cannot be taken as the stable warrant of discourse. There is no primordial "I" that is the undisputable or even independent source of speech. In *Lord Jim*, for example, Marlow's voice incorporates in an often undifferentiated way all the voices he heard, Jim's included, so that the text is marked by a constant oscillation or hesitation of the narrative origin and becomes indeed a "damaged kaleidoscope," wherein the several fragments undergo a kind of general effusion, and the subject, or the several subjects, become variables of the utterances, deriving from them rather than being their origin. Here as well, "it speaks" in the text, speech becomes collective, neutral, and the utterances diverge autonomously in this narrative ocean. "He was one of us," the origin of which is lost, becomes a drifting iridescent echo, and the subjects of enunciation are dissolved in this collective, undifferentiated utterance. Dialectical discourse, instead of being warranted by a stable subject of enunciation, becomes what Foucault calls "un grand bourdonnement incessant et désordonné du discours." (Deleuze, *Foucault*, 62). The final narrative destination of all these texts is not a first-person narration.

The Master of Ballantrae, Strange Case, Lord Jim, and *Heart of Darkness* all stage in a spectacular way the dispossession of the omniscient third-person narrator that occupies the narrative ground in the beginning and that is forced to give way to a first-person narrator in a staged and ritual wreckage of the realist's favored narrative standpoint. But they go a step further, since their first person is not stable but extremely porous, as the floating "I" of Dr. Jekyll makes clear. The effusion of the self brings about an effusion of speech and an eventual neutralization from the grammatical point of view: "I" and "he" become interchangeable and equally inadequate; the subject of enunciation becomes a random variable, an empty grammatical wreck. In this respect I think the French lieutenant's testimony in *Lord Jim* may be read as an ironic instance of self-effusion and thus of textual oscillation. Though the French lieutenant seems to be a solid figure of speech, though Marlow cannot resist his apparently final arguments and cutting verdict—"Hang the fellow! he had pricked the bubble" (*LJ* 91)—a whole network of dissonant clues is built by Conrad to present him as an unstable, in-between hybrid. There is indeed a strong suspicion that this character, who staunchly defends the idea of a stable identity, who repudiates any wavering of the self on the grounds of honor, might be the most fluctuating, the most incoherent impostor of the novel. In between land and sea he may easily pass as a grotesque avatar of the stereotype of the drunken retired sailor, always ready to blab away with strangers in port taverns, so that the Gospel truth he dispenses to Marlow, "looking more priest-like than ever," might amount to nothing more than an alcoholic mania (*LJ* 145). "Sitting drowsily over a tumbler half-full of some dark liquid," "without raising his eyelids," he keeps "taking up his tumbler" and "putting down the glass awkwardly" throughout the interview, "[drinking] carelessly," "[draining] his glass" (*LJ* 138, 145, 146, 146, 147). Such physical dissolution is doubled by his speech, which is at times totally incoherent, precisely characterized by the erratic effusion of the two languages he mixes up, French and English. His jarring translations, his random shortcuts, result in a kind of linguistic magma, with French disguised as fake English.

Two stable axiomatic linguistic systems are then mixed up and deterritorialized to result in random fanciful, divagating utterances with no stable subject of enunciation and no stable code, either: "I have rolled my hump (*roulé ma bosse*)" or "One's courage does not come of itself (*ne vient pas tout seul*)," he first says, thus signaling the gap, formally separating the two systems through translation (*LJ* 146, 148); but then the effusion is more erratic and may go unnoticed: "This is always to be seen" (*LJ* 146), which does not mean much in English but is a word-for-word translation of "C'est encore à voir," that is, "Nothing is settled yet"; or "I have made my proofs," another effusion in English of the phrase "J'ai fait mes preuves," which should in proper English be, "I proved myself, I showed my ability." The stability of the subject is shaken further through the French lieutenant's highly symptomatic use of the neutral pronoun "one": "One is always afraid. One may talk but"; "One talks, one talks"; "One does not die of it"; "One puts up with it"; "One's courage does not come of itself"; "At my age, one knows what one is talking about" (*LJ* 146–48). Rashly borrowed from the French impersonal *on*, and lavishly spilled on the text, the neutral pronoun used in an improper way ridicules the lieutenant's attempts to define himself as a reference and results in a massive neutralization, an active dissolution of the "I" pronoun as the reliable warrant of speech—the more ironic since it contam-

inates the apparently staunchest viewpoint in the novel, Marlow's most
reliable narrative compass.

But Conrad and Stevenson go a step further: they radicalize these
processes in a kind of submarine way, through apparently negligible inner
texts that seem very transitory but that eventually board the frame texts. I
have established elsewhere the process of inner textual proliferation that
ritually takes place in these novels, the sense of textual effusion that is
present in both writers, as if they were eager to open numerous and rhizomatic lines of escape so that the text could never be a solid, coherent,
finished product but always, as we have already seen, a transitory process
with many possibilities of inner divagations, many ways out.[6] In a fascinating way, Conrad and Stevenson thus clandestinely introduce in their
novels textual stowaways that constitute intratextual prototypes, concen-
trates of Stevenson's and Conrad's ideal literary form. They are the ultimate aims of the texts, their embedded solution and literary aspiration,
and I will concentrate on a few of these uncompromising literary divagations, namely Jim's final letter, Jekyll's manuscript, and above all the two
logbooks, Kurtz's journal and Captain Flint's papers, whose form is literally conditioned by the unpredictable, irregular progress of the boats on
the river or on the sea.

These inner doubles constitute the actual loot of the text. In
Stevenson's novels Jekyll's or Mackellar's manuscripts are carefully preserved at the bottom of chests, dutifully guarded by lawyers, preciously
packed and sealed. In *Treasure Island* the bundle of papers found in the
chest totally eclipses the canvas bag that gives "the jingle of gold" (*WRLS*
5:44). In *Heart of Darkness*, ivory is only the screen treasure, and Kurtz's
journal is the true object of everyone's desire. No less than four literary
scavengers try to plunder the remnants of Kurtz's journals: "A clean-
shaved man with an official manner and wearing gold-rimmed spectacles
called on me one day and made inquiries, at first circuitous, afterwards
suavely pressing, about what he was pleased to denominate certain 'documents.' I was not surprised because I had had two rows with the Manager
on the subject out there. I had refused to give up the smallest scrap out of
that package, and I took the same attitude with the spectacled man" (*HD*

71). He manages to go away with a meager mutilated report: "I offered him the report on the 'Suppression of Savage Customs,' with the post-script torn off" (*HD* 71). Then one of Kurtz's cousins tries his luck and does not leave empty-handed either, "bearing off some family letters and memoranda without importance" (*HD* 72). Eventually, a journalist gets another fragment: "[I] forthwith handed him the famous Report for publication if he thought fit. He glanced through it hurriedly, mumbling all the time, judging 'it would do,' and took himself off with this plunder. Thus, I was left at last with a slim packet of letters and the girl's portrait" (*HD* 72).

At the end of the process, two elements are clear. First, Kurtz's journal constitutes the actual stake of the novel, just as its fellow literary stow-aways do, and it is an experimental, ever-evading center. Indeed, Marlow explains that he is not sure he was given the right bundle of papers: "I rather suspect he wanted me to take care of another batch of his papers which after his death I saw the Manager examining under the lamp" (*HD* 75). What the episode of the papers thus forcefully demonstrates, in a final twist of deconstruction, is that a text is never a finished product but always a transitory version, always a fake, always a manipulation, and that there is always an irreducible remainder, always a way out. Even more radically than *Heart of Darkness* as a whole, this inner concentrate is characterized by an accelerated tendency to dissemination, by a process of emptying, of escape, of wandering—by a total loss of integrity. Kurtz's journal, both loot and efficient pirate, empties *Heart of Darkness* and leaves it with mere scraps, with fragments that might even be fake, with a transitory impostor that annuls the frame text: "'We have lost the first of the ebb,' said the Director, suddenly" (*HD* 77). The story of the *Nellie* will forever remain suspended, and the ideal of the open, transitory text will have been fulfilled.

Second, the vocabulary used by Conrad is so close to that used by Stevenson for Captain Flint's papers that one wonders whether the scene is not a tribute to *Treasure Island*. In both cases "a bundle of papers" is found; in both cases it is "tied" along with a flat, panoramic surface, a map in the first case, a photograph in the second; in both cases they are referred to as "scraps" and "fragments." Without a doubt this hidden log-book is the other pirate of the text, Long John Silver's literary twin. The literary solution it proposes scuppers Jim's text and radically accelerates some of its more daring tendencies.[7] The topological juxtaposition of Jim's and the doctor's viewpoints, both written in an unassuming first person, constituted a celebrated effort at horizontality and expressed a wish to flatten the text, seen "from the level of a nursery-fender." Stevenson also deliberately inserted blank spaces in his textual map, unreferenced, escaping fragments left for the reader to explore, as when Jim swoons on the boat and leaves the text missing.

Yet Captain Flint's logbook is much more uncompromising; here horizontal progression is the only way through the closely related fragments that compose it and that can be read randomly. The course through the logbook is utterly free; there is no beginning and no ending, none of the traditional narrative compasses: no chronology, no identifiable system of narration or narrative structure, an extreme opacity of language ("I can't make head or tail of this" [*WRLS* 5:61]), and above all no referenced narrator that could act as guide. All the utterances are fragmentary—"No more rum," "Off Palm Key he got itt"—the reader progresses by mere random juxtaposition, and the neutral forms colonize the text ("I could not help wondering who it was that had 'got itt,' and what 'itt' was that he got" [*WRLS* 5:60]), with no narrative beacon at all. Stevenson both pays a tribute and totally pirates the venerable literary form of the diary here. Instead of an ever-present first-person narrator, Stevenson proposes a nonperson, a neutral absentee that rules nothing, that merely records some transitory traces of his journey. The captain opens irreducible leaks in the archetypal form of the diary, literally wrecks and floods the text. What the reader finally gets is indeed a successful logbook, a crossbreed that situates itself within the literary tradition but bears the mark of the sea as well, an open, infinite, shapeless, nomadic textual surface that has actually been transformed into a maritime map: "the name of a place would be added, as 'Offe Caraccas'; or a mere entry of latitude and longitude, as '62° 17′ 20″, 19° 2′ 40″'" (*WRLS* 5:61). The final section, "a few bearings of places noted in the blank leaves towards the end," pushes to a theoretical extreme Stevenson's literary ideal and thus uses as a very efficient textual weapon the sea metaphor (*WRLS* 5:62). Dissolution and eventual neutrality of the viewpoint and dispersion and effusion of the text lead to the eventual creation of a maritime opaque surface containing only directions, opening random ways.

Jim's abortive final letter, his "sheet of greyish foolscap," just like the blank pages of the logbook, contains a spatial bearing, "The Fort, Patusan," but no temporal situation; topology once more replaces ordering chronology, "no date, as you observe," and consists of two "lines of escape," two intensive dimensions that lead nowhere before the paper is flooded by spluttering ink (*LJ* 340). "'An awful thing has happened,' he wrote before he flung the pen down for the first time; look at the ink blot resembling the head of an arrow under these words. After a while he had tried again, scrawling heavily, as if with a hand of lead, another line. 'I must now at once . . .' The pen had spluttered, and that time he gave it up" (*LJ* 340–41). Thus dissolved in ink, Jim's final letter, just like the captain's blank textual map, places the reader where the authors wanted him to be, in a Deleuzian intensive middle space. Conrad and Stevenson give substance to transit and find their literary power there, "all in the blue."

NOTES

1. "L'aventure, c'est la forme de l'œuvre plutôt que sa matière" is the exact quotation.

2. In the preface to *The Shorter Tales of Joseph Conrad* (ed. Richard Curle [New York: Doubleday, 1926]), when Conrad feels he has to return to the early years "when I launched my first paper boats in the days of my literary childhood," p. 143.

3. In *Robert Louis Stevenson and the Appearance of Modernism*, Sandison seems to apologize for the fact that Stevenson does not come up with an achieved version of modernism: "But Stevenson is not writing in the age of Roland Barthes. He is a transitional writer" (Sandison 312). And yet we could say that Stevenson's taste for transit is precisely what makes him very Barthesian, neutral in the sense Barthes and Blanchot developed, away from paradigms, systems, and ideospheres.

4. "I was informed a long time after by an elderly French lieutenant whom I came across one afternoon in Sydney, by the merest chance . . ." (*LJ* 84).

5. A phrase that Freud borrowed from Romain Rolland and that he develops in *Civilisation and Its Discontents*.

6. I developed the point in a paper at the Gargnano Conference on Stevenson, 2002: "Stevenson's Stories as Textual Greenhouses."

7. For a full analysis of Captain Flint's papers, see Nathalie Jaëck, "*Treasure Island*: l'immanence de la surface contre l'aplomb naturaliste," in Conférence on "La Surface," Chambéry, 2003.

Telling Them Apart:
Conrad, Stevenson, and the Social Double

LAURENCE DAVIES

$\mathcal{F}$ICTIONAL DOUBLES wear a literary history on their backs. They come to us dressed for a life of eeriness, transgression, solitude. Greater and greater loneliness is their fate; three's a crowd for them, and two no decent company at all. Their abandoned behavior leads them into ever narrower, dirtier byways. Their wicked deeds align them with their fellows in uncanniness: ghosts, vampires, werewolves, ghouls, and necromancers. In short, the most familiar version of literary doubling derives from the romantic doppelgänger as manifested in the work of Poe and Hoffman. If the Gothic clothes fall off or split a seam, the wearer stands exposed as a divided self of another kind, the psychoanalytic subject. Freudian, Kleinian, or Lacanian, this subject is notably more secular but no less isolated. Thus, in the other familiar reading of the double he (only occasionally she) is an antisocial character in an asocial narrative.[1] Yet one may propose alternative histories. My plan is to read the *Strange Case of Dr. Jekyll and Mr. Hyde* and "The Secret Sharer" against other varieties of doubling that became increasingly visible, or rather legible, in the late nineteenth and early twentieth centuries. Although often dramatizing the isolation of the central character (or pair of characters), these varieties have a louder and more persistent communal resonance than their predecessors. This chapter is a contribution toward a history of social doubling and the social double.[2]

One kind of social doubling revives the ancient tropes of twinning, mirroring, turning upside down, and changing places.[3] Two examples just slightly earlier than the *Strange Case* are Mark Twain's *The Prince and the Pauper* (1881) and F. Anstey Guthrie's *Vice Versa; or, a Lesson to Fathers* (1882, revised 1883 and 1894).[4] In Twain's story, a boy from the London slums changes identities for a while with his look-alike the prince, to the great moral benefit of the latter. *Vice Versa* transposes a father and a son; the father, magicked into his son's body, must now endure the various tyrannies and privations of a junior boarding school while the son works his way through the father's stock of port and choice cigars. Primarily, these books were meant for youngsters, but another Twain novel, *Pudd'nhead Wilson* (1894), with its account of racial and sexual privilege, is as clearly meant for adults. In these works and many more, the author turns at least one daunting hierarchy upside down so that the previously fortunate one is now the wretch: pauper becomes prince; son, father; legally black, legally white. The reversals in all these plots depend upon the physical resemblance of two characters, but in others, whole classes of people change place, as in Mary Cholmondeley's *Votes for Men!* (1909), a play about men's struggle to win the vote in a matriarchal Britain.

Another kind of social doubling retains the idea of the fissured self while to some degree acknowledging the fissures in the body politic. Such are the stories that dwell on lives chosen and not chosen. Again, there are obvious antecedents, such as Dickens's *A Christmas Carol* (1843) or, less obviously, Poe's "William Wilson," but from the 1880s onward, as lives increasingly become careers and the notion of a common culture is undermined by a warren of subcultures, paths not taken and paths walked in tandem feature more prominently on the map of human lives.[5] Such is the case in Wilde's *The Picture of Dorian Gray*, with its glimpses of clandestine London and its emphasis on a will bounded by the human rather than the divine; such is the case with James's stories of artistic life. In some examples, such as "The Jolly Corner," the spectral is an essential—

and unforgettable—narrative force, but even here the personal haunting and the individual psychomachia are set against and in a sense depend upon public history and geography in a way quite alien to, say, "William Wilson."

A purist might object that the first of these types of social doubling has no business in a history of doubles precisely because it deals with a split in society, not the individual. An objection to the second type might be that unless the narrative is uncanny, it is nothing; by exaggerating, perhaps tendentiously, a minor aspect of the major theme, a social reading strips the eerie (and/or psychoanalytic) glamour from the topos, leaving us only with a banal rationalism. Why, in other words, confuse a venerable comic motif like mistaken identity with the story of a haunted and conflicted soul? Two answers come to mind. First, much depends upon the treatment; if the resolution of the mistaken identity involves some awareness of affinity, of shared humanity or inhumanity beyond the artifice of disguise or the vagaries of misprision, then the recognition is akin to doubling.[6] Second, one cannot answer purity with more purity. The narrative of doubling is an impure genre dependent on a curious arithmetic.

What, then, is the arithmetic of literary doubling? To pose this question might seem like the trivial pursuit of the dazzlingly clear, the equivalent of asking how many beans make five or, in this case, what do we get by adding one and one? Yet even if we find the obvious answer satisfying, are we talking about two wholes or two halves, mirroring effects or fissures? It is at least hypothetically possible, moreover, for a literary double to go on doubling. That certainly happens whenever critical discourse prescribes itself a set of new lenses: in its career so far, *Strange Case of Dr. Jekyll and Mr. Hyde* has been viewed at its simplest as a confrontation between good and evil, or id and superego, or straight and gay, or criminal and law-abiding. Is *confrontation between* the right phrase, however? Or might we substitute *collusion between*, or *recognition of the power or existence of*, or *forcible separation of*? By arranging these pairs more symmetrically (for example, aligning *good* with *superego* and *evil* with *id*) or more hierarchically (for example, by making the legal subordinate to the metaphysical), or by admitting their sheer diversity, could we see a larger and more complex picture? As the presence of so many *or*s suggests, the history of reading works such as *Strange Case* and "The Secret Sharer" is as much a narrative of the One and the Many as it is of the One and the Dual.

The texts themselves acknowledge multiplicities. Here is a passage from "The Secret Sharer." The unnamed mate and the unnamed captain are talking, just after Captain Archbold returns to the *Sephora*:

> "I suppose he did drown himself. Don't you, sir?"
>
> "I don't suppose anything.'
>
> "You have no doubt in the matter, sir?"
>
> "None whatever."
>
> I left him suddenly. I felt I was producing a bad impression, but with my double down there it was most trying to be on deck. And it was almost as trying to be below. Altogether a nerve-trying situation. But on the whole I felt less torn in two when I was with him. (*TLS* 123)

The naming of Leggatt as the narrator's double is explicit, seemingly unequivocal. On the grounds that a title such as "*The Secret Sharer . . .* may be *too* enigmatic," Conrad suggested "*The Secret Self* or *The Other Self*" (*CL* 4:300). The relation between these selves, however, is not antagonistic—it is not even agonistic. Apropos of the captain and his hidden guest, the words that come to mind are recognition, kinship, affinity, bonding. Yes, there is difference as well, an acknowledgement of disparate fates, but not a contest, not a struggle for mastery. The presence of this complementary double does all the same drive two rifts: one between the captain and his crew, and the other in the captain's own psyche. In effect, we have one double but three dualities. For "The Secret Sharer," at least, literary doubling resembles mitosis: cells divide, then each divided cell divides—division cannot stop at two. Writing to another Pole, Conrad saw the process in himself: "Both at sea and on land my point of view is English, from which the conclusion should not be drawn that I have become an Englishman. That is not the case Homo duplex has in my case more than one meaning. You will understand" (*CL* 3:89). It is not only in Conrad's case that "homo duplex" describes a multiple rather than dual condition. In its trajectory from the Hermetics to Buffon, on to Balzac and

Baudelaire, and then to Conrad, the phrase rarely holds a steady state for long.[7]

What we might call the received or folk version of the Jekyll and Hyde story offers something more straightforward than these Conradesque ambivalences. In the vivid light of popular tradition, this is a tale that gives us a good, old-fashioned Manichaean conflict, a battle to the death 'twixt pure virtue and damnation.[8] Yet one of the fascinations of Dr. Jekyll's "Statement" is that he himself complicates the idea of doubling, and who can speak of doubling more authoritatively than Henry Jekyll? According to him, human nature remains uncompromisingly dual, but, true to his scientific training, he will not insist upon this being the final answer to the mystery. Further research, he speculates, may show us to be not doubles but multiples. The relevant passage comes from the lengthy first paragraph of Dr. Jekyll's "Full Statement of the Case":

> With every day, and from both sides of my intelligence, the moral and the intellectual, I thus drew steadily nearer to that truth, by whose partial discovery I have been doomed to such a dreadful shipwreck: that man is not truly one, but truly two. I say two, because the state of my own knowledge does not pass beyond that point. Others will follow, others will outstrip me on the same lines; and I hazard the guess that man will be ultimately known for a mere polity of multifarious, incongruous and independent denizens. (*JH* 59)

In just a couple of sentences, Jekyll leaps from black and white to polychrome, from the Manichaean (or, to oversimplify, Victorian) to what looks remarkably like some version of the modernist or postmodernist subject, from the dualistic to the rhizomatic.

Doubles enter the world through ruptures in the everyday. Enjoying a few minutes of intimate seclusion with his first command, the captain sees Leggatt as a "A headless corpse!" floating in a "greenish cadaverous glow" (*TLS* 97); arriving at his school, an ancient and labyrinthine "palace of enchantment," William Wilson meets another new boy identical in name, age, and physiognomy (Poe 340); stepping out of his careful and regular habits as a civil servant, Golyadkin encounters his double and tormentor-to-be one foul night in Saint Petersburg. Burning with spiritual pride and toxic theology, Robert Wringhim meets Gil-Martin, his dia- bolical nemesis, on the very day that Wringhim has been freshly dedi- cated to the Lord in the full assurance of salvation. In these examples from Conrad, Poe, Dostoevsky, and Hogg, an uncanny timing is at work. A crisis provokes an apparent coincidence, not desired but in some way brought upon the victim. Although he is ignorant of the consequences, Jekyll's transformation, on the other hand, is willed: "[L]ate one accursed night, I compounded the elements, watched them boil and smoke together in the glass, and when the ebullition had subsided, with a strong glow of courage, drank off the potion" (*JH* 60). Willed or not, all these are cases where an initial singularity, physical, metaphysical, or both, leads not to a newly defined stability but to an unpredictable, often astonishing series of mutations.

Why dwell on such instabilities? Whether in psychoanalytic or in theological terms, doesn't the power of literary doubling inhere in its vir- tually tragic sense of consequence? Yes and no, the emphasis falling on the *and*. Doppelgänger stories from Hoffman and before to Conrad and after lend themselves easily—and productively—to strong interpreta- tions, schematics in high contrast, narratives of light and dark, id and superego, salvation and damnation. Yet these readings base themselves on an ever-shifting array of tropes. Consider some of the forms doubles take: the reflection, the distortion, the projection, the guardian angel or the guardian demon, the buried self, the resurrected self, the ghost, the split, the twin, the mask, the scapegoat, the inversion. When we come up against satirical absurdity in Dostoevsky or satirical grotesquerie in Hogg, even the affinity with tragedy is not a reliable interpretative guide. If it is a genre at all, rather than a tangle of motifs, literary doubling works through dualistic metaphors, but metonymically it is plural, and its name is legion.

My purpose in venturing through this taxonomic thicket is not so much to play the now traditional game of hacking binaries to pieces as to emphasize both the protean resourcefulness (or, more formally, the onto- logical instability) and the social resonance of doubles narratives. In Wai

Chee Dimock's formulation, it is resonance, the capacity to be heard in manifold voices over time and space, that rescues texts from being either captive to the conditions of their origin or sent naked into an ahistorical limbo (Dimock 1060–71). Thus, trying to hear a work as a writer's contemporaries might have heard it is an antiquarian or confining project only when it cramps the work's interpretative openness instead of expanding it. The same principle operates with interpretations that take the work entirely outside the bounds of time, either as an illustration of some enduring critical problem or as a statement on some supposedly timeless (and placeless) topic such as the battle of Good and Evil or the nature of human nature. An alertness to resonance thickens and enriches the text whether we think of its readers as the author's contemporaries or as ours. Readers rather than reader: implied, recuperated, hypothecated, or observed readership is better understood not as a unanimity but as a collective whose membership and patterns of thinking are volatile and whose identity often consists of an agreement to disagree. It is a resonance of our own cultural world that "timeless" or "placeless" readings of the *Strange Case* and "The Secret Sharer" are much less common than they were a quarter of a century ago, but they are still often read as though there were no shift in the function or perception of doubling during the nineteenth century.

Truth to tell, the story of doubling has always had some element of social reference. Like his predecessor Gogol, who worked with kinds of the fantastic other than the double, Dostoevsky mocks the pretensions and rigidities of Saint Petersburg life. Writing twenty years before the Disruption, the great rift in the Scottish Kirk, Hogg shows a keen sense that the fiercely argumentative politics of church and state in late-seventeenth-century Scotland are not so very different from those of the early nineteenth century. In other words, although the social double became more prominent by the end of the nineteenth century, he or she was not quite a novelty. What changes is the understanding of what constitutes transgression, which becomes increasingly an offense not so much against divine prescription as against human community and, at the same time, increasingly a challenge to those supposedly fixed human categories, such as those of class and gender, that religion has been known to sanction, even naturalize. With the gradual secularization of society came a more and more powerful sense that social barriers are unjust but often permeable.

The work of Stevenson and Conrad originated in a time of epistemic shifts. One of the period's master figures is the voluntary or involuntary swapping of roles, visible for example in Shaw's womanly men and manly women, Wilde's inverted epigrams, and Wells's transformation of Londoners under siege into Tasmanians; another figure, closely related, is the recognition of a shared humanity across the fences of gender, sexuality, class, or race, as in Marlow's moments of solidarity with the BaKongo or Quatermain's with Umslopagaas.

The discontent with present-day civilization as contemporary writers knew it also welled up in stories of the supernatural, for example those by Edith Nesbit or the Benson brothers, and an association with the uncanny has often enough distracted attention from what else is going on in fictions of doubling. As the following short discussion of exemplary works may illustrate, the uncanny infuses a good few, but not all, narratives of social doubling, including those by Stevenson and Conrad; sometimes, as in some of James's stories, it suffuses every corner of them. In its evocation of dream states, unsettling resemblances, bizarre mysteries, fateful chances, sudden metamorphoses, and quasi-paranoid experiences, doubling tends toward the weird in all its senses (fateful, bizarre, uncanny) because its narrative patterns threaten the comforting but fragile mental structures of the everyday with the suggestion that to think rationally is to think parochially

By the late nineteenth century, however, the metaphysics of the doubling story had undergone a change. *The Picture of Dorian Gray* turns on a kind of symbolic magic; the encounter with the other self in "The Jolly Corner" is ghostly. Nevertheless, the language of these quasi-supernatural stories is seldom theological; the doctrines of salvation or damnation, Heaven or Hell, have faded, replaced by a fervent agnosticism. What remains of traditional belief consists in those echoes of hymns, prayer books, and the Bible in King James's version that persisted long after writers such as Stevenson and Wilde had turned away from orthodoxy. What remains of traditional morality, especially in Twain, is the do-as-you-would-be-done-by ethic of the Golden Rule.[9] If Hell has survived in these end-of-the-century works, it is in places like the slums of London,

Dublin, Edinburgh, and New York—or in the deceptive folksiness of the American South.

In Twain's *The Prince and the Pauper*, Offal Court is a sixteenth-century equivalent of Five Points and Seven Dials. One of its inhabitants, Tom, switches places with Edward, heir to the throne of England, who is his body-double. Like *A Connecticut Yankee*, this novel looks on its surface like a glorification of the modern and the American at the expense of the British and archaic, but, as usual with Twain, his preoccupation with human rights and his critique of arrogance and servitude also proffered a mirror to American readers, especially those who felt that wealth or breeding made them more virtuous, more important, more entitled than their poor compatriots.

Doubling fascinated Twain, who tried to write a satirical novel about Siamese twins and spoke of Stevenson's *Strange Case* even on his deathbed (Kaplan 340–41). With *Pudd'nhead Wilson* (1894), Twain returned to his attack on hierarchy and inherited privilege, this time in a racial context. In Missouri during the 1830s a slave nurse switches the identities of two white-skinned babies, one her own child, and thus legally black and a slave, the other destined by birth to be a slave owner. Scholars argue vigorously about the racial politics of this novel (see Gilman and Robinson, especially the essays by James M. Cox, Eric J. Sundquist, and Forrest G. Robinson), but in most readings nurture trumps nature: the African American brought up as white becomes a braggart, bully, thief, and ultimately murderer because, as soon as he can walk and talk, he learns to exploit his racial privileges. With this kind of social doubling, human destiny is neither entirely autonomous nor entirely innate. So much depends on how the world perceives the social subject—as white or black, lord or commoner, man or woman. *Pudd'nhead Wilson* ridicules the whole notion of the Southern gentleman, not least by making the pseudogentlemanly villain a cross-dresser. In an age of biology inflected by racial prejudice and social Darwinist ideas of fitness, Twain asserts the Shakespearean principle that a dog's obeyed in office.

Other kinds of social doubling dwell on lives chosen or not chosen. That is the case with Oscar Wilde; that is the case, especially, with James's stories. "The Private Life" (*Atlantic Monthly*, 1892) shows a pair of artist figures: one is Lord Mellifont, a painter who, whenever out of the public eye, simply ceases to exist; the other, Clare Vawdrey, a writer who delights his friends with amiable banalities even as his other self sits writing in the dark, magnificently.

James's most powerful version of the dual career is "The Jolly Corner" (*English Review*, 1908). Here the hidden life is the life not taken. Coming back to New York after an absence of thirty-three years in Europe, Spencer Brydon first stalks and then recoils from the specter of the self that stayed behind in the old family home, becoming over time completely alien to the self that left. The homely, or New York, self has become unreachably and dangerously alien to the expatriated one. The narrative point of view is that of the cosmopolitan self, the more domesticated of the two. The threat to sanity and stability, the threat of the alien, comes from the self that has thrived amid the rough and tumble of Manhattan. Biographical readings of "The Jolly Corner" link it with James's brief return to the United States (as recorded in *The American Scene* of 1906), which confirmed him in the conviction of choices well made while stirring up nostalgia for the long-gone past, guilt about what he had put behind him, and a fearful sense of what he might have become had he remained. These feelings of loss, guilt, and dread lend themselves well to readings that bring out the narrative's uncanniness; this is one of James's ghostly stories and, in that guise, a favorite in anthologies. It is also, however, a social narrative, a tale of communal rupture and upheaval: a response to the hustling world of the late Gilded Age in which aggression came, more than ever, to be the mark of promise and the index of success, and the genteel came to envision themselves as an endangered species—endangered not only by militant commercialism but by, as it seemed to them, promiscuous immigration.

Not every late Victorian or Edwardian story of an identity mistaken or a life not chosen fits comfortably into a pattern of social doubling. A novel like Conrad's *An Outcast of the Islands* is a narrative of dammed-up lives but not of serious confrontation with any free-flowing alternatives; after his disgrace, Willems yearns for his former life and has fantasies about a new one with Aïssa but is too ineffectual to pursue any goal with sufficient

passion. "The Secret Sharer," however, vigorously engages with both diver-
gent histories and concealed identities. Written in ten days in order to pay
the hospital expenses of Nellie Lyons, the silent sufferer of the Conrads'
life—a maid who had concealed the painful evidence of a gastric ulcer lest
she disturb the household—"The Secret Sharer" dates from 1909 (*CL*
4:297–98). This was little more than a year after "The Jolly Corner" was
serialized in the *English Review* alongside episodes of Conrad's "Some
Reminiscences," the memoir later known as *A Personal Record*.

For readers versed in the tradition of the doppelgänger, much in "The
Secret Sharer" sounds familiar: the eerie and grotesque first sighting,
Leggatt's disruption of the captain's life, their physical resemblance, the
captain's having to keep up appearances, the awareness of being watched,
the stabs of paranoia, the existential Angst: "[A]n irresistible doubt of his
bodily existence flitted through my mind. Can it be, I asked myself, that
he is not visible to other eyes than mine? It was like being haunted.... I
think I had come creeping quietly as near insanity as any man who has
not actually gone over the border" (*TLS* 130). But that last qualification is
significant. He has not "actually gone over the border." In giving Captain
Archbold such an extended tour of the ship, he has gambled, like Poe's
murderers, against the chance of discovery; by taking his vessel so close to
Koh-ring, he has not so much flirted with danger as grabbed it by the
neck. Yet he has not gone mad, he has not been arrested for aiding and
abetting, he has not run his ship aground. Instead, he has enabled the
escape of a fugitive guilty at the least of manslaughter. Whereas James's
Spencer Brydon can only perceive his other self as a violent and terrifying
stranger, Conrad's narrator does the opposite: he sees a violent stranger as
his other self.

Artistically speaking, "The Secret Sharer" resembles *Hamlet* more
than it does "William Wilson" or the *Private Memoirs and Confessions*. It
is, in other words, a moral conundrum rather than a moral fable. Hogg no
more endorses fratricide than Poe endorses card-sharping. In Conrad's
story, the frequent allusions to Cain's being "[d]riven off the face of the
earth" (*TLS* 132) remind us that *fratricide* is one way to describe the
killing of the mutinous sailor.[10] Yet for the killer's host, any theoretical
notion of the brotherhood of man carries far less weight than the need to
enforce discipline in a frightful storm: "And I knew well enough the pes-

tiferous danger of such a character where there are no means of legal repression. And I knew well enough also that my double there was no homicidal ruffian. I did not think of asking him for details, and he told me the story roughly in brusque, disconnected sentences. I needed no more. I saw it all going on as though I were myself inside that other sleeping-suit" (*TLS* 102). This is one of Conrad's not-quite-reliable narrators, who needs to be assessed even as he assesses, speaking the prose equivalent of a dramatic monologue. In two ways his is a case of social doubling. Rather than across the lines of race, or class, or gender, he has recognized his other across the line of criminality, seeing not a homicidal ruffian but a man much like himself. Both of them are officers and gentlemen, linked by shared assumptions about caste. By this recognition he has also had to contemplate an alternative life for himself, one in which he too has crossed the line. Yet this understanding of Leggatt and the ties that bind the captain to him do not extend to humanity at large. Although he speaks slightingly of landsmen, he is not exactly complimentary about other sailors. He saves his concern for Leggatt, who, with his talk of further mayhem, makes a hard case even harder to defend.

In spite of Leggatt's rebarbative affect, his protector risks not only his crew, who do not seem to matter much to him, but also his ship, his precious first command. The anonymous master exemplifies two nautical truisms: that a captain's life is lonely and that a captain is loyal to his ship even to the point of sinking with her. As so often with truisms in Conrad, they are tested almost to destruction. There is something excessive in the narrator's devotion to his ship, something excessive in his devotion to Leggatt, as if this fugitive officer mattered more than the complement of his own vessel. In making these claims I am not thinking exclusively, or even first, of erotics, even though the triangle of captain, ship, and runaway is very queer indeed. The strongest force working here is doubling's ability to run away with itself, to extend, instead of narrowing, the possibilities. Consider the ending, for example, which is itself a double one. Whatever the symbolic power of the celebrated floating hat in the penultimate paragraph (and that hat draws interpretations as a honeycomb draws bears), the last paragraph veers in a new direction. The captain has become free to love his ship, if not his crew; the fugitive, free to swim away: "the secret sharer of my cabin and of my thoughts, as though he were my second self, had lowered himself into the water to take his punishment: a free man, a proud swimmer striking out for a new destiny" (*TLS* 143).

Is this famous sentence an opening up or a closing in? The crisis gone by, the captain's risky gamble has paid off, his unsettling double has consigned himself to the deeps, and the final cadence resolves into a major chord. Yet certain questions can't be silenced. Why should freedom be a punishment? What in the world, not least the world of late-nineteenth-century Southeast Asia, with its intricate definitions of identity and its many hierarchies both indigenous and colonial, might this freedom mean? What echo is there here of that schoolmasterly exhortation, "Take your punishment like a man"? Is there, all the same, a note of envy in the captain's voice? Is staying with the ship his punishment, a confinement in a floating prison, or is it too some kind of liberation? In what sense could his experience with Leggatt make him a better captain? Or a worse? Has he expelled something of himself or learned to recognize, even to accept it? Are we to see the ground between good and bad behavior as slippery indeed, contingent upon circumstance and necessity? "The Secret Sharer" embeds an inner narrative that is Leggatt's confession, but is the entire story a confession? Or, in the old sense of a reasonable presentation of one's life, an apologia? Could it be, perhaps, another case of haunting, a metaphorical one, the story of a story that will not go away? Like many of Conrad's more powerful stories, "The Secret Sharer" attracts interpretations and repels them with equal verve. It particularly resists that most traditional mode of reading doubly, the allegorical.

Short by Conrad's standards, the small scale of "The Secret Sharer" enabled him to write a crossover story, one readable for plot and for perplexity. It offers secrets, drama, and suspense; it also offers entry to a disorienting moral labyrinth. Instead of providing a map, "social" readings further complicate it, because even as the affinities crisscross, the hairline fractures in society multiply, setting one kind of solidarity, the loyalty of shipmates or the claims of humanity in general, against another, the bonds among ship's officers and gentlemen. This, one might say, more categorically than suits an anticategorical reading, is doubling in a modernist style.

*

As a potential source of social doubling, the *Strange Case* looks unpromising. The tradition of reading the book allegorically, often in terms of cosmic hostilities between damned and saved, dates back to its inception. Although seeing distant perspectives of multiplicity, Jekyll insists that, in his own experience "man is truly two" (*JH* 59). His anguish and Hyde's refusal to be anguished are intensely private. Jekyll's studies in "transcendental medicine" (*JH* 56) evoke the even stranger cases that attract J. Sheridan Le Fanu's Dr. Heselius, not least "Green Tea," the story of an Anglican clergyman who, by excessive consumption of a drink then valued more for its visionary than its antioxidant powers, is terrified by a familiar spirit in the form of a monkey. Above all, the *Strange Case* is a chamber of Biblical echoes. In Stevenson's day and ours, other stories such as "Markheim," "Olalla," "Thrawn Janet," and "The Body Snatcher" confirm the impression that he had a gift for metaphysical drama. Listening for social resonances in these circumstances seems like discussing *The Pilgrim's Progress* as a lesson in physical geography.

Whatever the furtive and brutal pleasures of Mr. Hyde's existence, no one could envy the experience of his better half, whose "Full Statement" embodies the metaphysical drama at its highest: "A change had come over me. It was no longer the fear of the gallows, it was the horror of being Hyde that racked me . . . I became, in my own person, a creature eaten up and emptied by fever, languidly weak both in body and mind, and solely occupied by one thought: the horror of my other self " (*JH* 71). With language of this sort, there seems little room for ambiguity and none at all for the social double. Nevertheless, Jekyll's written confession is framed by the experiences and qualified by the judgment of two men who take their professions seriously. What they judge is a case of professional deformation, a career gone bad. Dr. Jekyll is a remarkably gifted man, and, hypocrisies and moral inconsistencies notwithstanding, he has belonged to a community—two communities, closely linked, the one of professionals, the other of public benefactors, both these communities firmly ensconced in upper-middle-class London.[11] He has made a life, and a distinguished one. Whatever his conduct by night, he has "laboured, in the eye of day, at the furtherance of knowledge or the relief of sorrow and suffering" (*JH* 58). He has had much to lose, and what he throws away is society's loss as well as his.

Like other stories of social doubling, then, this narrative articulates a notion of the common good, that good that Hyde so crassly wants to smirch and Jekyll wants to disassemble in the interests of a higher virtue: "If each, I told myself, could but be housed in separate identities ... the unjust might go his way, delivered from the aspirations and remorse of his more upright twin; and the just could walk steadfastly and securely on his upward path, doing the good things in which he found his pleasure" (*JH* 59). Blind to the power of his desires, Jekyll thus positions himself as a dangerously naïve reformer eager to inflict yet another rift on an already fragmentary world. If there were no such fragmentation, the philanthropy of Jekyll and his friends would be superfluous.

Both plot and setting depend on this fragmentation, on the distinction between prosperous and poor districts, on the existence of areas such as Soho with a reputation for louche conduct. Every evocation of Hyde's bad behavior has its place in metropolitan geography, as does every evocation of social misery. The juxtapositions of poverty and wealth, the proximity of vice to virtue, are not just symbolic; they reflect the conjunctions of an actual city.[12] R. B. Cunninghame Graham's claim that "there is a Darker Continent east of Temple Bar than that through which the Zambezi, the Congo, and the Limpopo flow" expresses a common perception that the most miserable parts of London stood well apart from the comfortable ones, but that was not entirely the case (Watts and Davies 112). Clare Market, for example, a stench-ridden slum hostile to strangers, lay between Drury Lane and Lincolns Inn Fields, bounded by legal, theatrical, and commercial London. Accounts of such districts by campaigning journalists such as George R. Sims imply that such scenes are alien to polite readers, yet the abundance of such exposés in the eighties surely meant that most of Stevenson's readers would be aware, if only from their reading, of the scandalous closeness of poverty and wealth.[13]

These are not the only permeable categories. Beneath the agonistic language of polarity so audible in this novella are whispers of other business, hints that barriers of all sorts are leaking. Hyde's clothes do not fit him as a gentleman's should; he lives in a shady part of town; he lacks the restraint expected of his status and his nationality; he slinks back and forth across the class divide; he weeps, he minces; his sexuality and gender are ambiguous, his habits detestable and brutish.[14] On top of all these failings he's an overreacher and a fraud, an aging man in disguise, seeking out a youngster's thrills. This, with the right admixture of chemicals, is what might become of the most respectable of persons. We are back to social standing as contingency.

Other allusions hook the narrative to the fears, anxieties, and scandals of the late Victorian world.[15] Although much of Hyde's behavior (and Jekyll's too) is left to the reader's imagination, we have some clues. There is the matter of the migratory cheval glass, for example, an item of furniture associated with brothels and houses of assignation, but the most resonant allusions are those to various kinds of violence. Hyde runs over a child like a juggernaut and fatally batters an M.P. Certainly these are diabolical activities, but they also imply a whole inventory of social panics. Street attacks with cudgel or garrotte were acknowledged dangers of Victorian life.[16] Hyde's Irish name and his "ape-like" tricks summon up both racist caricatures of Fenians in the press and the distressing idea that biological evolution might go into reverse. The allusion to the juggernaut brings in another colonial trope: the cruelties of Hinduism.[17] Above all, brutality toward a child evokes Victorian contradictions. Throughout the period there were serious efforts to protect children, such as the legislation restricting child labor, the founding of the Great Ormond Street Hospital and of Doctor Barnardo's Homes—not to mention the cult of childhood innocence in fiction. Yet the episode of the juggernaut serves as a reminder of how much more there was to do regarding brutal school and prison discipline and those implicitly reproachful figures of the child prostitute, the crossing sweeper, and the mudlark.[18] *Strange Case* is by no means a plea for social reform, but it frames its iniquities in a recognizably quotidian milieu.

For the most part, Stevenson does not specify the precise nature of Jekyll's debaucheries or Hyde's iniquities. Like the contents of the pit in Poe's story, or the full nature of Mr. Kurtz's midnight ceremonies, they are left to the imagination. Before patronizing this imprecision as nineteenth-century prissiness—something we would never find in Clive Barker or Stephen King—we might remember Baudelaire's invocation of readerly complicity: "Hypocrite lecteur, mon semblable, mon frère." Leaving the schedule of abominations vague enhances the possibilities while delivering one or another of them more securely to the reader's door.

I have suggested that the implied reader of this text might be one attuned to social as well as metaphysical abominations. An emphasis on the social has certainly characterized the response of current academic readers, but in a culture suspicious of the transcendental, that is not surprising. What about Stevenson himself? It is tempting to propose a model of overlapping literary consciousness, one in which the worldly and the transcendental coexist. Stevenson, in his own antidoctrinal way, remained a believer, as the Vailima prayers attest. He had been steeped in a vigorous Scottish tradition of the uncanny—indeed a double tradition, Celtic and Germanic. All the same, he read widely in contemporary British, American, and French fiction and was well aware of literary and scientific trends. Although professing to a strong dislike, he knew his Zola, for example, and would have read enough of the Rougon-Macquart cycle to encounter Zola's streak of genetic determinism and his demonstration that two closely related families could head in opposite moral directions, one toward distinction, the other toward destruction.[19] In Stevenson's day, a new mode of horror fiction was emerging, one that might be called materialist Gothic—a mode whose horrors have more to do with physics, biology, and psychology than with metaphysics or theology. Here was a way of looking at the world, indeed the universe, that appealed to Maupassant, later, Wells, and even to some extent Stevenson. Jekyll "thought of Hyde, for all his energy, as of something not only hellish but inorganic. This was the shocking thing; that the slime of the pit seemed to utter cries and voices" (*JH* 72). To judge by the popularity of this phobic mode in the work of Stevenson's successors, such as Machen, E. F. Benson, M. P. Shiel, and Bernard Capes, a substantial section of the reading public must have shared this dual consciousness, a kind of existential nausea before its time.

The secularization of horror accompanied the secularization of the double. Max Weber's concept of *Entzauberung* (usually translated as "disenchantment") speaks to what was going on—a process, as he saw it, that had started centuries before but accelerated toward the end of the nineteenth century, a time when "there are no mysterious incalculable forces that come into play, but rather . . . one can, in principle, master all things by calculation. This means that the world is disenchanted. One need no longer have recourse to magical means in order to master or implore the spirits, as did the savage, for whom such mysterious powers existed."[20] Although secular horror and secular doubling may appear in the same narrative, and speak to the same phobias, especially sexual and racial ones, their proximate causes differ a little. The horror comes from a sense of life's blind energy in a universe bereft of religious certainty; in doubling, the missing certainty is social. This social uncertainty is deeply involved with uncertainties of identity, with a fracturing of social rules that leads to a fracturing of the sense of self—and vice versa—the one encouraging the other.[21] Yet the social bones may be reset and grow, perhaps more healthily than they did before. If there is a master narrative of secular horror, it concerns preserving sanity by turning one's back upon the unspeakable. The narrative of social doubling is one of recognition, of seeing what is wrong with human beings and their world but not abandoning them.

Nevertheless, texts such as "The Secret Sharer," "The Jolly Corner," *Strange Case*, or *The Picture of Dorian Gray* do not reflect social relationships in the manner of realist novels. Not even *Pudd'nhead Wilson* does that. Dependent on wild invention, their plots do not belong in the everyday world. In every case but Twain's, they bear a powerful scent of the uncanny, and all of them, Twain's novel included, are too extravagant in conception to obey the sober constraints of realism. Thanks to doubling's ability to keep on multiplying, the extraordinary and the social coexist; the resonance of one intensifies the resonance of the other. The aura of uncanniness flickers around what whole societies as much as individuals have repressed. Social doubling is both a way of holding the mirror up to nature and a departure from the naturalistic. Doubling remains a wonder, and in that sense the magicking persists.

NOTES

1. Asocial to the extent that, as well as claiming the center of the stage, the double blocks the view of any social mise-en-scène: this is not to deny the presence in the narrative of well-meaning friends or the expectation that the reader will make some kind of moral judgement.

2. To claim any originality in noticing that Stevenson's novella and Conrad's long

short story lend themselves to "social" readings would, of course, be shameless. What I try to offer here is a wider literary context for these readings.

3. As, for example, in *Twelfth Night* or the tale of Pwyll, Prince of Dyfed, in the *Mabinogion*.

4. Wildly popular in its day and frequently reprinted, *Vice Versa* is now seldom read, but *The Prince and the Pauper* has lasted well enough to be turned into a Classic Comics and adapted as *The Princess and the Pauper* (2004), a full-length animated film starring Barbie in both roles. My thanks go to Lorna Modeen for drawing my attention to the latter.

5. Any story of doubling is likely to make us ask about the life not lived, but in "William Wilson," the other self—"my admonisher at Eton . . . the destroyer of my honor at Oxford" (Poe 354)—follows not so much an alternative life of virtue as a career of foiling his original.

6. Anthony Hope's best-selling *The Prisoner of Zenda* (1894) is one example of a novel in which confused identity is a plot device (and something of a joke) rather than a cause of wonder, anguish, or reflection.

7. See *Asclepius* VII, Buffon's *Histoire naturelle*, vol. 4; the Preface to Balzac's *Cousine Bette*; and Baudelaire's essay "La Double Vie."

8. In his review of the 1941 film, Jorge Luis Borges observed that Dr. Jekyll had become a paragon of virtue, whereas in the original he "is morally duplicitous in the way all men are double" (Borges 259–60).

9. The phrase "Do-as-you-would-be-done-by" comes from Charles Kingsley's *The Water Babies* (1863), one of the earlier children's tales of role reversal, far more committed to Christian doctrine than its successors.

10. Conrad had taken a hostile line toward fraternity ten years earlier. One cannot, of course, assume consistency, and the occasion was an invitation to attend a meeting with a group of Russian dissidents whom Conrad loathed for their nationality. Nevertheless, his comments further complicate readings of "The Secret Sharer": "What does fraternity mean. Abnegation-self-sacrifice means something. Fraternity means nothing unless the Cain-Abel business" (to R. B. Cunninghame Graham, February 8, 1899, *CL* 2:159). Are the Captain's actions, then, a form of abnegation?

11. He is unlikely to have followed two careers, as some commentators suggest (*JH* 87n13); his doctorates in law are the traditional marks of approbation for the public figure renowned outside his professional sphere.

12. For a fuller discussion, see Dryden, *The Modern Gothic*, 102–8.

13. George R. Sims describes Clare Market at length in chapter 13 of *How the Poor Live* (London: Chatto & Windus, 1883), compiled from articles written for the *Pictorial World*. Descriptions of this district also appear in *Dickens's Dictionary of London* (1879) and the Reverend D. Rice-Jones's *In the Slums* (1884). The nine volumes of Charles Booth's *Life and Labour of the People in London* (1889–92) show a similarly patchy social geography in areas such as Pimlico and Soho.

14. See Doane and Hodges 63–74. Karl Miller characterizes the eighties and nineties as "an age tormented by genders . . . by the 'he' and 'she' of it all" (Miller 209).

15. Much recent scholarship is devoted to such issues. See, for example, Dryden, *The Modern Gothic*, 76–88, on Jack the Ripper, atavism, and the dread of crowds.

16. And, with mandatory flogging for garrotters, provoked a violent legal response.

17. As portrayed in Meadows Taylor's *Confessions of a Thug* (1839) or the juggernaut scene in C. R. Maturin's *Melmoth the Wanderer* (1820).

18. Often read as a metaphor for sexual abuse, the episode of the trampled girl can also be taken more broadly. It signifies a cruel disregard for anybody standing in the way of any manifestation of the overweening self, whether in the form of sexual desire, greed, the joy of power, or self-importance.

19. For Stevenson on Zola, see *SL* 5 311.

20. Max Weber, *Essays in Sociology*, trans. and ed. H. H. Gerth and C. Wright Mills (London: Routledge, 1948), 139; this passage comes from "Wissenschaft als Beruf," first published in 1919. The word *disenchantment* is potentially confusing; by *Entzauberung* Weber meant not so much disillusionment as a growing lack of sympathy with the magical.

21. In this context, the most suggestive discussion of doubling as a problem of the social self is an essay by the anthropologist George E. Marcus: "Doubled, Divided, and Crossed Selves in *Pudd'nhead Wilson*," in Gilman and Robinson 190–210. Marcus's argument presents late-nineteenth-century stories of identity exchange as a critique of "hegemonic autonomous individualism" (193).

PART TWO

Stevenson and Conrad: Writing the Empire

Allegories of the Self and of Empire: A Study of Stevenson's *Strange Case of Dr. Jekyll and Mr. Hyde* and of Conrad's "A Smile of Fortune"

ANDREA WHITE

*I*T IS TEMPTING to read Conrad's "A Smile of Fortune" as another island tale in the tradition of *The Tempest, Robinson Crusoe,* or *The Coral Island,* especially in the story's initial paragraphs, which narrate our approach to "a fertile and beautiful island of the tropics," the "Pearl of the Ocean." But if we do so, our horizon of expectation soon suffers a shock, for this story tells of belatedness and darkness, of self-deception and self-destruction. Its complex doublings and withheld mysteries are illuminated less by an island story such as *Treasure Island* than by *Strange Case of Dr. Jekyll and Mr. Hyde.* Not only does the Victorian story famously concern the decentering of the sovereign self in a way that anticipates "A Smile of Fortune," but it also depicts 1880s London as a dark place, an image replicated and intensified in Conrad's story. London, as "home" to both fictions' protagonists, is represented as indeed one of the dark places of the earth, a metropolitan center with fissures and repressions of its own that interestingly repeats the figure of the decentered self common to both Stevenson's and Conrad's texts.

In the nineteenth-century European imaginary, the capital cities served to justify the imperial incursion as beacons of light and oases of civilization, although increasingly late Victorian and early-twentieth-century cities—London especially—were represented as places of urban pathology, poverty, crime, and violence. This essay will demonstrate how the instability and violence that served imperial discourse in the construction of the colonized Other are used in these fictions to characterize the metropolitan center itself. It will explore the implications of the basic Derridean tenet that only through acts of exclusion are the structures that organize our experience—empire and its mercantile service, the metropolitan center, and subjectivity itself—made possible. As both fictions make clear, that which is excluded is repressed, and what is repressed returns.

The subversion of the coherent, sovereign self has long been a concern of modern and postmodern fiction. While the split Lacanian subject had not yet been theorized, in Victorian fiction the heterogeneous self was represented by images of the double; this sense of inherent human duality was a staple feature of gothic literature that attempted "to channel unconscious thought processes into literary creativity" (Daly 14–15). Contemporary reviews of *Jekyll and Hyde* noticed its gothic features and particularly this phenomenon of the double self; one critic described it as "a marvelous exploration into the recesses of human nature" (*JH* 95).[1] Another saw Jekyll as "a feeble but kindly nature steadily and inevitably succumbing to the sinister influences of besetting weaknesses," reading the tale as a parable of the dark double within (*JH* 98). Andrew Lang noticed Stevenson's unique use of the double: it did not "take the form of a personified conscience, the doppelgänger of the sinner," but was a "'separable self'" with a vitality all its own (Lang in *JH* 93). Most missed Stevenson's point in a letter to John Paul Bocock, that Jekyll's own repression of his Hydelike qualities turned him into something truly diabolical (*JH* 86). Jekyll initiates his experiment believing his selves are separable but comes to understand that identity is neither static nor unified but composed of multiple, antithetical selves. Glimpsing himself as Hyde in the mirror, Jekyll "was conscious of no repugnance, rather of a leap of welcome. This, too, was myself," "my familiar that I called out of my own soul" (*JH* 51, 53). The jubilation is Lacanian: his "leap of welcome" uncannily anticipates the mirror stage, but he can no more give a full account of himself than can any other Lacanian subject.

Jekyll likens this discovery to a "dreadful shipwreck." Having to accept as his own qualities he tried to assign to another, "foreign" subjectivity devastates his sense of self as though a violent act of nature had occurred. He goes on to acknowledge, in a prescient anticipation of the postmodern understanding of the subject's heterogeneity, his own "composite nature": "I say two because the state of my own knowledge does not pass beyond that point. Others will follow, others will outstrip me on the same lines; and I hazard the guess that man will be ultimately known for a mere polity of multifarious, incongruous and independent denizens." His scientific quest to separate "these polar twins" is doomed, not because our selves are so disparate, but because they are so imbricated one with another (*JH* 59).

Edwin Eigner argues that popular interpretations of the novel are facile and often off the mark. Stage and screen dramatizations largely had it wrong (Eigner 148). Jekyll initiates the experiment not to put an end to his pleasure-loving self but to sequester it so that the daytime, self-denying, respectable professional could work dutifully, undisturbed. Jekyll cannot reconcile his pleasure-seeking self with the one that desires "the respect of the wise and good" because of "the high views" he had set before himself, views shaped largely by Calvinist discourses—of a particularly virulent Lowland strain (*JH* 58; Eigner 155). Stevenson objected to Bocock that the American dramatization misrepresented Hyde as an evil sexual predator:

> The harm is in Jekyll, because he was a hypocrite—not because he was fond of women . . . ; but people are so filled full of folly and inverted lust, that they can think of nothing but sexuality. The Hypocrite let out the beast Hyde—who is no more sexual than another, but who is the essence of cruelty and malice, and selfishness and cowardice: and these are the diabolic in man. (*JH* 86)

After "conceal[ing] [his] pleasures" for twenty years, Jekyll hopes to end his "profound duplicity" and to obviate "the curse of mankind that these incongruous faggots were thus bound together"; instead, he comes to understand the futility of his experiment, for he "was radically both." Hyde was "knit to him, closer than a wife, closer than an eye" (*JH* 58–59, 72).

The attempt to "dissociate" these disparate elements is doomed to failure, and Hyde's transformation from indifferent hedonist to vicious murderer results from the artificially induced separation. Jekyll grants Hyde an independent existence, but the more he insists upon separate selves, the more stripped of his "balancing instincts," the more destructive Hyde becomes and the more intent Jekyll is on renouncing him (Eigner 158–59). Jekyll learns that "the doom and burthen of our life is bound forever on man's shoulders, and when the attempt is made to cast it off, it but returns upon us with more unfamiliar and more awful pressure" (*JH* 60). The price of "the awful pressure" of self-alienation is self-destruction.

Unlike most earlier treatments of literary doubles, Stevenson's novella enacts the drama of alternating personalities that cannot coexist. Traditional doubles, like Poe's "William Wilson," Harry Geduld argues, coexist with the hero as physically distinct individuals; here we have two selves "alternately claiming ownership of Jekyll's soul—prepared to fight to the death for domination" (Geduld 11). Stevenson thus complicates notions of self-alienation and destabilizes assumptions of a coherent sovereign self. Peter Garrett's analysis of the tangle of Hyde's many voices, and the confusion of personal pronouns, argues against any simple duality at work here. Rather, "[o]n the level of character and action as well as on the level of narration, we find neither unity nor purified duality but a complex weave of voices that resists conservative simplification" (in Veeder and Hirsch 67). Ronald Thomas argues for the literary subversiveness of Hyde, for while "the gothic tradition's doppelganger tale" informed the novel, Hyde is more subversive; it is a "schizo-text" prefiguring much modern and postmodern fiction (in Veeder and Hirsch 83). Here, the subject admits rather than denies his darker self. *Jekyll and Hyde* argues that the war between the members should desist and our multifaceted selves be reconciled, or at least accepted.

Freud's description of our psychic life as a "civil war" was anticipated by Stevenson's "war among the members," informed by "the Calvinist view that man must maintain a constant struggle with evil" (Calder in *JH* 127). This martial imagery is echoed as Jekyll sees identity as a "fortress," suggesting his perceived vulnerability to threats and the need for vigilance against armed assailants, that which has been repressed and excluded in the identity's construction. The assault Jekyll fears is Hyde's, but the enemy is already within the gates, turning Jekyll's fortress as a respectable, temperate gentleman into a "city of refuge," where as a "cavern" serves the "mountain bandit," he will be safe from the scaffold, fear of which helps "buttress and guard" his "better impulses" (*JH* 66). Jekyll's fortress of respectability becomes Hyde's city of refuge.

Hyde's presence results from Jekyll's repression, caused by Victorian hypocrisy in terms interestingly anticipating Derrida's "hospitality." For Derrida the term "city of refuge" is central to those who "cultivate an ethic of hospitality":

> Insofar as it has to do with the *ethos*, that is, the residence, one's home, the familiar place of dwelling, inasmuch as it is a manner of being there, the manner in which we relate to ourselves and to others, to others as our own or as foreigners, *ethics is hospitality*. . . . But for this very reason, and because being at home with oneself (. . . the other within oneself) supposes a reception or inclusion of the other which one seeks to appropriate, control, and master . . . there is a history of hospitality, an always possible perversion of *the* law of hospitality. . . . (Derrida 16–17)

Thus Jekyll's inhospitality to foreign "selves" is shown to be futile. This attempted inhospitality has dangerous repercussions, for, as Katherine Linehan argues, Stevenson is concerned to demonstrate the "damage that can be done to the psyche by the sexual puritanism rampant in Victorian society," a hypocritical puritanism that demands the destructive self-alienation his story thematizes (*JH* 210).

That Derrida places his discussion in an essay on twenty-first-century issues of immigration and political refugees does not lessen its usefulness. Jekyll is looked to—by Hyde—as a city of refuge and as "a mountain cavern." Sequestering his disparate selves, an inhospitality to the Other par excellence, brings Hyde forth. The refuge that Hyde, described appropriately as "troglodytic" by Utterson, seeks shelter in is Soho, a district crowded with poor immigrants (*JH* 18). Stevenson anticipates Freud's understanding of the repressed as a "foreign body" to suggest a parallel between Hyde, the cave-dweller/foreigner, and the alien populations of Soho and the East End who threatened the respectable West End. Like subjectivity itself, the city, and especially London's East End, is populated by elements foreign to such Cavendish Square sensibilities as Utterson's. As studies of the novel's gothic elements show, London is a shadowy place usually seen at night, gas-lit and often sinister. Enfield's narrative emphasizes the ominous silence of the nocturnal city in the moments preceding the "hellish" sight of Hyde's trampling of the girl and those London streets "that made you long for the sight of a policeman" (*JH* 9). As Linda Dryden observes, *Jekyll and Hyde* belongs to an emerging modern Gothic, a form that no longer demands "a geographically remote and historically distanced narrative" but that relocates "the scene of horror to the metropolitan streets" (Dryden, *The Modern Gothic*, 32).

Those streets witnessed scenes of violent crime, notably the 1888 Ripper murders. Dryden notices the geographical duality that these crimes and their representations pointed up, demonstrating how London was described in the press of the day as "a city divided along its East/West axis" (Dryden, *The Modern Gothic*, 36). *Jekyll and Hyde's* drama of antagonistic selves is played out in London's geography; from his home in fashionable Cavendish Square Utterson leads Inspector Newcomen, after Carew's murder, to Hyde's Soho apartment, "the dismal quarter . . . with its muddy ways, and slatternly passengers . . . like a district of some city in a nightmare, a dingy street, a gin palace, a low French eating house, a shop, ragged children huddled in doorways, and many women of many different nationalities passing out—to have a morning glass" (*JH* 26). The newspapers reported West Enders' anxieties about demos, and fears of its incursions mounted with the apprehension of the proximity of crime, poverty, and the alien Other. The West End, Judith Walkowitz notes, had become the "bureaucratic center of empire" and scene of Jubilee celebrations in 1887 and 1897, while "another kind of imperial spectacle was staged in the East End where the docks and railway termini were international entrepots for succeeding waves of immigrants" who competed with the indigenous laboring poor (Walkowitz 26). Increased migration from the countryside, as well as foreign immigration, exacerbated the already critical condition of London, hard hit by economic depression. Gareth Stedman Jones argues that social critics of the day, such as William Booth, theorized that the problems of unemployment, urban poverty, and unrest could be alleviated by state-aided colonization and the prohibition of "alien immigration" (Stedman Jones 310).

That *Jekyll and Hyde* is Stevenson's allegory of our double, even heterogeneous selves was recognized from its beginning. Dryden, Walkowitz and others read it as an allegory of empire, of England and its racial, cultural, and economic other flooding the metropolis and changing the face of Old England. The press characterized London as a divided city of contrasts, and this opposition "took on imperial and racial dimensions, as the two parts of London imaginatively doubled for England and its Empire" (Walkowitz 26). As a critique of empire, the novella deconstructs that sturdy line between them and us, between the metropolis and the colonial margin, and the myth that energized and redeemed the imperial intrusions, the supremacy of European civilization. Europe, particularly London, is depicted in Stevenson's tale, as well as in Conrad's, as dark indeed, and hardly the place of light that could underwrite and justify military invasions, impositions of culture and religion, and the merchant service traveling on the Queen's imperial business.

In the 1880s London was the largest city in the world, metropolitan center of the greatest empire of the day, but contemporary crime reports and fictional representations make us aware of its dark side. Two years after the publication of *Jekyll and Hyde,* and days after its dramatic adaptation starring Richard Mansfield, the first of Jack the Ripper's mutilation murders occurred on August 31, 1888. So connected in the popular mind was the self's dark double, as rendered in Stevenson's novella and the city's own dark self, that newspapers reported that "[h]igh on the list of suspects was Richard Mansfield" (Geduld 6).

Such newspapers surface in Alfred Jacobus's store, in Conrad's "A Smile of Fortune," and form his daughter's reading. Police reports and accounts of crimes convince Alice that European cities—London and Paris—are "sinks of abomination' (*TLS* 60). How far from such a dark, fog-enshrouded city as London seems the Pearl of the Indian Ocean, Mauritius. First published in *London Magazine* in 1911 and a year later in *'Twixt Land and Sea,* "A Smile of Fortune" also uncovers the difference that constitutes identity, and although the epiphany belongs more to the reader than to the self-deceived young narrator, his fortress of identity certainly suffers a shock, a kind of shipwreck indeed. Like Jekyll, this young captain refuses to acknowledge a vital part of his complex self in order to realize his ideal self-conception. But readers of Conrad recognize the perils of idealism gone awry: the captain undergoes a transformation in hopes of living up to those ideals. It could be argued that Stevenson's novel, set at approximately the same time in the 1880s, is this story's unconscious. Alice is as much "the ghost of some old sin" as Utterson supposes Hyde to be (*JH* 19). As Jekyll pays for "the capers of his youth," so Conrad's narrator thinks of Alfred Jacobus upon hearing his story of abandoning wife and child to follow a circus woman (*JH* 11). It is hard to believe this taciturn man capable of such aberrance, but Alice is a disruptive trace of that history. Though she is present physically, she is as Other to this island and its inhabitants as Hyde was to Jekyll and as the captain's submerged selves are, for he also suffers when the fortress of identity is assailed. That identity so carefully constructed as a humane, helpful fellow—he has saved his mate's life at some expense to himself—given to philosophical musings gives way under the pressures of an antithetical, powerfully shaping discourse, the imperial business he must tend to, and becomes someone unrecognizable to himself. He achieves commercial success, but at a price. His behavior, increasingly unaccountable to himself, his callous insensitivity, and his violent outbursts constitute for him a kind of shipwreck, costing his command, career, and self-respect. At story's end, dropping his letter of resignation to his owners into the mailbox felt to him as if he "were plucking out [his] very heart" (*TLS* 77).

In pursuit of "high views," Jekyll consigns Hyde to the nethermost regions of his psyche, of London, and of the night. What Conrad's story confronts us with is much less schematized, less conscious, and more complex. Publicly, Conrad disparaged Stevenson, bristling at comparisons that seemed reductive. Yet Stevenson prepared the way for Conrad in important respects. As *Almayer's Folly* seems to take up where *Ebb-Tide* and "Beach of Falesá" leave off, so "A Smile of Fortune" continues and complicates notions central to *Jekyll and Hyde*. Like its predecessor, Conrad's story has been viewed as Gothic. Monika Elbert reads it "as

Conrad's Gothic sea story": the Conradian "struggle for self-possession . . . is shifted to the setting of an old slumbering house in the countryside," whose dark passages, occupied by the sullen, passive Alice and her "old sorceress" of an aunt, the narrator comes to haunt against his conscious will (Elbert 2, 140). Arguing for some degree of subjective coherence amid the shaping influences of ideology, Beth Sharon Ash writes, "[P]eople create themselves to some extent from the basic material of their given conditions." If the subject is an effect of signifying practices, it also enjoys some autonomy. Her illuminating analysis of Conrad as a "psychosocial subject" examines the shaping influence of the three most powerful—yet often conflicting—discourses of his day: organicism, imperialism, and politics (Ash 5). The captain's ideal self-conception is built in great part upon repressions and exclusions shaped by his "given conditions," the desires of imperial trade. That the protagonist is a "composite being" becomes clear to us but remains an unrealized source of repressed consternation to the captain, increasingly acting out of a self he hardly recognizes. Readers of Conrad know that subjectivity is always a dangerous site, its unknowableness likened in *Lord Jim* to the constant threat of ambush by a snake. And yet some self-shaping is also apparent, for at the story's end he chooses not to return to the Pearl, asserting a self outside the discursive structures of commerce and trade.

He approaches the island with two antithetical wishes: that the sea remain unspoiled by commerce and war and that his commercial dealings on the island be successful. This attests to an impossible division, one that Conrad's captain narrators often achieve through repressing knowledge of the merchant service's commercial imperatives. It is usual in Conrad that the sea as the site of romantic adventure and of the work that redeems is kept apart from that work's purpose and driving motive—imperial commerce, the sea as a link in the commodity chain. In the midst of his reverie about the ever-nearing "Pearl," an entrancing "blue, pinnacled apparition," the captain's "horrid thoughts of business interfered with my enjoyment of an accomplished passage," for he is collecting "a cargo of sugar in the hope of the crop having been good and of the freights being high" (*TLS* 3–4). These ships—from the *Judea* to the *Nan Shan* to the *Roi des Belges*—as emblems of empire and its economies and the "pristine" Pearl exist because of each other. As Cedric Watts observes, Conrad's "maritime pastoral" worked to veil "the dependence of maritime life on the commercial activities of the city." The *Narcissus*, while imagined by the narrator as "a center of virtue" as opposed to its ugly, soulless dockland berth, would cease to exist without them: "If there were no cranes and warehouses, there would be no ship either; each is as soulless as the other" (Watts in Moore, 20). The captain's stance on deck, anticipating landfall, is a condition of his imperial trade. The fissure is immediately apparent to us, although repressed by him, turning away wistfully from that complicating impasse and reasserting his identity as a good employee making the most of his opportunities for his owners' sakes: "I was anxious for success and I wished, too, to do justice to the flattering latitude of my owners' instructions" (*TLS* 4). But he is as much a stranger to himself as is the captain/narrator of the volume's next story, "The Secret Sharer," which Karl Miller describes as "a crucial text of the dualistic tradition." For Miller "Conrad's dualistic practice" entails "a contest between suicide and survival, defection and community" (Miller 225–26). "A Smile of Fortune" thus doubles "The Secret Sharer"; it too charts a passage from youth to maturity and concerns a young man's "opening life," but the latter story externalizes the double; the complexity of the heterogeneous self is narrated. He arrives a kind of self-deceived, untested innocent, desirous of the success of his task, one he believes, Marlow-like, constitutes "real work." To learn the commercial ropes of this place and do the best job possible seems a way of realizing his ideal self-conception. The events reveal a composite self fissured by desire and uncertainty; commercial fortune smiles upon the captain, but at great personal cost. The moment his ship moors, a complication arises. His company's recommended agent comes aboard, and he wonders at this surprising early morning visit. It unsettles his already shaky confidence in his business abilities, and he suspects black magic, "some dark design against my commercial innocence" (*TLS* 6). Was it, he wondered, "white magic or some black trick of trade?" (*TLS* 7). The breakfast strikes him dumb by its splendor: "I had expected the usual sea-breakfast, whereas I beheld spread before us a veritable feast of shore provisions: eggs, sausages, butter which plainly did not come from a Danish tin, cutlets, and even a dish of potatoes" (TLS 8). The potatoes, he is grieved to learn, didn't come from the island, as he at first assumed, but had been imported.

The agent's actions and talk of trade unsettle him. The entertainment feels more like an assault, a kind of preemptive strike on his inexperience. That and his misrecognition of his host's identity—it was the "wrong" Jacobus, Albert, not the recommended Ernest—as well as of the commercial realities of potato dealing throw him off balance. He blames "these commercial interests" for

> spoiling the finest life under the sun. Why must the sea be used for trade—and for war as well? Why kill and traffic on it, pursuing selfish aims of no great importance after all? It would have been so much nicer just to sail about with here and there a port and a bit of land to stretch one's legs on, buy a few books and get a change of cooking for a while. (*TLS* 6)

He turns away from the threatening commercial work and evokes the purity of the sea, positing a self congruent with the disinterested traveler rather than the calculating, savvy merchant. Of course, these two are each other's necessary condition, knit as closely as Jekyll is to Hyde. But the captain can only conclude that, "living in a world more or less homicidal and desperately mercantile," it was his duty "to make the best of its opportunities" (*TLS* 11). He appears to put away that other self, to leave it behind in his cabin out of sight along with his more philosophical musings.

In his preface to *The Nigger of the "Narcissus"* Conrad speaks of our dividedness and of the artist's appeal "to our less obvious capacities: to that part of our nature which, because of the warlike conditions of existence, is necessarily kept out of sight within the more resisting and hard qualities—like the vulnerable body within a steel armor. . . . The artist appeals . . . to that in us which is a gift and not an acquisition—and, therefore, more permanently enduring" (*NNTOS* viii).

Conrad speaks of that part of us that has been given, not acquired—an unworldly secret sharer to be hidden and protected. The captain's less obvious capacities—the gift for appreciating disinterested beauty, for fragrant gardens, and for unacquisitive adventure—must be kept hidden. This captain would not think of expressing these thoughts to Burns, his mate, burying them under his "more resisting and hard qualities" and trying to forget them as intruders inappropriate to his commercial tasks. The commercial force makes itself felt from the moment the lavish breakfast he thought a gift turned out to be—as was everything else here—"in the way of business" (*TLS* 32). This early instance of the reigning ethic on the Pearl puts him on guard and strengthens those "resisting and hard qualities." Again, the consequences of self-division are calamitous, engendering such self-deception that he is prey to feelings he does not suspect and cannot anticipate.

That this unease and lack of self-knowledge is gendered reveals a further dimension of the identity's instability. Marianne deKoven speaks of "Lord" Jim's failure to accept his feminized self as his undoing (DeKoven 155ff). This captain also sees that self as a sensibility that needs to be left behind, the "vulnerable body within a steel armor" (*NNTOS*). Even his status as ship's master is threatened by Jacobus's present of garden flowers: "I assured him . . . that he made me feel as if I were a pretty girl, and that he mustn't be surprised if I blushed" (*TLS* 22–23). Is he being courted or bought? What is the difference when "everything here is bound to be in the way of business," as Jacobus assures him (*TLS* 32)? The confusion between wooing and buying is rendered and felt in terms that will later sound and reverberate when the proposed transaction between the captain and Alice's father makes the commerce of courtship explicit. Alice, too, is an object of exchange; the flowers come from that enchanted garden where Alice was isolated, a garden marking the social boundaries of Mauritius her father has transgressed. Jacobus had listened once to that vulnerable self—one motivated by eros rather than the logos of a society bound by the economics of patriarchal imperialism. He too has learned to put away that self and subject himself to the commercial symbolic where kisses are paid for. The captain will realize that the flowers are no gift, but an enticement into that garden in a commercial transaction that turns him into someone unrecognizable to himself and the garden into a prison "buried in darkness" (*TLS* 79).

We understand from his response that it is that vulnerable, "feminized" "part of our nature" the captain feels we must repress or keep "out of sight." Neither women nor the feminized self belong on a ship or in a sailor's life, he firmly believes; they deflect one from purposeful engagement with meaningful work, and the narrative chronicles the gradual

relinquishing or repression of those "less obvious capacities." By the end
of the first section the captain can still remark scornfully on the hypocritical and transient sympathy his consignees' clerk momentarily works up
for an infant's death and imminent burial and his speedy shift to business
matters, "dismissing from this workaday world the baby" (*TLS* 14). But at
the funeral he notices with self-contempt that he has no tears, only
thoughts "of commercial success, of ships, freights, business" (*TLS* 16).
He has "become outrageous to [himself]," ashamed of his callousness as
he listens to the burial rites in critical detachment (*TLS* 16). He remarks
on "the instability of his emotions," for he has not quite lost all vestiges of
sympathetic imagination (*TLS* 15). Along with commercial preoccupations, some sense of shame lingers, for "indeed I had preserved some
decency of feeling. It was only the mind which—" (*TLS* 16). He acknowledges the split between decency and his commercially preoccupied mind
with a dash, a gap he cannot account for. Moments later "accosted" by the
Hilda's captain, who laments—ludicrously, our narrator feels—the loss of
his ship's figurehead, he suggests that "surely another figure of a woman
could be procured" (*TLS* 18–20). The grieving man reprimands him for
his insensitivity, comparing him to Jacobus—who had made a similar
suggestion—that "figurehead-procuring bloodsucker" (*TLS* 20). This
wooden figurehead suggests his own increasing wooden unfeeling-
ness and prefigures the resentment he will feel at Alice's treatment of
him. His violent outburst of passion seems to be precipitated by her
"movement to pass by me as if I were a wooden post or a piece of furniture" (*TLS* 69).

By the time he meets Alice, that vulnerable, sympathetic self is so successfully repressed that his callous response to her surprises even himself.
He has not just put the other self away, but the hardened self has taken
over. He continues to return to Jacobus's house, where he feels exquisite
moral discomfort and exclaims, "How weak, irrational, and absurd we
are! How easily carried away whenever our awakened imagination brings
us the irritating hint of a desire." and proceeds, several days later, to fall
upon Alice aggressively with violent kisses (*TLS* 56). He has become an
unfeeling voyeur and predator, and as though forgetting his regret that
the world was "more or less homicidal and desperately mercantile," he
dismisses Alice's suspicions about the evils of European cities she has

gleaned from newspapers. He insists that "these horrors on which she fed her imagination" were "like a few drops of blood in the ocean," "lost in the mass of orderly life" (*TLS* 61). But despite his protests, these newspaper accounts effectively tether this far-flung trading outpost to the great metropolitan centers that had always posited order and unity. This imperial outpost is not Other to London; both are the products of the same "desperately mercantile" force. As the normative male European self, constructed in colonial discourse vis-à-vis racial and gendered others, is here unraveled, so is the imperial metropolis as the civilized center; both are revealed as fictions. The captain is blind to this decentering, dismissing these reports as extravagant, such an interpellated subject of Her Majesty's Merchant Service has he become. These newspapers, having recently "reported a series of crimes in the East End of London"—Jack the Ripper? Sir Danvers Carew?—effectively decenter London as the civilized site that justifies its colonization of the margins (*TLS* 61). On the basis of this reading, Alice

> had formed for herself a notion of the civilised world as a scene of murders, abductions, burglaries, stabbing affrays, and every sort of desperate violence. England and France, Paris and London . . . appeared to her sinks of abomination, reeking with blood, in contrast to her little island where petty larceny was about the standard of current misdeeds, with, now and then, some more pronounced crime—and that only among the imported coolie labourers on sugar estates or the Negroes of the town. But in Europe these things were being done daily by a wicked population of white men among whom . . . the wandering sailors, the associates of her precious papa, were the lowest of the low. (*TLS* 60–61)

These accounts confirm the captain's regretful admission that the world was "more or less homicidal and desperately mercantile" and make clear that "civilized" white men and sailors in Her Majesty's Merchant Service are the perpetrators. Dryden's assertion that "identity and the city are crucial to the imaginative representation of the divided self in *Jekyll and Hyde*" is provocative here, for it is at this point as a product of that urban wickedness that the captain's self-alienation is complete (Dryden, *The*

Modern Gothic, 17). Against his promise to himself, to Jacobus, and to Alice, he does indeed trade. The self that carefully distinguished between company's business and cutting his own deals evaporates, and another self acts in a way that surprises him, so unknown to himself is he. "I don't go in for trade" (*TLS* 31), and then he does and makes a fortune in the bargain. His dream that night—of a girl being buried under a pile of gold—records his own loss and exposes the greed that results from and feeds capitalism's imperial desire.

Historically, imperial desire—first Dutch, then French, and then English—designated Mauritius as a sugar production colony entailing rapid importation of African and Madagascaran slaves. The island's sweetness is tempered by traces of a dark imperial past lingering in the story's representation of cultural spaces fissured by complex divisions of race, class, and geography: "imported coolie labourers on sugar estates," the "Negroes of the town," some remaining Dutch families, French planters living "a narrow domestic life in dull, dignified decay," and the English traders and colonial rulers (*TLS* 34, 61). The business of Mauritius, "so isolated and so exclusively trading," had always been business (*TLS* 15). The island and everything on it, even its daughters, were commodities, such is the force of the commercial in the civilized metropolitan world. Daly could be describing Conrad's story when he observes that "through the increasing dominance of commodity production, relations between people appear as relations between the objects they exchange" (Daly 91). Even the aunt's attendance upon Alice is an economic arrangement, and from their first interview Jacobus regards the bachelor captain as a negotiating partner. Social relations are material relations: potatoes, sugar bags, daughters. Potatoes are a better deal than Alice, who is seemingly a commercial disaster: Jacobus and Alice are social castaways, and there is not enough money for "anyone to come forward" (*TLS* 39).

Mauritius's identity is achieved through silences, suppressions, and strangenesses occupying the story's margins: the "other" Jacobus's much abused mulatto son, the bewitching circus woman and her death, the doubling of Jacobus's daughters, the repeated murmurs of "burials," "graves," "cemeteries." While Lawrence Graver fault the story for withheld, unexplained "mysteries" (Graver 160–61), Watts feels its enigmatic

quality made it "one of Conrad's most brilliant yet most neglected" stories
(Watts, "Narrative Enigma," 131). Conrad's suppression of the specifics of
longitude and latitude, and of names, works to make this story an allegory, effectively challenging the discourse of imperial trade and progress
that produced this captain as a historical subject. Thus, the story marks a
falling off from the "adventure" Conrad gestures toward in his dedication
of *'Twixt Land and Sea* to Captain C. M. Marris, "in memory of those
old days of adventure." Conrad remembers those days in "Geography and
Some Explorers," recalling his 1888 voyage from Sydney to Mauritius,
thrilled to follow in the wake of those explorers he admired as selfless
searchers of the truth, sailing "through the heart of the old Pacific mystery" he regarded as part of a tradition bound more to the ideals of
organicism than to imperialism (*LE* 18). A rereading of that essay confirms Conrad's conviction that trade's overmastering acquisitive spirit in
the late nineteenth century signaled the transition of adventurous exploration from geography triumphant to "the merry dance of death and
trade" (*HD* 14). His 1911 story chronicles this degeneration, caused in
great part by the self-division the discourse of imperial trade necessitates.
Speaking of *Heart of Darkness* and Conrad's awareness of his audience as
represented by the men on board the *Nellie,* Edward Said observes that
"during the 1890s the business of empire, once an adventurous and often
individualistic enterprise, had become the empire of business" (Said 23).
This story records that shift and its self-alienating effects on its interpellated subjects.

Stevenson insists to Bocock that "there is no harm in a voluptuary,"
"hand on my heart and in the sight of God," arguing that the frequent
misinterpretations of *Jekyll and Hyde* probably resulted from the fact that
it is "the sexual field and the business field [that] are perhaps the two
best fitted for the display of cruelty and cowardice and selfishness" (*JH*
87). The consequence of both Calvinist and colonialist discourses, these
fictions reveal, is a pressure toward self-division rather than self-
integration. Both imagine identity as complex for protagonists who deny
the self's multiple nature, subject to multiple, often conflicting, discourses. Neither wants to acknowledge the self's contradictory heterogeneity or understand the discourses shaping their conflicting desires,
better understood in terms of their mutual complicity rather than oppo-

sition. The idea of a stable subject about whom final revelations will be made and for whom epiphanic moments will disclose a true, unified self that can finally be known undergoes a radical revision. The center that posits order and unity, of the self and of the imperial metropolis, is revealed as, indeed, fictional. Both suggest the darkness at the heart of the imperial center and open the structures of civilization, its metropolitan centers, and the self to their repressed differences.

NOTE

1. All references to *Strange Case of Dr. Jekyll and Mr. Hyde* in this chapter are to the Linehan edition (New York: Norton, 2003).

Cross-Cultural Encounters in
In the South Seas and *Heart of Darkness*

MONICA BUNGARO

*T*HE WRITING from the period when colonialism was at its height and already exhausting its forward movement was inevitably informed by the relation of Self to the Other. Between 1870 and 1900 the British Empire "annexed thirty-nine separate areas adding 88 million new subjects for Queen and Empress Victoria" (Ledger and Luckurst 133). However, despite the official policy of forward expansion bolstered through new media, "the case for colonialism was now having to be made more strongly because of increasing doubts about the project" (Booth and Rigby 3). The parallel with Rome was frequently drawn, but that analogy was double-edged. If Seeley's *The Expansion of England* celebrated the might of Rome (1883), Froude's *Oceana* (1886) drew on the resemblance between the decay of English society and the late days of the Roman Empire. The economic recession of the 1880s, the death of General Gordon in Khartoum in 1885, a succession of rebellions in the colonies, and the traumatic losses inflicted on the British army by a ragged peasant army of Boers in 1899 instilled in the British cultural imagination a fear that imperialism's heyday might turn out to be short-lived.

The time-honored idea of historical decline, reinforced by the events and changes of the latter half of the nineteenth century, became associated with scientific theories of degeneration and extinction. Racial theory, with its insistence on white purity and supremacy, implied inevitable decline. Gobineau began *Essai sur l'inegalité des races humaines* (1853) thus: "The fall of civilization is the most striking and, at the same time, the most obscure of all phenomena of history" (in Brantlinger, *Bread and Circuses*, 142). If the 1850s were deeply shaken by Darwinian biological theories of evolution, ensuing decades brought fears about the permanence of the universe itself. William Thomson's theory of a cooling sun and dying earth and Max Nordau's apocalyptic vision of the earth wrapped in "shadows creeping with deepening gloom" feature prominently in French and British writing of the period: Flaubert, Loti, Wells (Ledger and Luckhurst 13). Others mirror and expose the moral, social, and psychological internalized terrors of the age. In *Ulysses* the narrator imagines "the annihilation of the world and consequent extermination of the human species, inevitable but unpredictable," and Wilde's Dorian Gray longs for the "*fin du globe*," anticipating the apocalyptic themes of Conrad's *Heart of Darkness* (Joyce 794; Wilde 138).

Stevenson's writing shares the modernist themes of imperial confidence and anxiety. *In the South Seas* highlights Stevenson's concerns over the decline and decay of civilization and contamination of the European race through close contact with the racial and colonized Other. Widespread belief in the extinction of other cultures was in part a displaced expression of fear of the extinction of European culture. Stevenson's contemplation of the death of other cultures raises the prospect of the death of his own: "I saw their case as ours, death coming in like a tide, and the day already numbered when there should be no more Beretani, and no more of any race whatever, and no more literary works, no more readers" (*WRLS* 15:34). At the leper colony on Molokai in the Hawaiian islands, Stevenson saw a potentially lethal threat to Europe: "[A] new variety of leprosy, cultivated in the virgin soil of Polynesian races, might prove more fatal than we dream" (*Travels in Hawaii* 84). As the world map was colored in by colonialism, the colonies themselves exercised destructive and regenerative power over the colonial psyche.

The idea of the inevitable extinction of native peoples underlines Western observers' obsession with forms of degeneration and decay, biological, cultural, and historical, and provided an ideological ground for the violence of colonization. If the imperial self is the target of physical and moral corruption through contact with the Other, the reverse is also true. Like Conrad, Stevenson shows that degeneration comes not from outside but from within. It is inherent in European civilization that threatens to destroy the invaded society: "[E]xperience begins to show us that change of habit is bloodier than a bombardment" (*WRLS* 15:49). European colonial enterprises proved that the colonial mission lacked morality and decency. In *Heart of Darkness* Marlow's recognition of the inhumanity of the work in Africa—"[T]he work was going on. The work!"—is a case in point (*HD* 20).[1] If the "uncivil" was in need of civilizing, then "civilized" humanity lacked precisely those qualities that made it human. Despite its missionary cover, Europe rivaled other cultures in savagery when defending its economic and political interests. Destruction/appropriation of other cultures and territories was instrumental to the project of maintaining and reinforcing national identity.

Stevenson's and Conrad's Conception of the Other

Societies such as the Samoans' had long survived natural calamities and internal wars by drawing on physical strength and self-controlling mechanisms, such as taboos, to guarantee unity and respect, but European ignorance often caused riots and brought about crises. "A Tale of a Tapu" describes how the whites disseminated degradation by convincing the king to raise the "tapu" against liquor: "For ten days the town had been passing the bottle or lying in hoggish sleep; and the king, moved by the Old Men and their own appetites, continued to squander his savings on liquor and to join in and lead the debauch. The whites were the authors of this crisis" (*WRLS* 15:235).

Conrad, in "An Outpost of Progress" and *Heart of Darkness*, shows that European progress in Africa is both a beacon "on the road towards better things" (*HD* 34) and the symbol of barbarism beneath the ideology of colonialism. For Conrad, the story of progress is not one of colonial mastery but of degeneration and atavism. His whites are both victims and perpetrators of their culture's desire to possess. The chief accountant is a hairdresser's dummy, "making correct entries of perfectly correct transactions" (*HD* 22); the station manager has "nothing within him" (*HD* 31). Conrad challenges his "superior" readers by returning humanity to the colonized Other: "No. They were not inhuman. . . . [W]hat thrilled you was just the thought of their humanity—like yours—the thought of your remote kinship with this wild and passionate uproar" (*HD* 37–38). Kinship, no matter how remote, remains kinship. "Ugly" as their shouting, leaping, spinning, and horrid faces still seem, Marlow recognizes a meaning: if the Other represents a threat, it is through sameness as much as difference. Like Marlow, Stevenson admits that savagery is part of human history, always available to subsume the civilized: "If I desired any detail of savage custom, or of superstitious belief, I cast back in the story of my fathers, and fished for what I wanted with some trait of equal barbarism" (*WRLS* 15:13).

A culturally relativistic outlook dominated Western thought in the early twentieth century, shared by Conrad and Stevenson. In Malinowski's new ethnography, distinctions between "civilized" and "savage" people became meaningless (Rossetti 486), so the trappings of civilization, "[p]rinciples, . . . [a]cquisitions, clothes, pretty rags" won't do against barbarity (*HD* 38). If Africans are figured in animal imagery, Europeans were inhuman: "[They] had opened with their Winchesters, and were simply squirting lead into that bush" (*HD* 46). Even cannibals appear more human: "I looked at them as you would on any human being, with a curiosity of their impulses, motives, capacities, weaknesses, when brought to the test of an inexorable physical necessity. Restraint! What possible restraint?" (*HD* 43). Stressing common ground between "us" and "them," Conrad offers a critique of Eurocentric discourse about superiority. If history reveals the kinship between the colonizer and the colonized, they may become either mutually parasitic or mutually enriching, center and margins locked together in a mutually reinforcing set of fears.

By the 1850s "the Enlightenment ethos of the equality of humankind could no longer be maintained in the face of the encounter with other human societies, and differences between Western and other cultures were treated as different stages in the same overall evolutionary process" (Young, *Colonial Desire*, 47). Cross-cultural encounters were thus conceptualized as "a process of deculturation of the less powerful and its transformation towards the norms of the West" (Young, *Colonial Desire*, 4). This involved appropriation of other cultures for assimilating "alien" elements into Western standards. However, in the struggle for dominance the colonizer remained caught in a dynamic of horror and fascination with the Other. Conrad's and Stevenson's conception of the encounter with the Other seems informed by the perception of the interaction and collision of antagonistic forces simultaneously at work in the "civilized" mind.

Stevenson apparently wrestles over whether the relation of Self to Other is ineluctably one of domination and appropriation or whether the Other offers an exhausted and tired West a way out. Engaging with racial and cultural otherness may offer a transformative encounter, if one is willing to adapt to the context. He urges missionaries "to seek rather the point of agreement than the points of difference; to proceed rather by confirmation and extension than by iconoclasm" ("Missions in the South Seas" 1). He came into direct contact with local chiefs and missionaries and gained some degree of familiarity with the local political, economic, and social organization and the changes wrought by colonialism.

Attwater, in *The Ebb-Tide*, epitomizes this mediation between Pacific and capitalist economies of exchange, reflecting the fractured identity of the colonial missionary project. He manifests the instability of the "civilized" values that Europeans were endeavoring to establish, highlighting a recidivist potential within their own societies. Attwater's theology combines with his accumulation of riches: "a whole curiosity shop of sea-curios, gross and solid, heavy to lift, ill to break, bound with brass and shod with iron."[2] Jean and John Camaroff's description of the relationship between the African missionary and capitalist enterprise can be equally applied here: "The impact of Protestant evangelists as harbingers of industrial capitalism lay in the fact that their civilizing mission was simultaneously symbolic and practical. The goods and techniques they brought with them . . . were both vehicles of a moral economy that celebrated the global spirit of commerce, the commodity, and the imperial marketplace" (Camaroff and Camaroff 12–13). Combining the imperial spirit of commerce with the reforming civilizing mission, missionaries in the Pacific embodied a new type of foreign subject, threatening the unique representative status of the beachcombers.

Attwater is a missionary liberated from dependence on the metropolitan article. At his dinner party he displays authority through appropriation of Polynesian cuisine: "Not a tin had been opened; and save for the oil and vinegar in the salad . . . not even the condiments were European" (*ET* 261). His ability to manipulate that slippery signifier, the bottle, is a supplementary sign of control: "Sherry, hock, and claret succeeded each other, and the 'Farallone' champagne brought up the rear with the dessert" (*ET* 261). As Vanessa Smith explains: "[B]y appropriating the beachcomber's strategy of cultural interaction, the missionary achieves ascendancy in the Pacific" (Smith 105).

For Conrad no adaptation to context or strategy of cultural interaction can provide the white man with knowledge about the Other, nor can the Other represent a way out for the colonizer. Robert Hampson's comments on Conrad's Malay fiction are pertinent: "After 'The Lagoon' and 'Karain,' Conrad moved away from attempts to represent Malay realities to an engagement instead with the problematics of representing another culture" (Hampson, *Cross-Cultural Encounters*, 162). Thus, Conrad's "strategy of ignorance" is an ethical response to the problem of knowing/representing another culture. Conrad's notion of imperial encounter moves from the vulgarly colonial to the humanity of the colonized, involving the impossibility of normalizing and appropriating the Other. Historical and cultural specificity is universalized: "There is a bond between us and that humanity so far away." Conrad is content "to sympathize with common mortals, no matter where they live in houses or in huts, in the streets under a fog, or in the forests" (Note to *OI*). He realizes that radically different realities cannot be subsumed under a hierarchizing of differences. Thus, Conrad avoids what Young calls "ontological imperialism," in which "the same constitutes itself through a form of negativity in relation to the Other, producing all knowledge by appropriating and sublating the Other within itself" (Young, *White Mythologies*, 13).

Stevenson's move to the Pacific changed his axes of novelistic practice: instead of adventures, he produced ethnographically authoritative accounts of island cultures, focusing on local politics; in place of idealized landscapes and characters, he wrote stories exposing the ugly legacies of colonial contact; ignoring the imperial model, he depicted humane Polynesian chiefs heroically negotiating opportunities for allegiances with European colonizers. Stevenson moves from romances, predicated upon detachment, to engagement with Polynesian life, at once critical of and informed by the colonial contract. His accounts of King Tembinok represent his willingness to access other subjectivities and his recognition that these subjectivities are often resistant to, instead of available for, inscription. Tembinok only appropriates those Western tools he considers useful for physical or political power, manipulating Western artifacts to his own advantage: "Collector, though he was, he did not collect useless information and all his questions had a purpose" (*WRLS* 15:310). The "native" in this case resists and subverts containment and restraint by moving from passive victim to agent and protagonist of cultural interaction and exchange.

Stevenson's presence serves Tembinok's purposes: "The king promised himself a vast amount of useful knowledge ere we left" (*WRLS* 15:286). Stevenson plays interpreter of historical data and events, only to be confronted with historical inconsistencies:

> Tembinok once brought me a difficulty of this kind which I was long of comprehending. A schooner had told him of Captain Cook; the king was much interested in the story and turned for more information—not to Mr. Stephen's dictionary, not to the "Britannica" but to the Bible in the Gilbert Island version. Here he sought long and earnestly; Paul he found and Festus, and Alexander the Coppersmith, no word of Cook. The inference was obvious: the explorer was a myth. (*WRLS* 15:310)

Tembinok cross-references between the Bible and the history of exploration, highlighting the gap between spiritual and imperial narratives. His knowledge is not just cumulative but involves a direct interrogation of Western society's values, legends, heroes, and beliefs, thus moving from mimic to interpreter and potential transgressor as Western cultural narcissism is exposed.

The same ambivalence between mimicry, mockery, and transgression is registered in the trading relationship that typifies the dialectical exchange between Europeans and Polynesians. Maude describes a society whose contact with European colonialism was regulated and mediated by its rulers: "[T]hough the traders frequently had to play the pipers, it was the islanders who in reality called the tunes" (Maude 213). The relationship between trader and Pacific islander was a performative one, dictated by local practices. Traders "had to ascertain and conform to local mores and etiquette, as well as to the consumer preferences of their customers if they were to succeed in their ventures" (Maude 213). Under Tembinok, traders promoted the circulation of metropolitan commodities, but success was dictated by local cultural objectives, not global market forces.[3] However, Tembinok's obsession with cultural acquisitions exposes him to foreign trading agendas:

> Among goods exported especially for Tembinok there is a beverage known as Hennessy's brandy. It is neither Hennessy nor even brandy. . . . The king . . . has grown used to this amazing brand, and rather prides himself upon the taste; and any substitution is a double offence, being at once to cheat him and to cast a doubt upon his palate. A similar weakness is to be observed in all connoisseurs. (*WRLS* 15:285)

Since both use and exchange values become irrelevant to Tembinok, he is a type of anticonnoisseur, whose collecting challenges norms of taste and value. Maude represents Tembinok's obsession as slavishly imitative and as a kind of cultural abdication to "ascertain and copy the conventions of civilized European society" (Maude 215). Maude, however, neglects elements of "bricolage" and "subversive mimicry" that emerge strongly in Stevenson's account.[4] Stevenson portrays Tembinok as a role-player whose costume changes ignore and ironize European dress conventions: "Now he wears a woman's frock, now a naval uniform; now . . . figures in a masquerade costume of his own design: trousers and a singular jacket with shirt tails" (*WRLS* 15:278). Tembinok, however, as absolute ruler, mimics but also embodies an imperialist presence. He supervises the building of the Stevensons' compound, with 'a pith helmet on his head, a meershaum pipe in his mouth" (*WRLS* 15:287). Thus, Tembinok's cross-dressing could be an experiment in imperialism, displaying his real and symbolic authority. Cross-dressing is emblematic of the impact of empire on the native, a "subject of difference" who through mimicry becomes "almost the same but not quite" (Bhabha 86). Tembinok's mimicry implies mockery, since he appropriates those items on his own terms: simple imitation threatens to transform the "original" beyond recognition.

Tembinok's inability to differentiate between male and female attire testifies to fluid Polynesian gender codes, intentionally imitating Europeans while resisting impositions of gendered identities, thus subverting European ideas of virility and superiority. Colonial imitation and appropriation result in a "proliferation of inappropriate objects" that ensure the failure of the civilizing mission, since "mimicry is at once resemblance and menace" (Bhabha 86). When Marlow observes "a bit of white worsted" around an African's neck, he suggests that Africans assimilate manufactured European objects into their own symbolic system: "Was it a badge—an ornament—a charm—a propitiatory act?" (*HD* 20–21). As Bhabha notes: "Marlow interrogates the odd, inappropriate, colonial transformation of a textile into an uncertain, textual sign, possibly a fetish" (Bhabha 105). Bhabha uses this moment as an example of the "hybrid" involving the appropriation of Western symbols. Marlow is at least willing to acknowledge this possibility, leading to the destabilizing of the symbol's meaning and to the colonizer's control over that meaning. The legitimacy of the hierarchical colonial relationship is disrupted as the familiar enters the catalog of the exotic. In the process of mimicking the colonizer, the colonized subject often surreptitiously misrepresents the colonial signifier, thereby creating alternative contexts of meanings. Mimicry then is articulated in the gap between the image of the "civilized" colonial and its distorted imitation. As Bhabha explains: "Between the Western sign and its colonial signification there emerges a gap of misreading" (Bhabha 95). By recognizing the Africans' difference, Conrad suggests that like Europeans, Africans have their own culture. As Abdul JanMohamed notes: "Marlow's equation between the function of African drumming with that of church bells in a Christian country" can be a rejection of "the traditional colonialist use of drumming as the emblem of the native's evil" (JanMohamed 90).

In Tembinok's museum of foreign artifacts, the practical equipment of
the European colonial enters a catalog of the exotic—"house after house
is crammed with clocks, medical boxes, blue spectacles, umbrellas, sewing
machines" (*WRLS* 15:282)—but Stevenson's collection of Polynesian
necklaces, fans, combs, practical tools, and items of dress displays a similar tendency to fetishize the everyday. Stevenson is invited to test the traditional power of the local artifact by offering his body as a touchstone
for Kiribati medicines. The medicine box cures Stevenson's cold, and he
confesses: "[M]y appetite for curiosities had been very strongly whetted
by the sacred box," reflecting Tembinok's eagerness to acquire items of
trade (*WRLS* 15:328). The object from an/other culture enters the metropolitan system of exchange, losing its sacred value: "[I]t was to pass from
its green medicine-tree reverend precinct and devout attendants to be
handled by the profane" (*WRLS* 15:332). The Other is reduced to an aesthetic category deprived of historical and cultural specificity. The gap
between Polynesian king and European traveler is bridged, acknowledging that colonizer and colonized participate in an exchange of economy,
not a one-way flow of meanings. As Bhabha puts it: "[T]he effect of the
colonial power is seen to be the production of hybridization rather than
the noisy command of colonialist authority or the silent repression of
native traditions" (Bhabha 112).

In "Karain," attention to European amulets signals Conrad's relativistic presentation of cultures. Again Conrad indicates shared human
predicaments. While the narrator empathizes with the native, Hollis
asserts racial distinctions. When Karain implores Hollis to take him with
him, "or else give me some of your strength—a charm" (*TU* 44), Hollis
produces a box containing "a bit of silk ribbon," "a bunch of flowers," "a
narrow white glove," "a slim packet of letters," "the photographs of a
young woman," and "a jubilee sixpence," all "charms and talismans" (*TU*
48). Hollis cuts the glove to make a pouch for the coin, creating a "charm"
for Karain. As with Tembinok, Karain is persuaded that the European
artifact has magic power. The protagonists posit the native as superstitious and gullible, and the "charm" asserts European superiority. More
importantly, it represents native belief in the supremacy of Western civilization and the Empire's ability to control its colonized subjects.
According to Linda Dryden: "Hollis's ability to persuade Karain of the

effectiveness of the 'charm' relies upon the 'Victoria myth' having already infected Karain's perception of the West" (Dryden, *Joseph Conrad* 130). Legally, however, he is still a Malay, a savage gentleman who, although indulged by Europeans, is still "a subject of a difference that is almost the same but not quite" (Bhabha 86). The victim of white scientific knowledge and trickery, Karain is confined to the Eastern world of exoticism where he belongs.

The European as watcher is strongly present in *In the South Seas* and *Heart of Darkness*. Stevenson watches the population from his balcony, but his observation post falls within the purview of other gazes. Butaritari is characterized by a multilayered voyeurism that destabilizes Stevenson's individual authority. Similarly, the hierarchy of perception and observation is constantly destabilized in *Heart of Darkness*. Marlow's Africans are "to be looked at" rather than "engaged with": "They wanted no excuse for being there. They were a great comfort to look at" (*HD* 17). However, the returned gaze of Africa is seductive and menacing: "I wondered whether the stillness on the face of the immensity looking at us two were meant as an appeal or as a menace" (*HD* 29). Stevenson expresses a comparable sense of frustration: "[T]he cabin was filled from end to end with Marquesans . . . regarding me in silence with embarrassing eyes. . . . A kind of despair came over me, to sit there helpless under all those staring orbs" (*WRLS* 15:16). The evocation of "first contact," in which Europeans think natives into objecthood, slides into the disappointed recognition that Stevenson is the object of the gaze.

Stevenson finds being observed—as Sartre perceives it—less comforting than observing:[5] "To be looked at is to apprehend oneself as the unknown object of unknowable appraisals—in particular, value judgements" (Sartre 276). The looking back of Africa or the Pacific could be a demand for intimacy and reciprocity. Being observed forces upon the object a realization of the Other's inviolable self. As the European reader proceeds further into the "heart of darkness," and as Marlow penetrates the heart of Africa, both experience the African gaze, and most importantly, their gaze is returned, as with the dying helmsman: "He looked at me anxiously. . . . I had to make an effort to free my eyes from his gaze and attend to the steering" (*HD* 47). An inverse relationship between power and intimacy is therein implicated: "And the intimate profundity of that look he gave me when he received his hurt remains to this day in my memory—like a claim of distant kinship affirmed in a supreme moment" (*HD* 51). The less power one assumes by looking at the Other, the more human intimacy is created. The helmsman's intimate look forces Marlow into a reciprocal looking that offers him refuge against the inhumane claims of the colonial project. Mutual looking asserts a common humanity that challenges oppression and inequality.[6]

Stevenson implies that positive engagements are possible when there is a willingness to interrogate essentialist notions of savagery. He tells of a Marquesan who "picked up a human foot, and provocatively staring at the stranger, grinned and nibbled at the heel" (*WRLS* 15:92). Playing the cannibal, the Marquesan strategically manipulates an image of difference to intimidate his audience; equally, the foreigner responds with a performance of power to establish a tenuous authority. The settler gathered "three other whites and ostentatiously practised rifle shooting by day upon the beach. Natives were often there to watch them; the practice was excellent; and the assault was never delivered" (*WRLS* 15:94). Stevenson seems to share William Arens's view that societies label other cultures cannibal in order "to define their sense of worth and draw the line between contemporary civilization and barbarism" (Arens 159).

Montaigne had argued of Brazilian cannibals: "[T]here was no more barbarism in their eating men alive than in some of the things he and his readers had lately seen in France" (in Banton 7). Similarly, Stevenson details European barbarism in the Pacific: "I believe that natives regard white blood as a kind of talisman against the powers of hell. In no other way can they explain the unpunished recklessness of Europeans" (*WRLS* 15:187). Although Stevenson, like Conrad, remains subject to the kind of ambiguity typical of his age, he realizes differences are not fixed but part of a fluid performance of identity: "[A] man can scarce be said to belong to a particular atoll; he belongs to several" (*WRLS* 15:163). Moreover, Stevenson knows that "hybridity" is a constant human characteristic:[7] "All men believe in ghosts, all men combine with their recent Christianity fear of and a lingering faith in the old island deities. So, in Europe, the gods of Olympus slowly dwindled into village bogies; so today the theological Highlander sneaks from under the eye of the Free Church divine to lay an offering by a sacred well" (*WRLS* 15:191).

Stevenson deconstructs Western hierarchies of practices and institutions by showing that what the West despises most in other cultures is also at the heart of its own history. "Hybridity" is thus a universal condition that rejects myths of pure origins, celebrating instead the cultural mutations caused by disruptive gaps in history. The encounter with colonialism has only perpetuated this historical and cultural condition of "in-betweenness" that challenges the expectations of "civilized" society by constructing "a political object that is new, neither the one nor the other" (Bhabha 25).

Nevertheless, a relativistic idea of the equivalence of histories and cultures runs through *In the South Seas*:

> Not much beyond a century has passed since the Highlands were in the same convulsive and transitionary state as the Marquesans of today. In both cases an alien authority enforced, the clans disarmed, the chiefs deposed, new customs introduced. . . . In one the cherished practice of tattooing, in the other a cherished costume, proscribed. In each a main luxury cut off: beef . . . denied to the meat-loving Highlander; long-pig, pirated from the next village, to the man-eating Kanaka. (*WRLS* 15:20)

Chiefs, such as Taipi-Kikino of Anaho, are some of the by-products of the encounter with colonialism. Taipi is representative of a detribalized native, "elegant at a table, skilled in the use of knife and fork," but a man of no substance, addressed by a nickname translated as "Beggar on Horseback" in the land of orality, where "a nickname destroys almost the memory of the original name" (*WRLS* 15:52–53). Hierarchies of power are imposed on local chiefs like Taipi, and this "marginalization has a profound influence on the psyche of the colonized" (Fanon 201). Taipi's marginalization is compared to George II's deposition of Highland chiefs (*WRLS* 15:53). As Ngugi affirms, "Economic and political control can never be complete or effective without mental control" (Ngugi 16). The chief is kept in power, but "he is a chief to the French" (*WRLS* 15:53). Thus, the colonized subject internalizes hierarchies of power through strategies of mental control enforced by the colonizer (Fanon 201).

For Conrad, the most vital Africans fit naturally into their environment: "They shouted, sang; . . . they had . . . a wild vitality, an intense energy of movement that was as natural and true as the surf along their coast" (*HD* 17). The least vital have abandoned their original environment. Such people lack reality and are mere shams, neither fully African nor fully European. To this group belong most of the Africans at the Outer Station as well as detribalized Africans like the Manager's boy and the fireman: "[T]o look at him was as edifying as seeing a dog in a parody of breeches and a feather hat, walking on his hind-legs" (*HD* 38).

Conrad knows that different societies have different mores and customs that do not lose honor or value by failing to conform to the European behavior. Hence, the cannibals are morally superior to the Belgians: "Fine fellows—cannibals. . . . They were men one could work with, and I am grateful to them" (*HD* 36). Censuring Kurtz for "unspeakable rites" is a different matter: "Kurtz after all belongs to a different tribe, to Marlow's tribe, one that has different customs—different but not necessarily better" (Firchow 117). The "subtle horrors" of Kurtz's rule are a crime, since they do not stand comparison with African custom, that "pure, uncomplicated savagery . . . being something that had a right to exist . . . in the sunshine" (*HD* 58).

Unlike Stevenson's view, for Conrad the colony is not the utopian space where Europeans can be regenerated. Although profoundly attracted to Africa's immensity and mystery, Marlow is troubled: its very aspect violates his concept of intelligibility and congruity. He senses "an implacable force brooding over an inscrutable intention" (*HD* 36). Africa's "empty stream," "great silence," "impenetrable forest" nullify the rational orderings of Western thought and threaten European identity (*HD* 35). Marlow says of Africa: "The inner truth is hidden. . . . But I felt it all the same" (*HD* 36). Africa, though a powerful presence, can be perceived but not contained within topographical schema typical of European modes of representation. Conrad's narrative style reflects the incapacity of language to represent this world and sanctions the failure of the linear, realist style depending on the existence of an intelligible universe.

Here we are confronted with two questions that are never quite resolved: What is savagery, and what makes one savage? What is human, and what makes human beings human? During his period of "ascendancy," Kurtz forced visiting chiefs literally to "crawl" on the ground (*HD* 58); later, Kurtz is forced to crawl just as ignominiously (*HD* 64). In Conrad's vision, civilization is power, and power generates political, economic, and social darkness. European conduct in Africa proves civilization a sham and Western sophistication a hoax. For Cesaire, "[a] nation which colonizes, . . . a civilization which justifies colonization . . . is already a sick civilization, a civilization which is already morally diseased, that irresistibly, progressing from one consequence to another . . . calls for its Hitler, I mean its punishment" (Cesaire 176). If the European falls victim to its Other, London, the uncontested center of the world, is qualified by its "mournful gloom brooding motionless" (*HD* 7): barbarism is located in the heart of respectable England. Stevenson's encounter with the Other confirms duplicity as "the curse of mankind" (*JH* 59), but it also proves that the South Seas are a locus of evil: "[N]owhere else . . . could I hope to see the evil of riches stand so legibly exposed" (*WRLS* 15:331).

Conclusions

In the South Seas and *Heart of Darkness* highlight a movement from an objectifying to a reciprocal and intimate exchange of gaze. Stevenson and Conrad understand that humanity and animality are not mutually exclusive. Using the motif of cross-cultural encounter, their narratives encode anxieties about "otherness" and "sameness": the Other is the other *outside* but also *within*. The fear of "the beast within" that the encounter with the Other exposes was the late nineteenth century's fear of itself. Although Conrad and Stevenson are aware of a multifaceted human identity and their narratives shake confidence in European superiority, they show different points of arrival in their conception of interracial encounters. Unlike Conrad, Stevenson *encounters* the Other and *engages with* it. For Conrad, the Other is unknowable and, therefore, "unrepresentable," and cultures are mutually unintelligible. The deeper Marlow moves into Africa, the more it appears impenetrable, and he realizes that "[t]here's no initiation . . . into such mysteries" (*HD* 10). Encounters with the Other represent encounters with "the fascination of the abomination," but as these inconsistencies and incompatibilities cannot be "known" or explained, so cannot the Other (*HD* 10). Despite their common origins, the Other maintains his radical alterity. As a consequence, Conrad's narrative illustrates the impossibility of fully knowing/representing an/other culture. It is no coincidence that the wilderness is constantly "silent," "still," "immense," "great." Conrad expresses not only the inability of language to express and represent the Other but also the Other's resistance to performances of power and acts of appropriation.

For Stevenson the Pacific landscape presents an impediment to authorial appropriation, "offering to the eye, even when perfect, only a ring of glittering beach and verdant foliage, enclosing and enclosed by the blue sea" (*WRLS* 15:124). However, Stevenson's accounts reveal personal experience where details of intimacy with the Other are offered: cannibals make brothers, friendship blossoms between Stevenson and Tembinoka, and islanders become family friends. Although Stevenson's narrative accounts, like Conrad's, display the gap between signs and meaning, he willingly bridges this gap by recognizing the power of "bricolage" inherent to Samoan cultures. Stevenson is forced to negotiate his authorial voice with Tembinoka's, realizing their mutual implication in the interrogation of fixed notions of cultural identity. He documents a comparable history of colonization and circumscription of cultural practices that contributes to a better understanding of his surroundings: "What I knew of the Clunny Macpherson, or the Appin Stewarts, enabled me to learn, and helped to understand, about the *Tevas* of Tahiti" (*WRLS* 15:13). Stevenson's attempt at a discursive equilibrium between his personal history and Polynesian history and culture reverses an unequal relationship. *In the South Seas* makes manifest the contract implicit in all writing about oral cultures that may seek to remain faithful to the "voice" of the "local" but that remains financially dependent upon a metropolitan audience. Stevenson's accounts are based on the conflicting witness of duplicitous voices: "The worth of native testimony is small, the worth of white testimony not overwhelming" (*WRLS* 15:187). For Conrad, any opening to the Other is an act of power by which one culture invades the other's boundaries. *In the South Seas* exposes the interplay between oral and written and the fluid relationship between Other and Self. This informs Stevenson's method of cross-cultural inquiry and offers opportunities for mutual intimacy and understanding. If for both Conrad and Stevenson races are united in humanity and bestiality, for Conrad the

Other and the Self possess mutually "hidden knowledge." This "hidden reality" can only be felt, never known. Both messages, Stevenson's *interpenetration of cultures* and Conrad's *plurality of cultures*, sound particularly relevant to today's debate about life in the village of globalization.

NOTES

1. All references to *Heart of Darkness* in this chapter are from the Kimbrough edition (New York: Norton, 1988).

2. All references to *The Ebb-Tide* in this chapter are from the Penguin edition of *Dr. Jekyll and Mr. Hyde and Other Stories*.

3. A shift is notable in recent accounts of barter between metropolitan and peripheral societies, from the representation of the triumph of global capitalism to the depiction of the impact of local agendas. See in particular Caroline Humphrey and Stephen Hugh Jones, eds., *Barter, Exchange, and Value* (Cambridge: Cambridge University Press, 1992).

4. Mimicry refers to the form of control whereby the colonizer requires the colonized to adopt and internalize "superior" forms and ideologies. Bhabha suggests that "mimicry is one of the most elusive and effective strategies of colonial power and knowledge" (Bhabha 85).

5. In the preface to an anthology of African texts edited by Leopold Senghor, Sartre tells his French readers: "I want you to feel, as I, the sensation of being seen. For the white man has enjoyed for three thousand years the privilege of seeing without being seen. It was a seeing pure and uncomplicated. . . . Today, these black men have fixed their gaze upon us and our gaze is thrown back in our eyes. . . . By this steady and corrosive gaze, we are picked to the bone" (Sartre, *Black Orpheus*, French and European Publications, 1976, 7–11).

6. See Todd Bender, *Literary Impressionism in Jean Rhys, Ford Madox Ford, Joseph Conrad, and Charlotte Bronte* (New York: Garland, 1997), 133, which points out that *Heart of Darkness* "is filled with references to eyes, with over sixty uses of the word or its cognates."

7. By "hybridity" I understand not just a mixing (as in the organic hybrid) but also a contestation of fixed and essentialized notions of identity.

Conrad, Stevenson, and Cannibalism: Journeying Out of the Comfort Zone

ANN C. COLLEY

$\mathcal{A}$LTHOUGH Conrad, in *Heart of Darkness*, was just as willing as Stevenson to recognize the discomfort associated with the leaching of the savage into "civilized" Western culture, he did not share Stevenson's anthropological perspective founded in his experiences of a particular time and place. This difference finds fullest expression through their response to cannibalism. In *Heart of Darkness* Conrad maintains little critical distance from the subject. He structures his text upon the scaffolding of its horror and suffuses his narrative with a Gothic, primitive gloom. Stevenson, however, grapples with the realities and complexities of anthropophagy, positioning cannibalism within the context of a specific island and its history. While cruising the South Seas, Stevenson learned that cannibalism varied from island to island. He visited the Gilbert Islands and the Marquesas, where the practice was well established until missionary priests supposedly persuaded the inhabitants to renounce it. Stevenson was aware that of all the Pacific islands, New Guinea was considered the most active in its continuation of the ritual.

Cannibalism had many purposes, such as revenge (ritual eating of an enemy) or as a part of a funeral rite. For example, the London Missionary Society representative Rev. G. Pratt took notes on his visit to the Tokelau, Ellis, and Gilbert group of islands, recording that upon death the head was separated and kept in the house, and on the third day the flesh gnawed and eaten (Pratt, LMS Notebook, 163).

Because of these differences, and because *Heart of Darkness* is fiction, not a semianthropological study of a place, its setting and the tone bear little resemblance to Stevenson's account of the Pacific islands. Conrad's story weaves through a mythic landscape ranging beyond the arena of central Africa and London in order to realize or reach a primeval, timeless darkness that conflates specific and varied practices, with the effect of almost pandering to images of cannibalism propagated in magazines, adventure stories, and travel narratives. Stevenson's narrative, however, represents a different generic mode: unlike Conrad's tale, *In the South Seas* requires its readers to remain within, not break through, the parameters of time and space. Stevenson's accounts of his brushes with cannibalism reflect an acute sensitivity to a particular moment and locale. This orientation overrides any sense of a larger, mythic view and distinguishes his treatment of cannibalism from Conrad's.

Cannibalism in Heart of Darkness

When Marlow navigates the narrowing river, the presence of the cannibal crew prejudices his perception so that the very landscape seems to be "butchered" (*HD* 41).[1] Marlow, "cut off" from his surroundings, regards the bodies of the natives as pieces of flesh (*HD* 35, 37). Severed limbs, detached glaring eyes, and incomplete forms of men float through the enclosing fog into his field of vision. Only sporadically does he detect the movements of "human forms gliding here and there" (*HD* 52). At Kurtz's house human heads are attached to poles (a conventional signifier of cannibalism), and Marlow notices the dying Kurtz's voracious mouth gaping "as though he had wanted to swallow all the air, all the earth, all the men before him" (*HD* 59). For Marlow, Kurtz is as cannibalistic as the African crew, who flash their "sharp teeth" and seem to long for the taste of human flesh (*HD* 42). Unlike the pilgrims, however, who practice "restraint" and control "the gnawing devils of hunger" (*HD* 42–43), Kurtz exhibits no restraint when it comes to "the gratification of his various lusts" (*HD* 57). Dominated by a rapacious appetite that echoes the imperialism of old Roman times and that of contemporary mercantile Europe, he absorbs everything into himself while performing "unspeakable rites" (*HD* 50). Conrad never elaborates but offers enough hints that cannibalism could be at play.

So affected is Marlow that, on returning to "the sepulchral city," he cannot help but remark on the "sight of people hurrying through the streets . . . to devour their infamous cookery" (*HD* 70). On hearing of Kurtz's death, Marlow continues his evening meal: "All the pilgrims rushed out to see. I remained and went on with my dinner" (*HD* 69). Such an orientation, emphasizing appetite and hunger, even clings to the narrative's end when Marlow is trapped not only by the horrific memory of Kurtz's gaping mouth but by the voracious, compulsive craving of his "Intended," who demands an account of Kurtz's final moments. She talks "as thirsty men drank" (*HD* 72). She too wants to possess, to devour. Throughout the narrative, someone is always ingesting something in the dark places of the earth, whether in the East or the West.

Eliciting the enduring trope of cannibalism to structure *Heart of Darkness*, Conrad frequently summons the imperialistic fantasy of the barbaric, letting its images resonate with horror. The young Conrad had dreamed of exploring faraway places, including Africa; he had read dramatic accounts of travel filled with half-gnawed limbs and singed remains (Firchow 8). Their atmosphere lingers and reveals itself in the figure of Marlow, who succumbs to the assumption that the more savage and remote a setting, the more the territory is peopled by those who crave the taste of human flesh: one cannot travel to primitive places without the threat of cannibalization. This fear pulsates in Marlow's consciousness like the distant sound of primal drums. Misunderstanding the ritualistic nature of cannibalism and, therefore, believing that the natives desire human flesh as a staple, Marlow wonders when his cannibal crew will grow tired of rancid meat and turn on him. Frances B. Singh remarks upon Marlow's erroneous belief that cannibals "eat human flesh out of greed or lust or even as a dietary staple" (Singh in *HD* 274).

Henry Morton Stanley's popular *Through the Dark Continent* (1898) did much to propagate this mythology and inform those, like Marlow, who let themselves be consumed by the notion of the primitive. Stanley is quick to characterize the Congo as "cursed by cannibalism, savagery, and despair" (Stanley in *HD* 79). When his two porters die, Stanley speaks of consigning their bodies "to the swift river, lest they become food" for his cannibal guides (Arens 87), an impulse that Marlow repeats when he tips the body of his helmsman overboard for fear of his cannibal crew: "I had made up my mind that if my late helmsman was to be eaten, the fishes should have him" (*HD* 52).

Cannibalism in the Congo

Conrad, of course, does not merely subscribe to a stereotype. He builds his narrative upon selective historical realities that ideally are supposed to be distinct from the fantasies of barbarism or savagery and are to some degree tied to time and place instead of some stereotypical landscape of savagery. Though Conrad was well acquainted with Central African practices, it is unclear whether he had more than a superficial and formulaic knowledge of Congolese culture. What needs more thorough recognition is Conrad's awareness not only of the trope but also of the established practices of anthropophagy. As Peter Edgerly Firchow remarks, critics often find it difficult or "repugnant" to recognize the existence of cannibalistic rites (Firchow 123). He avers that one must consider its traditional presence as well as its distorted replica among the Belgians and Arab slave owners who, like Kurtz, made a mockery of traditional and ritualistic anthropophagy. Barely six years after Conrad left the Congo, Lieutenant Dom, an official of King Leopold II, used human skulls decoratively (Davis in *HD* 126): "a Captain Rom, station commander of Stanley Falls—the equivalent of Kurtz's inner station—did in reality use the heads of twenty-one 'rebels' as a decorative border for the flower-bed in front of his house" (Firchow 112).

Although Conrad was in the Congo for less than six months, between mid-June and early December 1890, and does not write of seeing such acts, he must have been aware of cannibalism as more than an imaginary phenomenon. George Washington Williams's 1890 letters, in Kimbrough's edition of *Heart of Darkness*, attest to this possibility. As

Conrad wove his way downriver, Williams was studying conditions in the Congo for the railroad magnate Collis P. Huntington. His letters speak of African soldiers as "bloodthirsty cannibalistic Bangalas, who give no quarter to the aged grandmother or nursing child at the breast of his mother." Williams describes instances in which soldiers "have brought the head of their victims to their white officers . . . and afterwards eaten the bodies of slain children" (Williams in *HD* 110). Conrad's correspondence with Roger Casement, a British foreign service officer, reveals his understanding of such brutalities, especially those equally violent ones committed by foreign interests connected with the ivory and rubber trades. Conrad wrote to Casement that it was "an extraordinary thing that the conscience of Europe, which seventy years ago had put down the slave trade on humanitarian grounds, tolerates the Congo State today. It is as if the moral clock had been put back many hours" (Franklin in *HD* 124).

Mythical Time and Place

However, as much as one acknowledges this historical context, one has difficulty recalling its factual particulars within the larger context of Conrad's narrative. Through Marlow's voice, Conrad detaches his text from time and place, situating it within the trope of a mythic savage, brutal primitivism as well as within the legendary spaces of *The Aeneid* or Dante.[2] Removing his tale from the specific history of the Congo Free State, Conrad offers instead a narrative that constantly breaks out of defining boundaries. He writes "beyond the actual facts of the case," playing down evidence of civilization evident on his own trip upriver (Singh in *HD* 269). He makes the area more isolated and deliberately depopulates the riverbanks for his narrative purposes.[3]

Heart of Darkness begins with Marlow's stretching time and imagining how the Thames River must have appeared when the Romans invaded. As the narrative progresses, past and future blend to create a vista of shifting periods that throw a deflective gauze over regular chronological sense and remove us from time. Fog prevents clear vision, half revealing a mythic prospect that propels both Marlow and his audience back to the legendary primeval mud. The Essex marshes bordering the Thames and the impenetrable land bordering the Congo River merge as some distant alien place; each specific locale disappears from consciousness. Going up the river is "like traveling back to the earliest beginnings of the world" (*HD* 35). The "great wall of vegetation" becomes a rolling wave that crests and sweeps all away (*HD* 32). Specific time and place dissolve, and "truth is stripped of its cloak of time" (*HD* 38). Even the Intended is "one of those creatures that are not the playthings of Time" (*HD* 73).

In a context disrobed of time and place, cannibalism easily serves as a metaphor that plays into the expectations of the Western reader, who is anxious to equate its practice with the uncivilized. In *Heart of Darkness* cannibalism is not so much a matter for history and the exploring of a practice in the Congo during the 1890s as it is the means by which the author encapsulates the primitive. This discrepancy distinguishes Conrad's handling of cannibalism from Stevenson's reaction to its proximity when traveling, writing, and residing in the South Seas.

Stevenson and Cannibalism

Conrad's fixation on anthropophagy naturally leads one to Stevenson's response to the Western fascination with cannibalism: How did Stevenson react to its lingering presence in the Pacific while cruising among peoples reputed to savor the taste of "long-pig" (a tongue-in-cheek term for a cannibal victim)? On remote Pacific islands was Stevenson also listening for primitive drums? Did he, like Conrad, willingly subscribe to the equation between savagery and cannibalism?

Sections of *In the South Seas* almost replicate Conrad's obsession with linking the two, revealing how stimulated Stevenson's imagination could be by the Western addiction to the idea of cannibalism. As Gananath Obeyesekere observes, accounts of eating human flesh, such as Chevalier Peter Dillon's *Fijian Cannibal Adventures*, were often "command performances" simply "invented to show the savages cannibalism desired by his reading public, especially that of savage singing and dancing with joy over their prizes ... and the priests['] cutting up and dissecting these unfortunate people within sight of the Europeans on the hill" (Obeyesekere 77, 137). Although Stevenson was intent upon engaging a specific moment, he at times approaches Conrad's fascination with its general lore, especially since the Pacific, even more than Africa, was associated with the forbidden act.

The Popular Image of Cannibalism

Schooled by Robinson Crusoe's staring at a beach darkened by a victim's blood and by passages in *The Coral Island*, in which three British lads witness cannibal feasts and live in fear that they too will be "roasted alive and eaten," and impressed by Melville's experiences in *Typee*, Stevenson heeded the popular equation between cannibalism and the Pacific (Ballantyne 27). Consequently, he cannot but suspect that the gracious and converted Queen Vaekehu missed her "barbarous and stirring past." Images of her presiding over feasts supplied with "blood-stained baskets of long-pig" clutter his imagination (*SS* 58).[4] Stevenson casts his eye on the menacing tattooed hands and legs that emerge from the prim gown of the quiet and smooth queen, who years before was supposed to have tired of her husband and killed and eaten him.

The specter of cannibalism was often close at hand, for Stevenson docked at places described by naturalists, explorers, sailors, traders, and missionaries who accentuated the heathen qualities of the island cultures by inserting into their accounts hair-raising tales of people being eaten—additions that were, in part, responses to the demands of Western readers accustomed to and expecting tales of such carnage. Some of these, particularly the missionary reports, made the practice more abhorrent by domesticating the act. Ta'Unga, a native representing the London Missionary Society, told how New Caledonians prepared the body for cooking, carved it, and warmed up the leftovers in the oven—like a Sunday joint. He embellished his accounts by noting that in one case a woman ate a baby while holding it to her breast, and in another a native kissed his victim while cutting off his arm and proceeded to cook and eat it in front of his still conscious victim. Such texts emphasized the gruesome practice to justify their authors' efforts both to colonize and to convert. As a result, among the plethora of ethnographic details about an island's languages, plant life, and social structure, these travelers served up images of natives ravenous for the taste of human flesh. They packed their

narratives with descriptions of sliced pieces of long-pig strewn along the
beach, of genitals hanging from sacred trees, or of porters carrying man-
gled bodies in baskets oozing fluids that trickled over their backs and
down their legs.[5]

Stevenson traveled with memories of these stories. On his first voyage
he visited the Marquesas, islands notorious for their recent appreciation
for long-pig as well as raids on neighboring tribes to refurbish their supply
of human bodies. On board the *Casco*, Stevenson came to areas from
where, only twenty years before, a missionary had sent reports naming
individuals who had been slain, cooked, and eaten. Stevenson followed the
currents that in 1820 had taken the shipwrecked crew of the *Essex*, an
American whaling ship, close to the Marquesan coast where they might
have been rescued. Instead, fearful of being eaten alive, these sailors went
on; after 190 days at sea they resorted to drinking the blood of their com-
panions and cannibalizing each other—an episode that recalls Conrad's
"Falk," a story about survival cannibalism at sea that relies upon the fact
that cannibalism was common among shipwrecked Westerners.[6]
Cannibalism was accepted in such circumstances; reputedly there was a
system for managing it.[7]

Fed on such a diet of reading and expectation, it is not surprising that
when Stevenson initially approached the Marquesas, he brought with
him a general sense that he was entering "man-eating isles."
Consequently, during his first encounter with the natives he indulged his
fantasies and experienced some trepidation. Stevenson identified the
welcoming natives, who were advancing toward his yacht in canoes, not
by a tribal name but simply as "cannibals," and, in the spirit of *The Coral
Island*, he wondered if their leader "might leap from his hams" and "with
an ear-splitting signal, the ship be carried at a rush, and the ship's company butchered for the table" (*SS* 9–10). A few lines later, though, an
embarrassed, retrospective, and ironic Stevenson rushes to point out that
his supposition was both short lived and inappropriate: soon their leader,
Kauanui, became his friend.

Stevenson and Anthropophagy

Yet, in spite of this alteration, Stevenson never forgot that the
Marquesans were "so recently and so imperfectly redeemed from a

blood-boltered barbarism" (*SS* 10). Their ensanguined history never rested easily beneath his consciousness. Most of the time Stevenson could not, as his mother did, dismiss cannibalism as a done deed and trust that the Roman Catholic priests had "persuaded them to give up their constant wars and the practice of cannibalism" (Margaret Stevenson 86–87). He was sensitive to and searched for vestiges of it wherever he went. He felt a compulsion to inquire, repeatedly, about past cannibal practices and was often disappointed if none was to surface. He pestered natives, traders, and missionaries for as much as they could remember. At the Malua Institute he avidly took notes on the Reverend George Turner's observations about the "many cases of cannibalism ... in the whole Gilbert zone" (HM 2398, Huntington Library). He understood the rationale that the Marquesans ate part of an enemy's body as an expression "of hatred and revenge ... that was not occasioned by the mere relish for human flesh, such as obtains throughout the Fiji, New Hebrides, and New Caledonian groupes [*sic*]" (London Missionary Society Archives). Eagerly, if not voraciously, Stevenson listened to natives speak of cannibal ghosts making a terror of solitary, dark forest paths, quickly altering his attitude. This research removed him from Conrad's mythic orientation and slipped him into the particulars of time and place. As he continued his travels, cannibalism emerged as more than generic barbarity: it became a variegated practice dependent upon a specific epoch or moment in an island's culture.

The specter of cannibalism attracted as well as repelled him; consequently, as Stevenson registered disgust and spoke of cannibalism as being "worse than bestial vice" (*SS* 7), he also sought out the company of people such as the Reverend James Chalmers, who from 1877 until his death in 1901 worked in Papua, New Guinea, the most active cannibalistic culture in all the South Seas. Stevenson was spellbound by Chalmers, partially because this heroic man moved in the society of man-eaters and told of difficulties in getting through dinner because fresh skulls belonging to cannibalized inland natives surrounded the table, summoning images of the heads surrounding Kurtz's compound and recalling the extent to which cannibalism and head-hunting were linked in the imagination as well as in fact.[8] Indeed, such was Stevenson's enthusiasm for Chalmers and the idea of cannibalism that he planned to visit Chalmers in New Guinea. Stevenson's family was horrified and anxious at the prospect. Not only were they worried about fevers, but they also fretted over the proximity to a man-eating culture, a circumstance, according to Margaret Stevenson, that "rather attracted Lou than otherwise!" (Margaret Stevenson 301). Eventually in 1901 Chalmers was, in fact, murdered, cooked in sago, and eaten.

Despite the attraction, and because of his interest in the specific circumstances surrounding cannibalism in the South Seas, Stevenson's reception of these narratives could be somewhat cautious. He registered a modest amount of skepticism, acknowledged that there was a possibility of a faulty source or an unreliable witness—what Melville in *Typee* calls "humbuggery" (*Typee* 170)—and conceded that the cannibal stories often emerged from complex dialogues between Europeans and Polynesians: that they were the result of compounded histories and, therefore, could not fully be trusted.[9] Furthermore, he allowed Montaigne's sobering thoughts on the subject to moderate what at times resembles a moral highhandedness on Stevenson's part. As a result, following Montaigne's example and in the spirit of Conrad, Stevenson did remind his readers of equally disgusting and cannibalistic practices in their own culture. But Stevenson could not always sustain such fairness. Although he attempted to offer an objective taxonomy of cannibalism and emphasized a fact, often overlooked in nineteenth-century popular works on the Pacific, that many areas were free of cannibalism and that its form varied from region to region, the lure of the forbidden and the magnetism of adventure periodically seduced his imagination. During these moments Stevenson wanted to believe his informants and delve into the dark fantasies of their narratives. Adopting the rhetoric of cannibal narratives and the suspenseful rhythms of the boys' adventure stories, as well as anticipating *Heart of Darkness*, Stevenson sometimes abandoned the apparatus he had been willing to muster and immersed his prose in the pleasure of the tabooed. Discarding objectivity and morality, he submerged himself in the thrill of the primitive even when he claimed to be "diffident" or cautious in his retelling of Father Siméon's account of cannibal hunts in Hiva-oa. His description pulsates with growing excitement and places both him and his reader at the very ceremony (*SS* 75–76). Stevenson was always attracted to violence. He once admitted that terror was "one of the chief joys of living" (*SL* 7:374).

Stevenson, though, was not a Conrad and tended not to linger within the boundaries of the stereotypes associated with cannibalism so he might create the terror of his landscape. As Linda Dryden points out, even though Conrad subverted the imperial romance, he still did not go as far as Stevenson, who had a more complex and skeptical approach to that genre.[10] I suggest, because Stevenson was someone who lived as well as traveled among vestiges of a cannibalistic past, he had more of an impulse to reject the stereotypical representations of the subject. He was not content to mimic apocryphal accounts of cannibalism that concentrate on the horror, if not the pleasure, of the moment. Stevenson chose, instead, to consider the complexities of inhabiting a culture caught between its past and its present. Cannibalism was not primarily a symbol of the uncivilized (whether in the East or the West) to be exploited for narrative momentum, as it was for Conrad, who used cannibalism as a trope to explore Kurtz's descent into savagery. The heads on the poles in *Heart of Darkness* are the physical evidence of much that is left unsaid and testimony to the "horror" of Kurtz's effect on these people, not primarily, it should be added, as proof of the Africans' savagery, since Conrad makes a point of showing their restraint in refusing to indulge in the act.

Cannibalism offered Stevenson the opportunity to address the particular sense of alienation he experienced in the South Seas. This domain was alienating, for it placed him in an incongruous landscape, and it confirmed his own skepticism concerning evolutionary psychology.[11] Stevenson could not completely share the conviction of those who subscribed to the current theories of evolution that suggested mankind had progressed and was continuing to advance from a barbaric state of mind to a more and more civilized condition—an attitude that Conrad shares when he suggests that progress, through Kurtz's presence and the descriptions of London, does not mean the relinquishing of the savage.

Incongruity and Journeying Out of the Comfort Zone

From Stevenson's point of view, to be in a place that had a history of cannibalism was to expose oneself to the disturbing disorientation that results when one recognizes the troublesome disparity between an island's cannibalistic past and its relatively civilized present. It is this incongruity, and not cannibalism itself, that propels his journey out from what he termed "the comfort zone" (*SS* 9) and leads him away from a reassuring continuity. Seized by the incongruities of the barbaric past and the civilized present, he is uncomfortable staring at a native dressed in prim European clothing while simultaneously recalling that individual's former relish for human flesh. Rather than glory in the alteration (or conversion), as the missionaries did, Stevenson finds the utter contrast troublesome. He finds not only amusement, as did Marlow, at the comic figure of the "savage" who resembles "a dog in a parody of breeches and a feather hat walking on his hind legs" (*HD* 38) but also a sense of threatening confusion.

Throughout *In the South Seas* Stevenson remarks on the fact that he was visiting areas with a history of mutilated corpses, where there remains a latent longing for older practices. He writes of walking through the "dripping vault of the forest" where cannibal feasts had been held, all the while standing, incongruously, next to a native Catholic priest in a kilted gown and a "bright-eyed Marquesan schoolboy" in uniform (*SS* 76). The moment was unsettling. Similarly, when Stevenson met the chief of Hatchei, the "last eater of long-pig in Huka-hia," who reputedly greeted strangers by "striding on the beach of Anaho . . . with a dead man's arm across his shoulder" while biting the human flesh (*SS* 37), the chief was dressed as a European gentleman. Neither image presumes the acquaintance of the other. Similarly, Moipu, a chief of Atuona, revolted Stevenson because he represented a violent, recent cannibalistic past within the guise of a gracious, gentlemanly, and even sentimental present. Stevenson was neither amused nor charmed, as were his mother and Fanny, when Moipu, upon saying fond farewells, held Fanny's hands and looked at her with tearful eyes. Stevenson could not rid his memory of the fact that not long ago the human hand had been Moipu's favorite morsel, writing that his repugnance in Moipu's presence "was mingled with nausea" (*SS* 102).

As for the challenge to evolutionary psychology, what was worst for Stevenson was what happened when the spaces of time collapsed and the past and the present, in all their incompatibility, stood simultaneously before his consciousness. The comforting hierarchy of sequence and distance had gone. At such times the assumption that the human mind evolved appeared dubious at best. One such moment occurred when the Marquesans, having cannibalized an individual, carried portions of flesh back to their dwellings in "a Swedish match-box," not wanting the Europeans to see. The combination of the mutilated flesh packaged in the modern European matchbox startled Stevenson: "[T]he barbarous substance of the drama and the European properties employed offer a seizing contrast to the imagination" (*SS* 72). This image as well as the specter of Moipu dressed as a gentleman were discomforting for Stevenson, who could not eradicate his shadow figure as a notorious cannibal.

For Stevenson, to live within the comfort zone is to be in a place where these incongruities do not concurrently press themselves upon one's consciousness; they retain a respectable and reassuring distance from one another: physically or imaginatively neither touches the other. To journey out of the comfort zone, on the other hand, is to stare simultaneously at both the savage and the civilized. Instead of dealing with a sense of time in which one moves progressively from barbaric to civilized, both are concurrent and the savage is also in view—no mythic landscape, as in *Heart of Darkness*, envelopes, mediates, or correlates the two in the fog of its timelessness.

The Taking of Heads

Throughout his life in the South Seas, Stevenson faced vestiges of the past, and this condition, coupled with his anthropological interest, created the realism of his Pacific fiction. Such was the case once Stevenson settled in Samoa, supposedly far away from the arena of cannibalism. Samoa had never been actively associated with the practice. Commentators consistently exempted Samoa from their gory narratives, and missionaries such as the Reverend Turner insisted that revenge in Samoan culture was not occasioned by "the mere relish for human flesh," as it was in Melanesia (Turner, London Missionary Society Archives). However, when civil war broke out in 1893, the old Samoan custom of displaying an enemy's head was reinstituted. (One has to remember that head hunting and cannibalism were almost synonymous in the Western imagination. It was one of those fantasy sites that authors such as Conrad exploited to help mark the idea of the primitive.) Stevenson heard reports of heads being taken on both sides and listened to tragic stories of a man receiving a head, washing off its war paint, and discovering the face of his own brother. Stevenson learned the alarming fact that among eleven heads presented to a chief, one proved to be a girl's—a reality that disoriented and greatly disturbed him, for the killing of females in Western stories about cannibalism was a well-rehearsed device to emphasize the deed's inhumanity. After learning that there had actually been three female heads, he drafted a letter to the British consul general asking him to submit an official reprimand, adding that such acts are "only practiced among the most debased races" (*SL* 8:142).

Conclusion

Suddenly the past had rushed forward and Stevenson found himself once more journeying out of the comfort zone and confronting a barbaric history within the more settled, forward-looking, and enlightened present. There was no retreat to a mythic land to modify the vision. Such incongruity not only threatened his future and his life (there were fears of a massacre) but also undermined Samoa's superiority and promise. Horrified, yet fascinated, his imagination hearkened to the sound of drums and to shouts in the moonlight close to Vailima, and Stevenson fancied the worst—the cries, it turned out, were only his staff enjoying a game of cards. However, even if these particular noises were ultimately benign, the severed heads displayed outside the chiefs' dwellings were real. They were not the symbolic ones facing Kurtz's house: despite evidence suggesting the heads were based on historical fact, their presence in the novel is essentially symbolic. Stevenson's reading of missionary texts, travel narratives, and adventure stories reflecting the Western obsession with anthropophagy was no preparation for the actual thing. Now his penchant for the fantasy of violence and his fascination with its particulars approached too close to home. Rather than serving as grist for a stereotype of primitivism, as in Conrad, these spoils of war expressed the living reality of an incongruity that Stevenson was himself experiencing: the improbable struggle of a dying culture to coexist with one that had superseded it. Stevenson could not enclose what he beheld within the fiction of a mythic fog; nor could he spread a softening gauze over the harsh landscape of incongruity. His "horror" was time bound and within the borders of Samoa. He could not drown it in the legendary deep; nor could he relegate it to a shifting, amorphous landscape that is neither sea nor forest. He had to remain among its lingering traces.

NOTES

1. All references to *Heart of Darkness* in this chapter are to the Kimbrough edition (New York: Norton, 1988).

2. It is understandable why critics like Patrick Brantlinger and Chinua Achebe suggest that Conrad's narrative is racist through its deliberate vilification of the continent. See Achebe and Brantlinger, *Rule of Darkness* and "Victorians and Africans: The Genealogy of the Myth of the Dark Continent."

3. For a discussion of Conrad's adjustment of the landscape, see Firchow 62–63.

4. All references to *In the South Seas* in this chapter are to the Rennie edition (London: Penguin, 1998).

5. For examples of these bloody accounts, see Captain Porter's *Journal of a Cruise Made to the Pacific* (1815), Reverend Charles Stewart's *A Visit to the South Seas* (1831), George Hosking Wicks's pamphlet published by the London Missionary Society describing the practice of devouring corpses in New Caledonia and the Loyalty Islands, Reverend George Turner's *Nineteen Years in Polynesia* (1861), Reverend A. W. Murray's *The Martyrs of Polynesia* (1885), Reverend James Alexander's *The Islanders in the Pacific from the Old to the New* (1895), *The Works of Ta'Unga: Records of a Polynesian Traveller in the South Seas, 1833–1896* (1968), John Elphinstone Erskine's *Journal of a Cruise among the Islands of the Western Pacific* (1853), and the Earl and the Doctor's *South Sea Bubbles* (1872).

6. For the reputation of the Marquesas, see Herbert, *Marquesan Encounters*.

7. See Simpson's *Cannibalism and the Common Law*, in which he argues that cannibalism after shipwreck was so much taken for granted in England that often ordinary innocuous survivors denied it had taken place.

8. Chalmers writes:

In a large open space near to the sacred place were pins to hang skulls on. These during our visit were down, being cleaned and dressed; and, having a compartment close by, I had a good opportunity of seeing them—in fact, some being too new, I found a difficulty in getting through my light dinner prepared by Johnnie. The skulls were all carved, and done over with many colours. A feast would soon be on, and the heaps of skulls would disappear, because all would find their places on the skullery pins. That head-gear once belonged to inland natives, who were killed . . . , presented to the gods, then cooked and eaten. (Chalmers 9)

9. When Stevenson gave in to the drama of tales about cannibalism, he barely entertained the possibility, now current in debates among anthropologists, that these narratives might be constructed to meet the expectations of the audience. For current anthropological debates concerning the nature and existence of cannibalism, see, for example, Arens.

10. See Dryden, *Joseph Conrad,* for more discussion.

11. See Julia Reid, *Stevenson, Science, and the Fin de Siècle,* for more discussion of Stevenson's engagement with late Victorian theories of evolutionary psychology and his belief that savagery survives amid supposedly civilized societies.

The Geopolitics of Criticism:
The Sea as Liminal Symbol in Stevenson's
The Ebb-Tide and Conrad's *An Outcast of the Islands*

ROBBIE B. H. GOH

*I*N HIS INTRODUCTION to the *Oxford Book of the Sea*, Jonathan Raban writes that "the sea is one of the most 'universal' symbols in literature; it is certainly the most protean," so much so that "the sea in eighteenth-century literature is one place, the sea in nineteenth-century literature quite another," as it reflects the sociopolitical realities of the age (Raban 3). It is thus hardly surprising to find that the sea, which for several centuries was the element that both obstructed and enabled English commerce and imperialism, should come to reflect in both obvious and unconscious ways the flow and ebb of that commercial-political state of mind.

With only a few significant exceptions it seems fair to say that while the sea featured prominently in romantic poetry and Gothic literature in the first quarter of the nineteenth century, it largely recedes to the background in the literary works produced at the height of England's imperial power and domestic order at midcentury. Looking at the way in which the sea is used in pre-Victorian writing, it is easy to conclude that such writings reflect in complex ways the anxieties of the commercial state in an age of empire just as they explore the imaginative prehistory of the individual consciousness as it struggles against the growing authority of patriarchal and rational institutionalism (Sedgwick 3–4; Williams 182, 197; Goh 270–74). In contrast, there is little such use and representation of the sea in the majority of Victorian writings. The literary productions of the high Victorian period are by and large conspicuously absent from the *Oxford Book of the Sea*, and Tony Tanner's edition of the *Oxford Book of Sea Stories* begins with English writers about the turn of the century—with Conrad, Kipling, Wells, and the like.[1]

John Peck's observation that "most novelists do not make a connection between the characters, society, and values presented and the maritime economy that has helped bring such people, such a society and such values into existence" refers particularly to Victorian literature (Peck 3). Taken as a whole, Victorian novels offer little more than brief invocations of the sea as a symbol of acknowledged and yet marginalized or repressed commercial anxieties. The sea is imagined as an undifferentiated space connoting great distance, fickle fortune, ill-gotten gain, and tragic fate. There is little interest in the actual sea voyages undertaken, their conditions and destinations, in large part because the major characters do not undertake such voyages.

This occlusion is surprising in the context of England's expanding commercial and political horizons and its increasing share of world shipping and shipbuilding. The Great Exhibition of 1851 was intended to showcase London as "not simply the capital of a great nation, but the metropolis of the world," as a contemporary newspaper account puts it (cited in Golby 5). The expectation was indeed that other nations would acknowledge Britain's preeminence. London's status as the metropolis of the world could not, of course, be divorced from England's growing empire and the seaborne trade with which the empire was so closely associated. Britain's maritime trade and exports increased sharply in this period. Between 1837 and 1865 its tonnage of sailing ships more than doubled, and Britain also came to dominate the iron shipbuilding industry (Beales 169). In the latter part of the nineteenth century Britain came to be one of the largest consumer markets for primary products such as foodstuffs while also becoming the greatest exporter of industrial products. Thus "the City of London and British shipping became more central than ever to the world economy" (Hobsbawm 39).

Hobsbawm notes the "strange schizophrenia of the capitalist world economy" (Hobsbawm 40–41) to explain the curious split between the expanding English empire and the refusal to acknowledge its mechanisms in the literature of the day. While nationalism and capitalism in practice went about their business with a great deal of collusion and coincidence of functions, in terms of thinking and consciousness there was a noticeable split between the "internationalist" and "global" individual or firms on the one hand and the sociopolitical and cultural mechanisms of the "nation" on the other. Hobsbawm's formulation resembles Deleuze and Guattari's account of capitalism's "schizophrenic" tendency, in which the decoding and deterritorializing function of capitalist production—its reduction of signifying differences to the abstract equivalents of money and capital—runs up against (even as, at another level, it is reinforced by) the "regulative functions of the state" (Deleuze and Guattari 242–53). Hence writing—as the system of encoding social values, meanings, and "privileged references"—"has never been capitalism's thing" (Deleuze and Guattari 240). Victorian writers deferred a full awareness of the global machinery of the British Empire even as they sought to define social meaning and value within the domestic sphere.

By the last decades of the nineteenth century the geopolitical realities of the British Empire could no longer be ignored, and the intensely domestic nature of high Victorian literature had given way to an increasing concern with cultural difference and diversity. The terms *geopolitics* and *political geography* were coined at the end of the nineteenth century in the writings of the German geographer Friedrich Ratzel and the Swedish social scientist Rudolf Kjellén to describe a conception of the world in terms of competing political-cultural blocs (Parker 10–12; Blouet 26–30). The turn toward a competitively Darwinian global geography was certainly precipitated by the stage of late imperialism that saw all parts of the globe as "filled in" as a result of an "explosion of inter-imperial rivalries," but naval power and the speed of seaborne traffic in creating a connected global space were also important factors, as reflected in the opening chapter of Admiral Mahan's 1890 book *The Influence of Seapower upon History, 1660–1783* (Agnew and Corbridge 23; Blouet 25).

Writers such as Rudyard Kipling, H. Rider Haggard, Bram Stoker, Arthur Conan Doyle, Joseph Conrad, and Robert Louis Stevenson, among others, in some ways anticipated this geopolitical development, while in other ways they practiced a narrativized deferral or delaying of the changing tide of geopolitical awareness.

Chris Bongie refers to Conrad's writerly dilemma as "the problem of a truly *global* modernity" (in contrast to the high Victorian consciousness of an Other antithetical to the domestic self) in which capitalism creates a completely "undifferentiated world" (Bongie 269). Conrad's narrator/protagonist Marlow in *Heart of Darkness* has a cartographic rumination that registers this change to a new geopolitical awareness: from a childhood spent dreaming of the "glories of exploration" of the "many blank spaces on the earth," he grows up to realize that exotic places such as Africa "had got filled since my boyhood" and are now mapped with "all the colours of a rainbow" representing the various and complicated colonial-mercantile claims on them (*HD* 8, 10). This is not to say that Conrad and his contemporaries were any more keen to engage with capitalist processes than were the Victorians. A later form of capitalist schizophrenia obtained, to the extent that writing was a means of symbolizing a crisis of national culture and values instead of a crisis of the capitalist machinery and the violence it employed as such. In this regard Fredric Jameson's assessment of Conrad—that his writings involved "the construction of the bourgeois subject in emergent capitalism and its schizophrenic disintegration in our own time" (Jameson 12)—might also, *mutatis mutandis*, be applied to Stevenson.

Cedric Watts notes that there are "various points of similarity between Conrad's *Victory* and [Stevenson's] *The Ebb-Tide*" but that many of these similarities are at an ideological level and go beyond "intermittent resemblances in aspects of plot, location, and characterization" (Watts, *Joseph Conrad's Letters*, 33). Many of the novels and stories of both Conrad and Stevenson explicitly feature sailors and other inveterate voyagers, who prefer the restlessness and challenges of life at sea to the domestic sphere and who considered themselves during their time on dry land merely as "exiles in a strange isle," to borrow a phrase that Stevenson uses in *In the South Seas* (*WRLS* 16:223). The transient and unsettled nature of their time spent on land is not merely occupational or incidental but is often represented as part of a deeper (if inchoate) existential state, one that characters often attribute to fate, the supernatural, and other forces outside of human will and control. Yet beyond (and despite) these less choate supernatural attributions, the circumstances in which these characters are found imply another kind of signification, one that sees human action as the result of being caught between conflicting sociopolitical forces.

Conrad's and Stevenson's characters might thus be described as occupying liminal positions. While the threshold or border assumes a contingent reality to a viewer on either side of it—a viewer whose affiliations and location are clear-cut, if only temporarily—as a position and state of consciousness in itself the threshold poses all kinds of problems, dissolving into the imaginary and arbitrary construction that it actually is. In this sense a liminal position is as "unnatural" as the schizophrenic's time-space awareness, which is a kind of perpetual hyperpresent, attenuated and unresolved, cut off from succession in time (see Jameson 27; Heise 21, 26). Conrad's and Stevenson's prototypical characters might be said to inhabit schizophrenically the liminal spaces foregrounded by the emerging geopolitical order, which creates an acute consciousness of competing spaces without conferring the security of settled national sites. This liminality is already figured in the typical landscapes occupied by these characters—beaches, river mouth settlements, atolls, and other sites at the edges of land and sea whose boundaries and shape depend on tidal flows—as well as in the often barely seaworthy ships that transport these characters from place to place and often function as their domestic space or territory. In terms of narrative style, liminality is expressed as a kind of schizophrenic consciousness and discourse on the part of characters who attribute a range of unstable and varying (we might say, ebbing and flowing) significations to their immediate loci without recognizing or being able to articulate the larger cultural and political context in which they act and move.

Joseph Conrad's *An Outcast of the Islands* (1896) is, as the title suggests, one of the best embodiments of the author's evocation of the condition of geopolitical insularity and alienation. The liminal-schizophrenic nature of the text is underscored by the fact that it eschews the more overt political commentary found in novels such as *Heart of Darkness*. *An Outcast of the Islands* tells the tale of Willems, a Dutchman who, having run away from a merchant ship, becomes a successful clerk and factotum in the firm of Hudig and Co. in the Dutch-controlled city of Macassar on the Indonesian island of Celebes. Willems's arrogance and greed, as well as his contemptuous patronage of his half-caste wife, Joanna, and her family, lead to his betrayal, the loss of his position, and the end of his dreams of grandeur. With the aid of his mentor, the powerful and fearsome adventurer-trader Captain Lingard, Willems is given a second chance as a trader based in the isolated island settlement of Sambir. Unable to come to terms with the loss of his standing as "the rising man sure to climb very high" in colonial society (*OI* 4), Willems comes under the spell of a tormented native woman, Aïssa, becomes a pawn in Sambir politics, and is used to overthrow Lingard's monopolistic control of the island's trade and affairs. Condemned by Lingard to banishment on the island, he seizes on a visit by his estranged wife, Joanna, to attempt an escape, comes between the jealous Aïssa and Joanna, and is shot dead.

What leads to Willems's tragic career is his liminal condition of being caught between opposing poles of culture, politics, economics, and race. This liminal position is seen in part in the novel's treatment of race and color. On the one hand Willems exhibits racial hatred for the natives among whom he lives. He has a "tender contempt" for his own "pale yellow child," and his complex relationship with Joanna and her family rely on the satisfaction that comes from their dependence on him and their "awe-struck respect" for him (*OI* 3). Willems's in-laws are themselves racially hybrid, "dark-skinned" but bearing the Portuguese name Da Souza, constituting in Willems's eyes the "shabby multitude" of native life, but some of them with a penchant for "pink neckties and ... patent-leather boots" (*OI* 3, 4).

Although Willems's racial-cultural liminality differs significantly from the Da Souzas' racial hybridity, he too comes to exhibit something of the debilitating effects of being caught between the races. In what he sees as the uncivilized backwater of Sambir, Willems resentfully sees himself as "the outcast of [his] people" (*OI* 71), barred from civilized white company yet also repulsed by the alien ways of the native people. At this stage the isolating effect of the seas is symbolized as a tide of racial hatred within him: "He did not stop to ask himself whether he could escape, and how, and where. He was carried away by the flood of hate, disgust, and contempt of a white man for that blood which is not his blood, for that race which is not his race; for the brown skins; for the hearts false like the sea, blacker than night" (*OI* 152). Despite his racial hatred, he becomes obsessed with Aïssa and soon joins her to help a native faction, led by Abdulla, overthrow the power and trade monopoly of his friend and fellow white man Lingard. In the early throes of passion he can only reconcile his paradoxical love for Aïssa by conceiving of space in ideal Edenic terms, cut off from the realities of race and culture. He longs to go away with her to "some distant place" where he would "have her all to [himself] away from her people," where he would "be all the world to her" (*OI* 92).

This Edenic and romantic imagining relies on the sea as barrier, as a void space that neutralizes race and culture by keeping out their human representatives (except, of course, the lovers themselves). That it is an about-face from Willems's imagining of the "flood" of racial hatred provoked by native hearts "false like the sea" is as obvious as the fact that his obsession with Aïssa contradicts his attitude to and dealings with all other natives, including his estranged wife and her family. Unable to accept, or perhaps unaware of, this contradiction in himself, Willems (in Adamic fashion) blames Aïssa for his downfall, attributing to her a Satanic influence that would exonerate himself: "[S]he found out something in me . . . and I was lost"; "[I]sn't [my devil] pretty?"; "Take that woman away—she is sin" (*OI* 269, 273, 278). If Aïssa, in her dependent and vulnerable position, is unable to bring Willems's conflicting racial attitudes to his consciousness, the brute consequences of his actions cannot be ignored. Lingard, in exiling him on Sambir and pronouncing, "You are alone. . . . You are neither white nor brown" (*OI* 276), only concretizes Willems's liminal position, which exceeds and transgresses the cultural domains of both native and European spaces.

Although imagining himself "more sinned against than sinning" (King Lear–like in his self-dethronement, nurturing a treacherous cuckoo who is part of his undoing), Lingard is himself a liminal figure whose supposed freedom from colonial greed is only sustained by his imagination and pride. Lingard is initially quick to attribute Willems's downfall to the corrupt values of the petty bourgeois colonial traders, which he contrasts unfavorably with the life of the sea:

> "[Y]ou got yourself so crooked amongst those longshore quill-drivers that you could not run clear in any way. That's what comes of such talk as yours, and of such a life. A man sees so much false-hood that he begins to lie to himself. Pah!" he said in disgust, "there's only one place for an honest man. The sea, my boy, the sea! But you never would; didn't think there was enough money in it; and now—look!" (*OI* 41–42)

Lingard takes great pride in the sobriquet Rajah Laut (King of the Sea) and exults in the power and wealth that his seamanship has brought him: "D'ye see, I have them all in my pocket. The rajah is an old friend of mine. My word is law—and I am the only trader. . . . Keep mum about my river when you get amongst the traders again. There's many would give their ears for the knowledge of it. I'll tell you something: that's where I get all my guttah and rattans. Simply inexhaustible, my boy" (*OI* 43). Secure in the power of his brig *Flash* and in his sailor's craft and courage, Lingard imagines an older geography in which the lone white adventurer remains unchallenged lord of any space that he is plucky enough to find and lay claim to—space that is assumed to be empty, pliable, and uncon-tested. This is in turn a reflection of his outdated notion of the "sea of the past" as an "incomparably beautiful mistress" who protected and sus-tained the rare men (among whom Lingard numbers himself) who knew her secrets (*OI* 12–13). If the reader realizes that the sea today is a "used-up drudge, wrinkled and defaced by the churned-up wakes of brutal pro-pellers, robbed of the enslaving charm of its vastness" (*OI* 13), Lingard's hubris and tragedy lie in his inability to realize this. His careless and uncomprehending appointment of Willems into the volatile situation in Sambir ultimately leads to his own undoing as well; unable to continue as Rajah Laut when his unacknowledged land empire collapses, Lingard's fate is fittingly to disappear on dry land, becoming untraceable while on a visit back to England.

Geography and landscape in the novel speak more accurately of the human condition than do either Lingard or Willems. The settlement of Sambir, which was "born in a swamp and passed its youth in malodorous mud," forms an "unhealthy" and ill-defined shore with the river mouth (*OI* 65). Although Lingard's trading company owns a substantial piece of land, it is defined by the constant water traffic at its feet, "the up-country canoes discharging guttah or rattans, and loading rice or European goods on the little wharf" (*OI* 64). The trading settlement even comes to assume, in Willems's febrile disgruntlement, something of the ebb-and-flow character, the impermanence and instability, of the flowing water: "Round him everything stirred, moved, swept by in a rush; the earth under his feet and the heavens above his head" (*OI* 65).

The river's movements and flows are of course significant to the action in the novel as well. Lingard's superior position, which is the envy of both native and colonial merchants, is founded on his secret knowledge of the river-mouth entrance and its treacherous banks—a secret that turns against Lingard when Willems conveys it to Lingard's rival, Abdulla. Almayer, Lingard's incumbent agent and the enemy of Willems, uses the tides in plotting Willems's demise later in the novel, deliberately grounding his boat upriver during low tide so that he can appear to have obeyed Lingard's orders while actually facilitating the tragic meeting between Willems and Joanna. Willems's vacillating behavior is prefigured in his constant crossing and recrossing of the river early in his time at Sambir. Discontented with his position in relation to both the European trading post and the native settlement, he takes to canoeing across the river in search of a solitary spot of land, only to meet "the discouragement of thorny thickets," which leads him "to seek another opening, to find another deception" (*OI* 67).

The white men thus inhabit an inherently unstable site at the margin of water and land, which necessitates constant shifting and crossing, the establishment of new and likewise temporary positions, and betrayals and reversals of fortune. The riverfront settlement as a symbol of the liminal condition of colonial man is repeated in the ebb and flow of at least the nominal political affiliations of the island. When Willems acts as the pawn of the native faction led by Abdulla to seize control of Sambir, his defiance of Lingard's authority is signaled (among other things) by the hoisting of a Dutch flag over the native settlement and his forcing

Almayer to run down the Union Jack that hangs over the trading station
(*OI* 179). Yet the competing colonial factions do not truly reflect the
political complexities on Sambir—Abdulla himself is nominally British,
based as he is in the port island of Penang in British Malaya, while
Almayer's allegiance to the British flag is a result of his loyalty to
Lingard—indicating the split between capitalism and nationalism, individual profit and colonial boundaries. Willems's quasi-schizophrenic
position, characterized by his inability to occupy any stable and fixed
space, his contradictory racial attitudes, his vacillations of loyalties, is thus
symptomatic of the schizophrenic effect that the colonial economy has
on territories and individuals.

Significantly, many of the natives exhibit a realpolitik awareness quite
at odds with the untenable romanticism of the Europeans. Babalatchi,
the veteran warrior and advisor who plots the coup on Sambir, takes
pride in being one of the Orang Laut, or sea people, "vagabond[s] of the
seas" who live by "rapine and plunder of coasts and ships," "brave and
bloodthirsty without any affection" (*OI* 51–52). He can see, where Lingard
cannot, the violent rapacity of white colonial power: "What am I to be
angry? I am only an Orang Laut, and I have fled before your people many
times. . . . What am I, to be angry with a white man? What is anger without the power to strike? But you whites have taken all: the land, the sea,
and the power to strike! And there is nothing left for us in the islands but
your white men's justice; your great justice that knows not anger" (*OI*
229). Conrad's novel, ostensibly a story about tragic fate, can be read
against that grain. It is both a sub rosa invocation of a new geopolitical
world and a cautionary tale about the fate of individuals caught in that
world but refusing to see it for what it really is, clinging instead to outdated romantic geographies. In narrative terms the novel creates a kind of
split perspective in which the reader is pulled between the compelling
idealism of individual characters and the cold political scenario that
implicitly frames their discourses and actions.

Stevenson, more blunt in his articulation of harsh geopolitical realities, nevertheless constructs a similar kind of moral landscape in many of
his South Seas narratives. *The Ebb-Tide*, his 1894 collaboration with
Lloyd Osbourne, tells the story of a trio of desperate white characters—
the disgraced American ship's captain Davis, the vicious Cockney Huish,

and the English gentleman come down in life Herrick—who, despite their different backgrounds, end up together in a shady undertaking to scuttle a ship and blackmail its owners for a share of the insurance money. Like many of Conrad's protagonists, the trio are dislocated white men, taken to the far side of the earth (in this case the Pacific rather than Conrad's Indonesian islands) by colonial enterprise.

Where Conrad's characters supplant harsh commercial-political realities with romanticized narratives of adventure, honor, and love (in the process transforming the sea into symbols of fate and existential loneliness), Stevenson's characters are all too aware of the degraded motives and conditions of their world. The novel introduces the trio of degenerate characters with a sweeping indictment of colonialism's consequences in the South Seas: "Throughout the island world of the Pacific, scattered men of many European races and from almost every grade of society carry activity and disseminate disease. Some prosper, some vegetate. Some have mounted the steps of thrones and owned islands and navies. Others again must marry for a livelihood; a strapping, merry, chocolate-coloured dame supports them in sheer idleness" (*ET* 3).[2] The trio exemplifies the "diseased" state of European affairs in the Pacific, moving in the course of the novel from unscrupulous deal to unscrupulous deal. At one level a story of crime, repentance, and atonement, *The Ebb-Tide* is also a geopolitical account of enforced isolation and dislocation in a filled-in, heavily contested globe. The novel's action takes place on a series of liminal spaces, from the beach at Papeete, where we first encounter the trio, to Attwater's seemingly fragile and evanescent atoll: "The isle was like the rim of a great vessel sunken in the waters; . . . So slender it seemed amidst the outrageous breakers, so frail and pretty, [Herrick] would scarce have wondered to see it sink and disappear without a sound, and the waves close smoothly over its descent" (*ET* 68). The ship is likewise a kind of nonspace, non grata in the first place because of the deadly illness that kills some of the unfortunate crew but also deeply compromised by the fraudulent greed of its owners. Intended all along to be scuttled for the insurance money, it is paradoxically a sailing shipwreck and tellingly wanders off course and fetches up arbitrarily on land, first at Tahiti and then at Attwater's island. Its name, the *Farallone*, thus quite clearly signals isolation. Again tellingly, the ship's name becomes extended to the trio of white men who sail on it, when "the Farallones" (as they are then called) find their way to Attwater's atoll (*ET* 70).

The racial-cultural liminality of the trio is underscored early in the novel. In chapter one, Herrick's fairy tale of the magic carpet, on which he and the other characters imagine flying home "in the crack of a whip," instead of bringing comforting memories only confirms their exile in "hell" (*ET* 10, 11). Each of the trio has his fantasy interrupted (Herrick by imaginative paucity, Huish by a coughing fit, and Davis by the realization of his utter lack of knowledge of his family's fate), and the supernatural story takes a devilish turn when Huish, recalled inexorably to their present sufferings, rashly calls out, "I defy the devil to make me worse off," and a squall immediately bursts onto them (*ET* 12, 13). This inability to return, even imaginatively, to the homeland is exacerbated by their feeling of irremediable distance from the natives. After breaking their long fast through the kindness of a group of Kanaka sailors, Herrick is moved to the "passionate utterance," "I wish to God I was a Kanaka" (*ET* 16). Yet it is clear in this episode that their white man's pride, their shame at relying on the kindness of the natives, and their deeply ingrained racial prejudices make it impossible for them to live the native life.

Attwater, the fourth white man in this novel's "quartette," represents the only means of establishing a stable position in the colonial world order—namely, by the exercise of sheer, ruthless power. Attwater is in many ways the prototypical imperialist: his physical size symbolizes the overpowering control he exerts on the tiny atoll, he treats the merest hint of native disobedience with violent punishment (as seen in the story of his execution of the native who breaks "the regulations of the place" [*ET* 97]), and his regime aims at nothing more or less than gross profit. Attwater, unlike the trio (or Conrad's white characters), does not feel the dislocating liminality of place simply because he imposes a template of his own culture and values onto the colonized space. He names his ship the *Trinity Hall*, imports sherry from London at an exorbitant cost, and frightens his native servants into keeping an "excellent bearing" as they wait on his table (*ET* 95). Above all, he imposes Christianity as an all-embracing value system, moral code, and governing discourse on life on his atoll, even dispensing judgments and decision of life or death depending on whether the supplicant is in his eyes a "true penitent" (*ET* 127). By the end of the novel he has even colonized Davis, who is mouthing the rhetoric of the zealous convert and has become what Herrick calls "Attwater's spoiled darling and pet penitent" (*ET* 130).

Yet Attwater, as his name suggests, is, despite his vigorous and violent colonialism, as much at sea as the trio. If he is successful in the purely practical sense of exerting his authority on the island and extracting his treasure in pearls, this nevertheless comes at a certain moral and cultural cost. Attwater is perpetually exiled, living on an island whose existence must remain a secret from other white men (with the exception of the mysterious and unseen partner Dr. Symmonds) if his authority is to continue, limited to servile and cowed natives for company, and relying on a zealous and strangely "fatalistic" brand of Christianity to exonerate himself.[3] The novel's rather abrupt ending—in which Herrick is on the verge of sailing off to unknown parts on Attwater's ship *Trinity Hall*, which has been sighted on the offing, while Davis seeks to persuade him to "be one of us" on the island and "come to Jesus right away" so that they may all "meet in yon beautiful land" (*ET* 130)—reinforces the liminal location of Christianity in this colonial world order, that it can only find its place either in the remote island outside of society's interventions or else in the utopian heavenly kingdom.

Liminality ultimately cannot be described and takes its toll on narrative, confirming Deleuze and Guattari's observation that "writing . . . has never been capitalism's thing" (Deleuze and Guattari 240). The narrative gaps and fissures that characterize Stevenson's supernatural and surreal tales become in the geopolitical context of *The Ebb-Tide* the abrupt closures that register the ineffability of space. This is evident not only in the deferred religious space that Davis invokes at the end of the novel but also in the various attempts by the trio earlier in the novel to imagine, narrate, or correspond in writing to their homes. Herrick's epistolary experiment is particularly interesting as an exercise in capitalist schizophrenia. After "scratch[ing] out the beginning to [his] father" and addressing his sweetheart Emma instead, he turns from memories of their life together in England ("in the parlour" and "the day on Battersea Bridge") to a perpetual and idealized exile ("Think of me, at the last, here, on a bright beach, the sky and sea immoderately blue" [*ET* 19–20]). Apart from the extreme contrast this idealized tropical space forms to his actual miserable condition on the beach at Papeete, the domestic and foreign sites invoked in his letter are irrevocably, quasi-schizophrenically closed off: "Turn the key in the door; let no thought of me return; be done with the poor ghost that pretended he was a man and stole your love" (*ET* 20). As a colonial "ghost," Herrick can comfortably inhabit neither the sanitized domestic sphere nor the idealized tropical space. His space, such as it is, is the threshold or doorway, which, by his own inscription, must be closed and locked if the myths that sustain European imperialism are to be perpetuated.

The geopolitics of naval power were not to survive the advent of air power in World War II and the era of air travel and the very differently networked world order that these ushered in. As itself a kind of transitional order, seaborne geopolitics occupied a liminal position itself, which could envision a filled-in and intensely contested global order even while it clung to older narratives of protected domestic spaces and distinct cultures. Stevenson and Conrad, despite their many ideological and stylistic differences, were bound by a historical as much as an artistic consciousness in which space and landscape become heavily symbolic elements in their articulation of a particularly modern condition. Their narratives of liminal landscapes and the impossibility of human positionings within those landscapes not only spoke more eloquently of this naval geopolitics than did the political discourses of the day but also anticipated many of the features of postmodern writing in its own age of globalization.

NOTES

1. That American writers such as Herman Melville, Washington Irving, Francis Bret Harte, and others continue to engage explicitly with the sea in their writings throughout the nineteenth century—indeed, Tanner (xvii) insists that "the short story about the sea is, initially, a distinctively American genre"—confirms the specific sociopolitical significance of this symbolism, that it is a peculiar high Victorian imperial consciousness that causes the sea and its implications to recede from English cultural productions of that period.

2. All references to *The Ebb-Tide* in this chapter are to the Hinchcliffe and Kerrigan edition (Edinburgh: Edinburgh University Press, 1995).

3. A number of religious echoes resonate throughout the novel: the various water

images (including Attwater's name) suggest both the baptism and the imagery of the Holy Spirit as "living streams (or fountains, or springs) of water" (Revelation 7:17), the trio of protagonists echoes the Holy Trinity, Attwater's ship is called *Trinity Hall*, and the wrongly accused native who hangs himself suggests Christ's innocent execution on the cross, among other allusions. Yet in the light of the novel's narrative pattern as a whole, these references turn out to be ironic (just as the supposed champagne turns out to be water, a reversal of the Biblical miracle in which water is turned to wine), so that any invocation of religion becomes compromised by the colonial politics and greed in which it is located.

Treasure Island and *Victory*: Maps, Class, and Sexuality

ROBERT HAMPSON

$\mathcal{S}$TEVENSON BEGINS "A Gossip on Romance" with a description of the reading process as "absorbing and voluptuous," as a result of which we should "be rapt clean out of ourselves, and rise from the perusal, our mind filled with the busiest, kaleidoscopic dance of images, incapable of sleep or of continuous thought" (*MP* 247). To produce this reading experience, Stevenson asserts, the focus has to be on "the brute incident" (*MP* 249), not character, and to produce the right kind of incident the great creative writer obeys "the ideal laws of the daydream" (*MP* 255). One aspect of these "ideal laws" is "fitness in events and places" (*MP* 251): Stevenson demonstrates how the imagination responds to particular places and atmospheres with the expectation of particular kinds of incident. Stevenson's version of organic form thus begins from the basis that the "right kind of thing should fall out in the right kind of place" (*MP* 255).

Treasure Island is, in origin and genesis, a response to place and a demonstration of the narrative potential of place. Significantly, on seeing Treasure Island, Jim Hawkins describes its topography as something seen "almost in a dream," and at the end he is haunted by nightmares of that "accursed island" where he hears "the surf booming about its coasts" (*TI* 72, 220).[1] In his Note to the novel, Lloyd Osbourne recalls its origin in a map he had drawn and was tinting with a paint-box:

> Stevenson came in as I was finishing it, and with his affectionate interest in everything I was doing, leaned over my shoulder, and was soon elaborating the map, and naming it. I shall never forget the thrill of Skeleton Island, Spy-Glass Hill, nor the heart-stirring climax of the three red crosses! And the greater climax still when he wrote down the words "Treasure Island" at the top right-hand corner! And he seemed to know so much about it too—the pirates, the buried treasure, the man who had been marooned on the island. "Oh, for a story about it," I exclaimed in a heaven of enchantment. (*TI* xviii)

The following day Stevenson read him the opening chapter. In "My First Book," Stevenson confirms the priority of the map to the text but claims authorship of the map.[2] The map is an object of meditation, a prompt to the imagination: "As I pored upon my map of Treasure Island, the future characters of the book began to appear there visibly among imaginary woods, and their brown faces and bright weapons peeped out upon me from unexpected quarters, as they passed to and fro, fighting and hunting treasure, on these four square inches of a flat projection" (*TI* xxvi). Stevenson's narrative responds to the map, presenting a reading of its topographical features: "[I]t was because I had made two harbours that the *Hispaniola* was sent on her wanderings with Israel Hands" (*TI* xxx). The reader too is presented at the outset with a map, decoded and narrativized by the novel. Its ownership is a focus of the action, and the narrative climax is the pirates' reading of it against the island's spaces. Stevenson was thus doubly right when he observed: "The map was the chief point of my plot" (*TI* xxx).

The novel begins with Hawkins recording his motive for the ensuing narrative: "Squire Trelawney, Dr Livesey, and the rest of these gentlemen having asked me to write down the whole particulars about Treasure Island" (*TI* 3). This reveals the story's outcome—in particular, it names the group with which Hawkins aligns himself and by whom he is finally accepted. Hawkins's location of the time and place of the beginning ("the time when my father kept the 'Admiral Benbow' inn") situates him in class terms relative to "these gentlemen," who provide the social context for the writing. The social distance between him and these gentlemen is implicit in their asking and his obeying; at the same time, as Alan Sandison says, the assertion of authorship also affirms Hawkins's "accession to authority" (Sandison 48). The negotiation of these class positions and affiliations is one of the major issues in the narrative that follows.

The novel can be read as a bildungsroman, Hawkins's journey to maturity.[3] The first part kills off his natural father and all the prominent males associated with his life at the Admiral Benbow. The narrative provides, through Trelawney and Livesey, another male social world as the context for his process of maturation in a world of men, specifically in relation to a world of "gentlemen," exploring both the idea of the gentleman and issues of class. The second part introduces another male world, which also makes claims on his loyalty.[4] The dominant figure in this competing world is Long John Silver, who is the keeper of "a public house" like Hawkins's dead father, and is thus set up as a potential substitute father (*TI* 44).[5] This is reinforced by the emotional tone of Hawkins's last visit to his mother at the Benbow, which makes him aware of "the home that I was leaving," while the apprentice "boy" replacing him readily figures the self he leaves behind to undertake this adventure (*TI* 46). Hawkins never looks back nostalgically to his early life at the Benbow or to his mother: his development takes place entirely in relation to men. As Stevenson notes, "Women were excluded" (*TI* xxvi): Hawkins's achievement of independent mature identity involves the negotiation of a range of father figures and rival male groupings.

Whereas Part I begins with a scene of writing, Part II begins with a scene of reading. Left alone at the Hall, Hawkins indulges in "sea-dreams, and the most charming anticipations of strange islands and adventures" (*TI* 43). However, as with his namesake, "Lord" Jim, adolescent dreams are not realized in subsequent experience. For Lord Jim the adventures anticipated from reading "light literature" are systematically overturned by actual experience. From the start, as Conrad makes clear, when Lord Jim enters "the regions so well known to his imagination" he finds them "strangely barren of adventure"; instead, he endures "the pro-saic severity of the daily task that gives bread" (*LJ* 10). Jim Hawkins, on the other hand, experiences a very different relationship between his "sea-dreams" and reality: "Sometimes the isle was thick with savages, with whom we fought, sometimes full of dangerous animals that hunted us; but in all my fancies nothing occurred to me so strange and tragic as our actual adventures" (*TI* 43). Where, in *Lord Jim*, reality falls short of romantic expectations, Stevenson's romance world exceeds the boy's dream of adventure. Hawkins's narrative deciphering of the map falls short of the narrative deciphering that Stevenson provides. Most inter-estingly, Hawkins's experiences in the novel involve neither "savages" nor "dangerous animals" (as might be the case in R. M. Ballantyne): his adventures arise from conflicts between Europeans.

The opening chapters present Hawkins as a reader—reading Billy Bones's appearance and tattoos (*TI* 13) and, finally, reading "the map of an island, with latitude and longitude, soundings, names of hills, and bays and inlets" (*TI* 38). The reference to "The Spy-Glass" apparently confirms that he is reading the map that the reader has already seen. Hawkins's first encounter with Silver is also orchestrated through the reading—and often misreading—of signs. He is sent to find Silver "at the sign of the Spy-glass," decoded as a "little tavern with a large brass telescope for sign" (*TI* 48). The telescope is offered as the "sign" for the tavern, but any con-nection with the map's "Spy-Glass Hill" is resolutely ignored. Similarly, Hawkins's response to Silver reminds us of Bones's anxieties about a one-legged man while also refusing to make the connection: "From the very first mention of Long John in Squire Trelawney's letter, I had taken a fear in my mind that he might prove to be the very one-legged sailor whom I had watched for so long at the old 'Benbow'" (*TI* 48–49). Hawkins offers, in response to this memory, a not fully convincing counterreading: "I thought I knew what a buccaneer was like—a very different creature, according to me, from this clean and pleasant-tempered landlord" (*TI* 49).

Although Hawkins has left the Benbow, the Benbow hasn't left him. In the Spy-glass he runs into Black Dog, who had visited Bones at the Benbow. As the *Hispaniola* prepares to sail, the capstan song "carried me back to the old 'Admiral Benbow' in a second" (*TI* 60). Silver's parrot is

named after Captain Flint, the pirate whose treasure they seek, and even
the *Hispaniola* has obvious, but unremarked, piratical associations.[6] All of
these signs, eloquent for the reader, are recorded but ignored by Hawkins:
a gap is thus opened between Hawkins's narrative and the reader's awareness of narrative exclusions. Only when overhearing Silver's speech to the
crew toward the end do the scales fall from Hawkins's eyes. Even then he
seems most upset by personal betrayal when hearing another youth
praised as he had been by Silver: "You may imagine how I felt when I
heard this abominable old rogue addressing another in the very same
words of flattery as he had used to myself" (*TI* 67). Hawkins looks for
adult male recognition, and Silver had seemed to offer this. Among the
gentlemen, the Squire is too imperceptive, too gullible to carry sufficient
moral authority, and too self-involved to be aware of Hawkins's needs.
Captain Smollet from the start establishes himself as stern and uncompromising. Only Dr. Livesey shows any readiness to respond emotionally,
while, as Sandison suggests, his "confident authority" (*TI* 55), "innate
compassion," and demonstrable "integrity" (*TI* 56) set him up as an "alternative moral authority" (*TI* 57), gradually establishing him as the "good"
father figure.

Silver addresses the crew as "gentlemen of fortune" (*TI* 67) and out-
lines his plan, once returned, to "set up gentleman in earnest" on the
expected fortune. He foresees (or pretends to) a future "in Parlyment, and
riding in my coach" (*TI* 70). This establishes an opposition between the
two groups in the novel as gentlemen of fortune and gentlemen in
earnest (or "gen'lemen born" in Ben Gunn's version) while problematizing that opposition. Silver takes pains to differentiate himself from other
pirates—such as Flint and Pew, who "died a beggar man"—by emphasizing his married status and properly invested money (*TI* 70). Trelawney
introduces Silver as "a man of substance": "he has a banker's account
which has never been overdrawn" (*TI* 45). Silver boasts about financial
success: "I laid by nine hundred safe, from England, and two thousand
after Flint . . .—all safe in bank" (*TI* 66). Hawkins's introduction to the
pirate world was Bones, with his careful "account-book." These are amaz-
ingly bourgeois pirates: for all their bloodthirsty language and adventures, Bones and Silver have a keen eye for accounts and savings, just as
those pillars of the community, the doctor and the squire, are eager to get
their hands on pirate treasure.[7]

At landfall, Silver reads the salient features of the approaching island, narrativizing those features in terms of pirates: "That hill to the nor'ard they calls the Fore-mast Hill; there are three hills in a row running south'ard—fore, main, and mizzen, sir. But the main—that's the big 'un with the cloud on it—they usually calls the Spy-glass, by reason of a look-out they kept when they was in the anchorage cleaning . . ." (*TI* 73). Even before Smollett produces his copy of the chart, the island is identified with its representation. When the *Hispaniola* drops anchor "just where the anchor was in the chart" (*TI* 82), representation and reality converge. When the pirates read the landscape against the chart, mapping the island's spaces via their progress through them, the map's remaining details are finally realized.

"Treasure Island," however, is as William Gray observes, a place and no place (Gray 97). At the start, Hawkins was asked to keep back "the bearings of the island." Accordingly, the map has a scale, an orientation, and annotations of depth soundings but lacks indications of latitude and longitude that Hawkins describes on the chart in Bones's chest. Smollett shows Silver a copy of the chart from which information pertaining to the treasure has been removed, and the chart shown to the reader is another incomplete copy.[8] Nevertheless, it is clear that the island is in the Caribbean. The ship's name, the *Hispaniola*, points to this, as does the route taken ("We had run up the trades to get wind of the island" [*TI* 64]).[9] Nicholas McGuinn even identifies it with Norman Island in the Virgin Islands (*TI* 247).[10] However, onshore, the flora and fauna—willows, bullrushes, pines, live oaks, sea lions, and rattlesnakes—do not suggest the West Indies. Writing to Sidney Colvin (May 1884), Stevenson described the scenery as "Californian in part," and Wendy Katz notes the resemblance to the landscape of *The Silverado Squatters* (1882) (*SL* 300; *TI*, ed. Katz, xxxii). Like Prospero's island, Patusan, and the Round Island in *Victory*, "Treasure Island" is a heterotopic space (Hampson in Caplan, Mallios, and White, eds., 121–35).

Here, through his "shore adventure" and "sea adventure," Hawkins experiences tests of courage and moral character, the greatest being when he falls into Silver's hands. Hawkins is conscious of "the threat of death that overhung me" (*TI* 177), but his real test is Silver's renewed seduction (and his own continuing susceptibility). However, Hawkins's show of courage in refusing to join the pirates genuinely impresses Silver, who praises him over the surviving pirates in terms that focus on maturation: "I never seen a better boy than that. He's more a man than any pair of rats of you" (*TI* 180). Later, Hawkins's maturation seems complete. While the pirates are reduced to a status "more like charity-school children than blood-guilty mutineers and pirates," Hawkins is "a young gentleman": "for a young gentleman you are, although poor born" (*TI* 191). The pirates were "shouting at the oars like children" when raiding the *Hispaniola* (*TI* 118). Now the language of relative maturation is supplemented by precise social designations: the pirates are not just children but "charity-school children," while Hawkins is not just a man but a "young gentleman" who recognizes Silver as "twice the man the rest were" (*TI* 191–92). Even if Hawkins is merely being flattered, the terms of the flattery are revealing in relation to his aspirations. Thus, when tempted by Livesey to escape and save his life, Hawkins performs and justifies the identity Silver assigns him. This is not just a demonstration of moral behavior: "Silver trusted me; I passed my word, and back I go." His response to Livesey's suggestion also implicitly asserts social status: "[Y]ou know right well you wouldn't do the thing yourself; neither you, nor squire, nor captain; and no more will I" (*TI* 194). Hawkins's moral behavior, while acknowledging his debt of trust to Silver, aligns him firmly with the born gentlemen.

Katz suggests that, "at the level of ideology," *Treasure Island* "depicts a stable social structure being challenged from beneath by the rum-addled, impatient, and ill-educated rabble who practice a crude but intriguing democracy in a parallel counter-world" (*TI* xxxvii).[11] In depicting this counter-world, Stevenson drew on his reading about pirates—in particular, Captain Charles Johnson's *History of the Pyrates* (1724), which he read at Braemar.[12] Johnson provided references to pirates such as Teach, England, Davis, and Roberts. The names Hawkins, Hispaniola, Ben Gunn, and Israel Hands are from the same source. But Stevenson also drew from Johnson this picture of a quasi-democratic social organization with its own rules and procedures. Johnson's account of Captain England notes that "when the Pyrates came out to Sea, they put it to the Vote what Voyage to take." An extended account of the career of Captain Roberts asserts that "all good Governments had (like theirs) the supream Power lodged with the community" (Captain Johnson 194) and describes how Roberts was elected captain and quotes the "Set of Articles" Roberts drew up for the crew (Captain Johnson 211–12).[13]

Hawkins finally sees Flint's treasure, "that we had come so far to seek, and that had cost already the lives of seventeen men from the *Hispaniola*," leading him to speculate: "How many it had cost in the amassing, what blood and sorrow, what good ships scuttled on the deep, what brave men walking the plank blindfold, what shot of cannon, what shame and lies and cruelty. . . ." (*TI* 214). However, the money is calmly divided up among the victorious party. As Nicholas Rankin observes: "It is money severed from social relations, morally neutral, the treasure of a child's world of finders-keepers. The slaves who mined and minted it, the pirates who murdered to get it, the real price of Flint's treasure no longer matters when the righteous get their hands on it" (Rankin 159). We see perhaps, here, the limitation of the logic of the daydream. Hawkins shares with Pip in *Great Expectations* the fantasy of "clean money," a guilt-free fortune, and Stevenson, unlike Dickens, does not force him to confront the social relations of money.[14] However, Rankin overstates the case in describing the Squire's party as "the righteous." One of the unsettling elements of the novel is precisely that the motives of the "born gentlemen" seem no different from those of the "gentlemen of fortune." Having criticized the pirates ("What were these villains after but money? . . . For what would they risk their rascal carcasses but money?"), the Squire blithely announces: "I'll have that treasure if I search a year" (*TI* 36). In addition, the social relations of money are not completely ignored. Indeed, what Fredric Jameson calls the "repressed space of a world of work and history" returns and presses on the world of daydream (Jameson 207).

As McGuinn notes, the novel's setting, the eighteenth-century Spanish Main, is not simply a "romantic location": "At that time, the area was actually a bloody arena in which the colonial powers of Europe fought each other for the wealth of the new World" (McGuinn, *Treasure Island* introduction, 6–7). There had been semipiratical raids upon the Spanish New World shipping by English and French privateers since the sixteenth century, and in the seventeenth century English and French buccaneers raided Spanish shipping and plundered Spanish colonies.[15] The name *Hispaniola* bears testimony to this history, as do Silver's anecdotes: his reference to "Roberts' men" and the *Royal Fortune*, for example, or his account of his parrot's maritime career, a potted version of Roberts's pirate exploits (*TI* 66, 63). Bristol, from where the *Hispaniola* sails and returns, grew rich on the slave trade, and that trade leaves its traces in the novel. Trelawney's letter from Bristol describes how his old friend Blandly "literally slaved" in his interest (*TI* 44). Silver's wife is "a woman of colour" (*TI* 45). Livesey is "a slave to tobacco" (*TI* 74). The daydream of a treasure island and pirate gold is thus framed by traces of an untold story of everyday wealth acquisition by Bristol's respectable bourgeoisie through the slave trade.[16]

In *Lord Jim*, it is precisely the logic of the daydream that takes Jim to Patusan. On board the training ship, Jim lives beforehand "the sea-life of light literature" at the expense of a real-life rescue (*LJ* 6). On the *Patna*, Jim indulges in daydreams, while on duty, when the ship runs over an obstacle. Only in Patusan are Jim's romantic expectations on a level with the novel's own mode of writing. In *Lord Jim*, as in *Victory*, Conrad plays with elements of the treasure island story. At one point rumors spread along the coast of a European who has found a jewel of great worth (*LJ* 280). But this is only one of a number of competing narratives produced around the figure of Jim, and, like the legends of Jim's heroic feats (carrying the cannon on his back in the battle against Sherif Ali [*LJ* 266], for example), this narrative elaboration is not to be taken seriously but rather to reveal, by contrast, the veracity of Marlow's narrative even as Marlow's narrative engages with the romance world of daydreams.

Lord Jim, like *Treasure Island*, hinges on the protagonist's encounter with a pirate. "Lord" Jim, however, is no Jim Hawkins. Whereas Hawkins is a boy going through a process of adolescent identity formation, Jim, for all his boyishness, is already a young man when he enters the archipelago: his agelessness, his eternal boyishness, is part of the limitation of his character. Hawkins is caught on a cusp. The narrative focuses on his potential to become either a gentleman or a rogue, tracing his movement from lowly origins to wealth and affiliation with the gentlemen. The "genteel" Silver is the attractive Falstaff figure he must renounce. Jim's gentlemanly status, as a parson's son, is never in doubt—this is part of his identification by Marlow as "one of us." Yet Marlow glimpses his potential to go "to the bad." Jim's brawl with a Danish lieutenant in the Royal Siamese Navy in Schomberg's Bangkok hotel marks a limit. In Marlow's words, "[I]f his exquisite sensibilities were to go the length of involving him in pot-house shindies, he would lose his name of an inoffensive, if aggravating, fool, and acquire that of a common loafer" (*LJ* 200). Unchecked, Jim was on his way to becoming the kind of European flotsam represented in *The Ebb-Tide* and *The Beach of Falesá*. Patusan pulls Jim from this decline and places him in the romantic world of his popular-fiction dreams. Consequently, Jim's identity formation in Patusan comes under the law of the daydream, allowing him to achieve the heroic identity he dreamed of. Gentleman Brown's arrival into this dream world is both a disaster and the opportunity for confirming that identity.

Brown enters the narrative explicitly as a pirate, "a latter-day buccaneer" (*LJ* 352). He is associated with real-life pirates such as Pease and Bully Hayes (*LJ* 352), and his reported actions (gun-running and kidnapping) involve literally and legally an act of piracy: seizing a Spanish schooner (*LJ* 344). However, these actions have none of the glamour of romantic piracy. His challenges to his terrified victims to engage in shotgun duels are sadistic bullying. His adventures in Patusan—pinned down in a muddy creek with the prospect of death from thirst or starvation—are petty and sordid. Nevertheless, his encounter with Jim and their mutual bond, that "sickening suggestion of common guilt," questions not only Jim's ideal sense of himself but also the ethical bases of Jim's romantic daydreams of colonial adventure (*LJ* 387).

Victory, similarly, offers a counterversion of *Treasure Island*'s romance world; like *Treasure Island*, it has its treasure map, not a secret map but a public document whose potential value lies precisely in its public nature. This map has its imaginative dimension, but the daydreams it records and prompts have firm material bases. The map is produced by the Tropical Belt Coal Company, and its treasure is coal, not "Pieces of Eight," marking a further embourgeoisification of romance. More obviously than in *Lord Jim*, it also marks where romantic adventure becomes commercial exploitation. The dreams of wealth it records and promotes have a similarly firm materialist basis; they are rooted in the changeover from sail to steam. Likewise, Heyst gains the nickname "the Enemy" not through physical threats and acts of personal violence but through the discreet bourgeois violence of depriving other Europeans (the men involved in the local, sail-based trading networks) of their livelihoods.

The reversal of the romance world of *Treasure Island* is complete and thoroughgoing. Consider the process of coming to identity central to *Treasure Island*: this was a boy's movement through adolescence toward acceptance in the world of men. With Jim, Conrad had already considered an adult male, and that process of acceptance had been subtilized and psychologized as an exploration of identity formation through identification with an alterated identity.[17] In *Victory*, Conrad's protagonist is a middle-aged man. Heyst's counterpart, Schomberg, is at the dangerous age when he is aware of impending decline: "Forty-five is the age of recklessness for many men, as if in defiance of the decay and death waiting with open arms in the sinister valley, at the bottom of the inevitable hill" (*V* 94). Heyst himself has had a potentially adventurous life, with extended travels around the archipelago. However, we get no sense of adventures. As Heyst expresses it, he has neither "killed a man" nor "loved a woman" (*V* 212). His visit to the dangerous area of New Guinea stands in sharp contrast to Lingard's in *The Rescue*. Heyst's visit results in "a portfolio of sketches" (*V* 8); Lingard had to fight his way off the beach, forging a bond with a Sulawesi prince and his sister and forming the basis for further adventures. By these standards it is with relative success that Heyst carries out his program of drifting through life unnoticed. At the same time, this program is also a means of evading himself. Indeed, the very basis of the program has been a denial of self—not just in the sense that Heyst intends, but also in the self-deception implicit in its origin. Heyst records his response to his father's death: "He became aware of his eyes being wet. It was not that the man was his father. For him it was purely a matter of hearsay which could not in itself cause this emotion" (*V* 175). He asserts the rational belief on which he has founded his life. As Stephen Dedalus puts it, fatherhood (at least prior to DNA) is a fiction, and attachment to one's father in this context would be irrational. Nevertheless, Heyst is attached, and that attachment is the illogical basis for adopting his father's philosophy of detachment. Through Lena and the novel's events, Heyst is forced to confront the denied aspects of himself. However, in contrast to *Treasure Island*, the outcome of this "Island Tale" is not the fixing of identity but a despairing realization of failure. Heyst experiences the impossibility of overcoming the habit of distrust and denial while realizing the necessity of doing both. He loses his one opportunity of being loved.

This, in turn, emphasizes the very different role of women in Conrad's novel. *Treasure Island* is the story of a boy's adventure in a context that almost completely excludes women. Leaving his mother behind at the Admiral Benbow, Hawkins apparently encounters no other women. Trelawney and Livesey are "a pair of old bachelors" (*TI* 45). Silver is apparently the only married man. Here, identity formation is a homosocial activity: Hawkins becomes a man in the world of men. In *Victory*, by contrast, Lena is central to Heyst's questioning of his identity. Heyst's prior involvement with Morrison is relevant here: the novel is not concerned just with the issue of detachment; it comes to focus on sexuality and desire. Jeffrey Meyer's interest in sexual failure in the novel is exactly right, even if his assertion of Heyst's sexual impotence is crudely literal.[18] Conrad is more concerned with Heyst's emotional damage and the difficulty of establishing mature mutuality within a sexual relationship. This focus on sexuality is obviously a long way from *Treasure Island*.

Finally, we should consider pirates. *Lord Jim*, like *Treasure Island*, featured pirates, even if much less romantic ones. In *Victory*, Jones's search for Heyst's "treasure" involves a further diminution of the adventure romance theme. Whereas Brown was involved in acts of piracy, Jones and Ricardo are involved in small-scale crime: robbery, illegal gambling, intimidation, sexual assault. As with Brown, there is a deheroizing and deglamorizing of the outlaw. Furthermore, in line with Conrad's introduction of women, there is a more general sexualizing of the material. Jones's "pier-head jump" fixes him as a fugitive—probably from a homosexual scandal (*V* 127). Ricardo, with his polymorphous perversity, sexual violence, and concealed knife, is identified by Peter Bagnall as a possible "Jack-the-Ripper."[19] Conrad's outlaws take us into the area of what was regarded by the standards of the time as sexual deviance and sexual crime. They complicate the exploration of sexuality at the center of the novel.

This also impacts on the issue of the gentleman. In *Victory*, as in *Treasure Island*, the concept of the gentleman is explicitly questioned, particularly in Ricardo's commentary on Jones. Having told Schomberg that "a gentleman isn't to be sized up so easily," he attempts to explain the nature of "the gentleman," believing that gentlemen "don't lose their temper" because it is "bad form" (*V* 135–36). He repeats Jones's advice: "There's a proper way of doing things. You'll have to learn to be correct. There's also unnecessary exertion. That must be avoided too—if only for the look of the thing" (*V* 137). Ricardo's account of their adventures and his admiration for Jones's cool responses presents a satiric version of the figure. Jones's concern for "bad form" and "the look of things" combines with psychopathic violence towards others. Nevertheless, Jones, like Heyst, is undeniably a "gentleman born." As with *Treasure Island*, in the absence of the non-European Other, the island becomes the stage for exploring metropolitan issues, and class relations are foregrounded. Their different class backgrounds were already a complicating factor in Heyst and Lena's developing relationship. Lena had misread what for Heyst were merely "the forms of simple courtesy" (*V* 79). When Heyst's revolver goes missing, Lena's response—"It was what a servant might have said—an inferior open to suspicion" (*V* 253–54)—reveals how their relative class status is always present as a default position. Jones seeks to establish a bond with Heyst in part, at least, on the basis of their shared class background, while Ricardo asserts a bond with Lena on the basis of their common London working-class origins. Jones's diabolical version of "the gentleman" forces us to consider not only what may lie behind the "gentlemanly" sangfroid he shares with Heyst, or the implications of the "gentlemanly" aversion to "unnecessary exertion," but also the whole idea of "the gentleman."

In writing *Treasure Island*, Stevenson had a definite first audience in mind: his twelve-year-old stepson. Stevenson told the story to Lloyd but also drew on his own father for assistance. The homosocial world of the novel's composition is replicated in its fictional world. Martin Green describes *Treasure Island* as "palpably the fantasy of men-being-boys" but also a fantasy of how boys become men (Green 228). Boys become men through recognition by other men. But the world in which this recognition takes place is not purely fantasy: it is marked and divided by class.

Sandison demonstrates how Hawkins's process of *Bildung* involves negotiating a series of alternative father figures to arrive at "a mature independence" (Sandison 78). The fascinating Silver, with his power, intelligence, and freedom from principle, who apparently offers to deal with Jim as an equal, is ultimately revealed to be as disempowering as the authoritarian Smollett. However, one of the strengths of *Treasure Island* is that Silver is not simply judged and transcended; he remains as "a permanent fixture in psychic reality" (Sandison 79). Hawkins's process of

Bildung does not produce an integrated, unified self. Silver's escape from narrative closure and his continuing presence in Hawkins's dreams mark a fissure in his psychic makeup. In the same way, the company of civilized and respectable gentlemen is motivated by the same greed for wealth as that of the "gentlemen of fortune" and is further stained by their implication in the slave trading economy of Bristol. "Gentlemen born" and "gentlemen of fortune" have more in common than is at first apparent.

White identifies Stevenson's South Seas fictions as anticipating "the subversion of Conrad's island world" (White 5). Conrad's *Almayer's Folly* provides pirates and smuggling, search for treasure, plots and intrigues, and an exotic setting but "subverts the basic tenets of the genre" (White 120). The treasure, which, as Linda Dryden notes, "precipitates the action" in so many adventure romances, has a distinctly ambiguous status in Conrad's first novel (Dryden, *Joseph Conrad*, 38). In *Treasure Island* too the treasure hunt is displaced by adventures of another kind and the distribution of the spoils oddly deemphasized. What Hawkins gains materially from the final division is not clear. In the end there is an unsettling silence about Hawkins's situation and prospects. This could be read in terms either of the quest for identity displacing the quest for treasure or as a reticence about the material wealth gained. In *Victory*, the treasure map becomes a map of coaling stations, and the treasure the outlaws seek never existed. The focus falls instead on an exploration of class and sexuality.

Katz suggests that Stevenson's "concern with moral questions reveals itself in dilemmas rather than in readily solvable issues" (*TI*, ed. Katz, xxxvii). White notes that Stevenson "refused to moralize" in *Treasure Island* and refused to "include 'the sayings of [Hawkins's] father or his mother' and passages of a 'religious character' that Stevenson's father had advised him to add as a way 'of harking back to something higher than mere incident'" (White 50). This provides a context for Stevenson's insistence on "the brute incident" and makes clear that it is a form of resistance to the Victorian pressure to moralize. In *Victory*, Conrad too presents dilemmas rather than solutions. He draws on the Jamesian "scenic method" to present the reader with action unmediated by narratorial commentary, and those actions and their presentation force the reader to engage with the novel's exploration of class and sexuality.

NOTES

1. Unless otherwise stated, all references to *Treasure Island* in this chapter are to the Tusitala edition (London: William Heinemann, 1923).

2. This contestation over authorship of the map is ironic, given the importance of authorship in Hawkins's negotiation of his independence in relation to his various father figures.

3. See, for example, Sandison 48–81. The process of *Bildung* (in Goethe's *Wilhelm Meister*, for example) also involves social positioning.

4. This second world has been introduced through Bill Bones, Black Dog, and Blind Pew, though neither Hawkins nor the reader realizes it. As Sandison observes, Jim's responses to Bones, Blind Dog, and Pew hint at "a fluidity in the boundaries between Jim's and the pirates' moral world" (Sandison 52).

5. As Sandison notes (53), both Bones and Black Dog had tried to occupy this position.

6. Hispaniola (modern-day Haiti) was a notorious pirate stronghold. H. F. Watson notes that the map that accompanies the novel resembles the outline of Haiti turned at right angles, with Monte Christo as Spy-Glass, Gonave as a slightly damaged Skeleton Island, and the Bay of Ocoa as Rum Cove. See *Coasts of Treasure Island* (San Antonio, TX: The Naylor Company, 1969), 126.

7. Rogozinski suggests that "[a]way from Madagascar, buried treasure makes no sense" and that ambitious pirates "used their booty to buy sugar plantations." See Jan Rogozinski, *Honor among Thieves: Captain Kidd, Henry Every, and the Pirate Democracy in the Indian Ocean* (Mechanicsburg, PA: Stackpole Books, 2000), 233.

8. The map accompanying many editions was not the original but a later version by Stevenson's father.

9. The northeast trade winds circle around Madeira to the Caribbean.

10. McGuinn notes that Norman Island has a Spy-Glass Hill and that Spanish treasure was buried there in 1750.

11. Alistair Fowler offers a perceptive reading of *Treasure Island* in terms of "a series of contests for power." See "Parables of Adventure: The Debatable Novels of Robert Louis Stevenson," in *Nineteenth-Century Scottish Fiction*, ed. Ian Campbell (1979).

12. Captain Charles Johnson, *A General History of the Robberies and Murders of the Most Notorious Pyrates* (London, 1724; reprint, London: J. M. Dent, 1972). "Johnson" is now generally believed to be a pseudonym adopted by Daniel Defoe. Watson notes that Stevenson had written five chapters before he received this book: in those chapters Stevenson refers generally to buccaneers; only in later chapters does he refer to pirates and pirate lore. Bill Bones refers to the Dry Tortugas, a buccaneer stronghold, and the pride with which his exploits are received reflects the patriotic spin given to buccaneering. In the latter part of the novel, Stevenson has clearly absorbed a lot of information about pirates from "Johnson."

13. The first begins with the assertion that "Every Man has a Vote in Affairs of Moment" (211). Article IV stipulates "The Lights and Candles to be put out at eight a-clock at Night" (211), and Article VI begins "No Boy or Woman to be allowed amongst them" (212).

14. As Sandison points out, Jim's new status is "earned in the process, not bought by the proceeds" (Sandison 73).

15. See C. H. Haring, *The Buccaneers in the West Indies in the XVII Century* (London: Methuen, 1910).

16. At the same time, the orderly world established at the end continues to be haunted by nightmares of Silver (marked synecdochically by his parrot).

17. For a fuller account, see Hampson, *Joseph Conrad: Betrayal and Identity*.

18. Jeffrey Meyers, *Homosexuality and Literature, 1890–1930* (London: Athlone Press, 1977), 83ff.

19. Peter Bagnall, "Joseph Conrad and Jack the Ripper," Ph.D. thesis, University of Oxford, 1999.

PART THREE

Social and Psychological Contexts

Conrad, the Stevensons, and the Imagination of Urban Chaos

DEAGLÁN Ó'DONGHAILE

$\mathcal{M}$ ANY late-nineteenth-century popular fictions imagined London as the site of political conflict between subversives and the state. The war-torn metropolis is a familiar trope of fin-de-siècle fiction, appearing in Tom Greer's *A Modern Dædalus* (1885), E. Douglas Fawcett's *Hartmann the Anarchist* (1893), John Coulson Kernehan's *Captain Shannon* (1897), and Robert Louis and Fanny Van de Grift Stevenson's *The Dynamiter* (1885). These fictions, often written in the immediate aftermath of bomb-ings, addressed contemporary fears about terrorism. *Captain Shannon*, about a bomb attack on the London underground, appeared within weeks of a mysterious and unclaimed explosion at Aldersgate Station. *The Dynamiter* responded to a series of bombings in 1885, addressing "the ugly devil of crime," or, more precisely, political crime (*WRLS* 2:15). While other "urban disaster" novels of the period, such as H. G. Wells's *The War of the Worlds* (1898), receive widespread critical attention, these lesser-known fictions constitute an important genre in their own right. This essay examines *The Dynamiter* as an influential but overlooked

Stevenson novel, proposing that it influenced other shilling shockers. Moreover, by treating the political shocks of terrorism, it influenced literary modernism. While Conrad's *The Secret Agent* (1907) is considered a work of classical modernist fiction, his anarchists are based on earlier popular antecedents. The reflexive way in which mass-produced "yellowback" novels dealt with contemporary events receives a modernist revision in *The Secret Agent*. Conrad shared an interest in subversion, particularly in Irish political revolt, with the Stevensons, and although *The Secret Agent* and his 1906 short stories "An Anarchist" and "The Informer" focus upon the later phenomenon of anarchism, they reflect similar concerns about political unrest.

During the 1883–85 dynamite campaign a U.S.-based Irish separatist group, Clan na Gael, sent cells of dynamiters to Britain, giving rise to this literary phenomenon. Armed with dynamite bombs and TNT, the high explosive patented by Joseph Wilbrand in 1863, Clan na Gael believed the explosives gave them an edge over the might of the British Empire. Also called the "Scientific School of the Fenian Brotherhood," Clan na Gael used a variant of TNT manufactured by the Atlas Powder Company, a branch of DuPont, and by the Repauno Chemical Company of Philadelphia ("Irish Agitation" 11; Le Caron 243). Packaged in slabs, it was remarkably stable, allowing dynamiters to create "infernal machines," bombs with fuses and timed detonators that ticked or burned away while the perpetrators melted into the urban crowd. The dynamiters terrorized British cities for two years with explosive devices secreted inside Gladstone bags and suitcases and with simpler homemade hand grenades.

Sir Robert Anderson, an experienced Fenian hunter and senior Home Office counterterrorism official, described the Clan na Gael campaign as "formidable" (Anderson 125). High-profile attacks included the March 1883 bombings of the Whitehall Admiralty, the Carlton Club, and the *Times'* London offices. The last of these bombings appears in J. D. Maginn's *Fitzgerald the Fenian* (1889), in which dynamiters target the *Times*, "[t]hat filthy and most-offensively conducted organ [that] has been opposed to the demands and wishes of the Irish people." Their desire to "shatter into fragments that abominable Bastille" reminds us of the Jacobin origins of modern terrorism and of the antagonism between the dynamiters and the British press (Maginn, *Fenian* 224). In response to these attacks, the Special Irish Branch of the Criminal Investigation Department (known since as the Special Branch) was established in April 1883, and the Explosives Substances Bill was passed in the same month. This bill prevented the illegal use of any "explosive substance" and proscribed "any apparatus, machine, implement, or materials used . . . or adapted for causing, or aiding in causing, any explosion" ("Explosive" 10). As the *Times* noted, it was designed to "discourage the future visits to the United Kingdom of the disciples of O'Donovan Rossa," the leading U.S.-based Fenian ("Explosive" 10).

But bombings continued. The London Underground and railway line were targeted in the new year, the Scotland Yard CID headquarters was destroyed in May 1884, and in December one of the most committed bombers, William Mackey Lomasney, was blown up while placing a bomb underneath London Bridge. The dynamite campaign did not end until January 1885, with further attacks on the underground railway, the bombing of the House of Commons, and an explosion inside the armory at the Tower of London.

Throughout, Clan na Gael celebrated their explosives as "the organ of the scientific war": "Dynamite! A few years ago it was unheard of; now it is a household word. This new destructive agent is destined to revolution-ize warfare. . . . Dynamite! It is the fear of the oppressor, the hope of the oppressed, and their salvation if they will but use it. England especially, the hotbed of oppression, dreads it in the hands of a few determined Irishmen" ("Press Organ" 8). Dynamite terrorism became a feature of late Victorian modernity and a permanent fixture in the wider cycle of met-ropolitan distractions. While modernity proper can, as Marshall Berman argues, be dated back to the French Revolution and its awakening of "a great modern public," with its subsequent upheavals in personal, social, and political life, the late nineteenth century inaugurated a period of intensified modernization characterized more by the unbridled circula-tion of commodities and capital than by the stirrings of the political con-sciousness of the masses (Berman 17). Since midcentury competitive individualism had been on the increase, an atmosphere in which the city seemed a place where anything might happen. The Explosives Act was a reaction against a more subversive aspect of this process. This intensely competitive environment reached a critical mass late in the century, "an epoch of intense social dynamism," occupying and entertaining subjects to the point of "hyperstimulus" (Singer 8, 22, 26). In this environment of hothouse capitalism and saturation of the middle class by intense circulation of commodities, a sensation-linked flux of images, shocks, and urban jolts was communicated by mass media such as sensational newspapers and popular fictions. Shilling shockers such as *The Dynamiter* and its modernist revision *The Secret Agent* traded on these political shocks, exploiting the opportunities to cause chaos offered by the urban sprawl of London and its "new and artificial conditions" (*Heart of the Empire* vii).

Guy De Bord's theory of the modern Society of the Spectacle presents a network of systems characterized by "spectacular modernization," in which perception is integrated with history, image with experience. Thanks to the modern media, historical events are no longer interpreted by individuals but are filtered through the superstructure of commodity capitalism and reproduced as intelligible pieces of information. Modern society thus functions as "an immense accumulation of spectacles" governed by the overarching liberal capitalist system (De Bord 7–10). The mainstream press described the dynamite campaign as "a conspiracy that makes war on humanity" and even the leading Fenian, John Devoy, could not condone dynamiting, condemning it as "useless" because Britain had "the ear of the world and control of all the agencies of news supply," believing its shocks had been absorbed by the Victorian society of the spectacle (Devoy, *Illustrated*, 542). He considered the dynamiter "a fanatic of the deepest dye" who "wanted simply to strike terror into the Government and the governing class" (Devoy, *Recollections*, 212). Hence, dynamite was its own message, underlining Walter Laqueur's claim that, predicated on pure shock, terrorism is a "truly all-purpose and value-free" phenomenon: a tactic available to groups and individuals of any political persuasion or none (Laqueur, *Age of Terrorism*, 5). This process was taken a step further by the Stevensons and Conrad, who appropriated the shocks of political terror and recycled them as literary materiel.

Dynamite Fictions and the Cultural Significance of Terror

The Dynamiter was published in April 1885, nine months before *Strange Case of Dr. Jekyll and Mr. Hyde*. (Despite the elevation of Stevenson's novel to classical status, it shares generic origins with *The Dynamiter*: when he began writing it he wrote to Sidney Colvin, "I am penning forth a penny [twelve-penny] dreadful; it is dam dreadful" [*SL* 5:128].) The novel condemns dynamiting in terms similar to those found in the *Times* while also attempting to contain terrorism. Exercising literary restraint in describing terrorism, it differs from other popular dynamite fictions, such as Coulson Kernehan's imaginatively unrestrained novel, in which explosions cause mass death and destruction. *The Dynamiter* is dedicated to a pair of policemen injured while removing a bomb from the Crypt in Westminster Abbey the previous January. Claiming to have "touched upon the ugly devil of crime, with which it is your glory to have contended," the dedication points out the uniqueness of Irish "political crime" (*WRLS* 2:15). Beneath this fastidiousness is an acknowledgement that the imagination is changed by terrorism: despite its reputation as light parody, *The Dynamiter* opens only after constituting itself as an effort against the bombers. Plugged directly into the panicky zeitgeist of 1885, *The Dynamiter* was reprinted in May and July (McLynn 114). Its dedication carries an immediacy or "datability"—an instantaneous moment of cultural reference—to which contemporary readers could relate (Heidegger 387). Fulfilling a similar cultural role to the "ideologically charged and fragmented images" of the popular press, *The Dynamiter* is considered to be among Stevenson's least accomplished literary works, yet it remains his most politically "involved" novel (Curtis 9).

Random Encounters

The adventure opens in London, a "city of encounters, the Bagdad [*sic*] of the West," an Orientalized, lawless space where three idlers, Challoner, Somerset, and Desborough, meet in a Soho club (*WRLS* 2:19). They answer a newspaper advertisement seeking a suspicious man observed near Green Park and decide to delve into the chaotic "labyrinth" of London. The city "roars like the noise of battle," and in setting young men of means against a dynamite conspiracy the Stevensons make a literary intervention in the realm of "counterplot," or counterterrorism, as it is now known, popularizing its politics and methodology (*WRLS* 2:7, 8, 29; Anderson 127). This occurs as a series of random encounters, beginning with Challoner's adventure, starting with an explosion in a Soho lodging house. From its very opening the novel presents the metropolis as the locus of an unfamiliar conflict: an exoticized and unfamiliar metropolis draws him directly into its political underground. The lodging house, with its transient inhabitants, is the sufficiently gray area containing a bomb factory; terrorism, a symptom of the urban derangement that is induced by merely inhabiting "the Bagdad of the West," is the result. Meeting a young woman called Fonblanque, who is "thrilling with incommunicable terrors" (*WRLS* 2:36), Challoner agrees to deliver money on her behalf to a contact in Glasgow, the mysterious M'Guire, but on arrival he barely escapes arrest during a police raid.

With its inevitable movement toward adventure, Challoner's *flâneur*-ship underlines Walter Benjamin's notion that "it takes a heroic constitution to live modernism." For Benjamin, such idle wandering and observation lead inevitably towards the discovery of urban thrills and amateur detection (Benjamin 74, 69). The ease with which Challoner slips into the dynamiters' conspiracy points to a voyeuristic implication, akin to Jean Baudrillard's assertion that everyone is complicit in "the pure event" of terrorism and in the universality of "that (unwittingly) terroristic imagination which dwells in all of us" (Baudrillard 4). Baudrillard has argued that "we have dreamt of this event . . . , everyone without exception has dreamt of it—because no one can avoid dreaming of the destruction of any power that has become hegemonic to this degree." Because of this the imagination of urban chaos is invested with a "symbolic dimension" that exists "everywhere, like an obscure object of desire." "Without this deep-seated complicity," Baudrillard states, "the event would not have had the resonance it has, and in their symbolic strategy the terrorists doubtless know that they can count on this unavowable complicity" (Baudrillard 5–6). Here, as everywhere, Baudrillard's mode is hyperbolic, but his argument does indicate how modern and postmodern society have been thoroughly taken by the *idea* of terrorism. Twenty-first-century images of airplanes crashing into skyscrapers or nineteenth-century motifs such as the Gladstone bag containing an infernal machine are as emblematic of modernity as those of space flight and the Internet.

Terrorism's Private Aesthetic

Paul Somerset's adventure "The Superfluous Mansion" underlines Baudrillard's theory of implication. Somerset steps into the metropolitan swell, searching the urban crowd for any "mysterious and hopeful hieroglyph" that it might offer (*WRLS* 2:116). In a city overflowing with secrets, affections, and private despairs, he is as anonymous and invisible as the rest of the population. Somerset meets an elderly lady who asks him to look out for her estranged runaway daughter, a rather Conradian, romantic type: "Some whim about oppressed nationalities—Ireland, Poland, and the like—has turned her brain," and she uses pseudonyms, including Fonblanque (*WRLS* 2:139). Somerset even owns to having been tempted to join a conspiracy himself: "I held at one time very liberal opinions, and should certainly have joined a secret society if I had been able to find one" (*WRLS* 2:162). He agrees to look after the lady's mansion—the site of the assassination attempt on Prince Florizel in *New Arabian Nights*—and sublets it. His advertisement for a tenant is answered by a suspicious Mr. Jones and his Irish maid, whose visitors, including "a man of powerful figure, strong lineaments, and a chin-beard in the American fashion," provoke suspicion. The Yankee cut of this man's beard, along with his luggage, excites Somerset's imagination: "What, he asked himself, had been the contents of the black portmanteau? Stolen goods? the carcass of one murdered? Or—and at the thought he sat upright in bed—an infernal machine?" (*WRLS* 2:184).

A suburban "palace of delight," the mansion appears more urban the more the bourgeois world of conspicuous domestic display is introduced to the terrors of the Soho lodging houses. In becoming the site of manufacture of infernal machines, suburbia is subverted; domestic commodities such as clocks are transformed into destructive engines, and the house is filled with an "arsenal of diabolical explosives" (*WRLS* 2:191). The lodger reveals that he is the Irish bomber Zero, a "romantic" nationalist dedicated "to that more emphatic, more striking, and (if you please) more popular method of the explosive bomb," boasting: "I have something of the poet in my nature" (*WRLS* 2:193, 196). He views London as a "plain of battle" about to be "startled by the detonation of the judgment gun" (*WRLS* 2:221). Terrorism, with its emphasis upon the striking, the popular, and the emphatic, has a cultural and aesthetic appeal for Zero, who links the poetry of the explosion to the poetics of subversive propaganda. Within this verbal matrix language is as explosive as the dynamiter's infernal machines, and terrorism amounts to a form of verbal and political *avant-gardisme*. As Zero suggests, his bombs have an aesthetic purpose, as there is something distinctly different, and especially modern, about committing "a striking act of dynamite"; he asks: "[W]hat could be more pictorial, what more effective, than the explosion of a hansom cab as it sped rapidly along the streets of London?" (*WRLS* 2:210)

The closure of *The Dynamiter* shows how terrorism becomes a self-valorizing process of setting off explosions, enlivened by their consumption as urban spectacles. The novel ends with Zero's autodestruction on a railway platform when, reaching for a newspaper carrying a story about one of his explosions, he accidentally detonates his own bomb:

> [T]he attention of the plotter was attracted by a *Standard* broadside bearing the words: "Second Edition: Explosion in Golden Square." His eye lighted; groping in his pocket for the necessary coin, he sprang forward—his bag knocked sharply on the corner of the stall—and instantly, with a formidable report, the dynamite exploded. When the smoke cleared away the stall was seen much shattered, and the stall keeper running forth in terror from the ruins; but of the Irish patriot or the Gladstone bag no adequate remains were to be found. (*WRLS* 2:318)

Here the Stevensons suggest that terrorism is a self-reflexive phenomenon (*Captain Shannon* opens with a bomb exploding on the underground, killing dozens but leaving the newsboys unharmed). The terrorist's addiction to media coverage underlines the self-perpetuating nature of his political activity since, for Zero, causing explosions becomes its own reality. This is what makes terrorism a "truly all-purpose and value-free" phenomenon (Laqueur, *Age of Terrorism*, 5). The rhetorical stance adopted by "Number One" and by his fictional counterpart, Zero, explains why other Irish republicans such as Devoy could not support the dynamiters.

Zero is killed within the circulation of modernity and its media, where the train platform, bustling crowds, and newspaper stand converge. The final explosion marks terrorism's absorption within the schema of urban modernity, so that instead of ending the city's cycle, the terrorist is appropriated by it. Exploding amid the crowd on the platform, Zero is atomized, fusing with the scattered remains of the daily papers, and achieves not the destruction of the system that he opposes but a literal synchronicity with it; instead of disrupting the metropolis, the terrorist—and his spectacularly violent campaign—is "processed" within it. Zero's end is modeled on the fate of William Mackey Lomasney, the prodigious dynamiter and veteran of the Fenian uprising of 1867 who was killed in a premature explosion while planting a bomb underneath London Bridge on December 13, 1884. With Mackey's death, noted the *Times*, Irish republican subversion became "of merely historical interest"; the newspaper added: "[T]here is something reassuring in the demonstration that the criminals who act—whatever may be the case with those who merely plot—do not work with impunity . . . and that two, literally hoist with their own petard, lie dead at the bottom of the Thames" ("Dynamite Party" 8).

    The Dynamiter is less concerned with the politics of republican terrorism than it is with its sensation-effect, revealing how it contributes to "the noise of battle" that is the aural backdrop to the metropolitan experience. What makes *The Dynamiter* unique is the manner in which the novel explores the inherent modernity of dynamiting, a theme that it shares with *The Secret Agent,* as its voyeuristic fixation on terrorism and interactions with modern mass culture are mirrored in Conrad's modernist novel. This dualistic discourse on terrorism examines the immediacy of the dynamite campaign in squeamish, conservative terms while offering a sophisticated understanding of its relationship with modernity. This makes *The Dynamiter* a key text in the literature of terrorism, going some way in explaining its relationship with *The Secret Agent.*

Joseph Conrad and Urban Chaos

As evidenced by his "domestic" fictions, Conrad was obsessed by terrorism. Anarchism features prominently in *The Secret Agent* and in the short stories "The Informer" and "An Anarchist." *Under Western Eyes* (1911) focuses on a young idealist's involvement in a nihilist plot and draws heavily on Sergius Stepniak's fictionalized memoir of 1892, *Career of a*

Nihilist, which the Russian revolutionary wrote in exile in London. The British anarchist scare peaked in February 1894 with the event around which *The Secret Agent* is centered: the Greenwich Park explosion. While Conrad was in London, writing *Almayer's Folly*, a young French anarchist, Martial Bourdin, died when a bomb he was carrying to the Greenwich Observatory exploded prematurely. The device, containing iron shrapnel, was a glass-bottle bomb with an acid time fuse, sensitive to shock. It detonated when Bourdin stumbled, blowing off his hand and inflicting severe injuries to his stomach; he died later at the Seamen's Hospital. His remains revealed £13 in getaway money, bomb-making instructions, and a membership card for the Autonomie Club on the Tottenham Court Road, a noted meeting point for foreign anarchists. In the immediate aftermath of the explosion it emerged that Bourdin was a brother-in-law of the anarchist writer and pamphleteer H. B. Samuels ("Bourdin's" 5).

Following the explosion, the *Times* cited the incident as proof that "this is an age of vanishing illusions. . . . Anarchists do not care to exist in inglorious idleness." It claimed that the outrage would undermine "the comfortable belief that England is so very convenient as headquarters that Anarchists will do nothing to impair their asylum" ("Bourdin's" 5). Pointing to "the close connexion between Bourdin and the desperadoes who have waged war against society in Paris, in Barcelona, and in other places on the Continent" it claimed that "the toils are closing in upon more than one miscreant who might have continued to enjoy immunity so long as the actual 'operations' had been excluded from British soil" ("Bourdin's" 5). Indeed, the London anarchists were in touch with café bombers such as Émile Henry, who had bombed innocent boulevardiers at the Café Terminus in Paris, and even praised Salvador Franch, the bomber of the Liceo Theatre in Barcelona, who killed twenty spectators during a gala performance, as one who had done much "for the propaganda of Anarchy" ("Spain" 8).

The Greenwich Observatory explosion seemed to justify fears of the activities of foreign anarchists in London. Two years previously police claimed to have uncovered the "Walsall Plot" when detectives arrested five anarchists in possession of explosives, a revolver, chloroform, and a collection of "revolutionary documents," including a manuscript beginning: "Let us occupy ourselves with bombs." Such devices, it seemed, were "much more useful than barricades" ("Trial" 8). These events inspired a raft of popular novels and stories about the anarchist threat, the most hysterical being E. Douglas Fawcett's *Hartmann the Anarchist; or, the Doom of the Great City*. Here, the continuum between dynamiting and anarchism is made clear as London is pitted against Hartmann, who is both an anarchist and "a dynamitard" (Fawcett 42). After killing scores with a bomb on Westminster Bridge, Hartmann deploys the "incalculable force" of a flying ship, or "aeronef," the *Attila*, to "wreck civilization and hurl tyrannies into nothingness!" (Fawcett 12). Declaring, "We only exist now to act," the crew states that they "live for the roar of the dynamite" (Fawcett 63). Their plan to destroy London from the air is close in aesthetic mania to Zero's "popular" method of the explosive bomb, Rossa's notion of laying Britain "in waste and ruin" (Devoy 212), and Conrad's "perfect anarchist" and "true propagandist," the Professor, whose political imagination is saturated by "images of ruin and destruction" (*SA* 269). Other popular fictions inspired by anarchism include Harry Blythe's 1894 story "The Accusing Shadow," in which the detective Jules Gervaise uncovers a "nest" of anarchists out to destroy "our Government," and Edgar Wallace's hugely popular 1905 mystery *The Four Just Men* (Blythe 321). These stories sensationalized contemporary concerns found in the pages of the daily press and in political commentaries on the anarchist "threat." As late as 1908, one year after the publication of *The Secret Agent*, the French chronicler of anarchism, Peter Latouche, warned that the British capital had become "the Mecca of all revolutionary exiles" (Latouche 22).

Conrad's Irish Context

Although clearly inspired by the political context of anarchism, *The Secret Agent* also draws on the politics surrounding the Clan na Gael TNT campaign. As Conrad stated in his Author's Note, he was "arrested" by Robert Anderson's 1887 memoir, *Sidelights on the Home Rule Movement*. A Dublin-born lawyer, Anderson worked for the Secret Service and then for the Home Office as a special advisor on Fenianism; his most notable duties included handling Thomas Beach, or Henri Le Caron, the British agent who infiltrated Clan na Gael in the United States. He was also an antinationalist propagandist and anonymously published the book *Parnellism and Crime; or, the Bloody Work of the Two Leagues* (1887), along with various uncredited articles in the *Times*. In citing Anderson's book at the start of *The Secret Agent*, Conrad reveals how his novel shares its most important thematic and contextual concerns with *The Dynamiter*.

Conrad also owed an unacknowledged debt to Anderson's spy, Thomas Beach. Verloc's identity as "the celebrated agent" (*SA* 27) mirrors the three-man governing body of Clan na Gael, known as "the triangle," which adopted its name from the cipher signature on its documents, discussed by Beach in his memoir (Le Caron 219–20). Providing a further Irish context, Michaelis, the "ticket-of-leave apostle" of anarchism, is based on Michael Davitt, sentenced to fifteen years for arms smuggling in 1870 and conditionally released on a ticket-of-leave in 1877. The story of Michaelis's imprisonment is taken from the actual events surrounding the "smashing of the van," when Irish Fenians attempted to rescue one of their leaders, Captain Kelly, from a prison van in Manchester in 1867, resulting, as does Michaelis's botched rescue, in the death of a constable. Michael O'Brien, Michael Larkin, and William Allen—the Manchester Martyrs—were hanged for their part in the actual rescue.

Despite being a canonical modernist novel, *The Secret Agent* owes much to popular fictions such as *The Dynamiter*. Set in 1886, its very periodicity resonates with the Clan na Gael TNT campaign, and Vladimir's demand for attacks "against buildings" echoes the first sustained Irish bombing campaign on British soil (*SA* 30). Like Zero, who enjoys dynamiting for its own sake, Vladimir wants a "purely destructive" attack that will shock the British public into reacting against the libertarian underground (*SA* 32). So taken by the *idea* of terrorism, the diplomat underlines Baudrillard's theory of how the pure *event* of terrorism, with its appeal to the popular imagination, functions (Baudrillard 4). As he bluntly reminds Verloc: "[B]ombs are your means of expression" (*SA* 33).

As well as sharing this aesthetic concern with popular fiction, *The Secret Agent* even underwent a transformation in form, bringing it closer to the shilling shocker than its canonical status as a modernist novel would suggest. Cedric Watts has pointed out that because it was published serially in the sensational magazine *Ridgway's: A Militant Weekly for God and Country*, this remodeled version became a popular literary "commodity for the market," marking a "compromise between the claims of the literary market-place and the integrity of the author as innovator" (Watts, *Joseph Conrad*, 104). And like the novel itself, Conrad's most famous terrorist, the Professor, is also a literary hybrid based on an Irishman called Rogers, who gave lectures on explosives under the "ferocious title" of Professor Mezzeroff ("Irish Agitators" 11). This figure from the dynamite campaign of the 1880s appeared in fictional form as Professor Mellerkoff in Donald MacKay's 1888 novel *The Dynamite Ship*. *The Secret Agent* shares subject matter with shilling shockers based on Irish revolutionary affairs. By showcasing anarchism, Conrad updates the dynamite novel to deal with contemporary concerns surrounding the anarchist scare that followed the death of Martial Bourdin, investing his novel with aesthetic and political chic. While it could be argued that Conrad did this in order to distance himself from the potentially embarrassing situation of having to criticize British imperialism, his motivations were much more complex. Examining Stevie's shattered remains, Chief Inspector Heat reflects upon the clues left at the blast site and muses, "[T]he problem was unreadable," and in doing so he points to an exploration of the relationship between anarchism and the written word (*SA* 89).

The Secret Agent closely followed Conrad's other anarchist tales: "An Anarchist" was published in *Harper's Monthly Magazine* in August 1906, and "The Informer" appeared in the same magazine the following December. Both stories, with their melodramatic plots and doomed terrorists, provide a thematic and stylistic bridge between popular dynamite fictions of the 1880s and 1890s and this early modernist novel. "An Anarchist" centers on a Parisian mechanic arrested for drunkenly roaring anarchist slogans after succumbing to "[g]loomy ideas—*des idées noires*" during a drinking bout with a pair of revolutionaries and agreeing with them that "There was only one way of dealing with the rotten state of society. Demolish the whole *sacrée boutique*." He is jailed for yelling "*Vive l'anarchie!* Death to the capitalists!" and becomes a "*compagnon*" of the anarchists (*A Set of Six* 146–49). Deported after a botched bank robbery, he exacts revenge on two of the gang for ruining his life "with their phrases" (*A Set of Six* 58). He turns a warder's revolver on the pair who have destroyed the word "Comrade," making it "accursed":

"Mercy," he whispered, faintly. "Mercy for me!—comrade."

"Ah, comrade," I said, in a low tone. "Yes, comrade, of course. Well, then, shout *Vive l'anarchie.*"

He flung up his arms, his face up to the sky and his mouth wide open in a great shout of despair. "*Vive l'anarchie! Vive—*"

He collapsed all in a heap, with a bullet through his head. (*A Set of Six* 159)

The Professor

Returning to the Author's Note, we find Conrad's "vision" of the metropolis: "a monstrous" city, "a cruel devourer of the world's light" containing "depth enough for any passion" and "darkness enough to bury five millions of lives." Here the modernist tendency to stress the politically alienated individual against the mass is blended with a fascination with the urban labyrinth, as in *The Dynamiter*. The Professor exemplifies this literary type. He first appears in "The Informer," where he works in an anarchist safe house on "perfecting some new detonators": "Explosives were his faith, his hope, his weapon, and his shield" (*A Set of Six* 88). (Conrad also suggests in this story that the Professor carries a personalized bomb.) Mirroring the terrorist described by Sergei Nechaev in his 1869 pamphlet *Catechism of the Revolutionist*, the Professor distinguishes himself from the rest of the anarchists, whom he derides as mere "revolutionists." Nechaev shared this elitism, believing the true revolutionary to be a pitiless opponent "of the State, of class, and of so-called culture," one who "knows of only one science, the science of destruction" and engages in an "unceasing and irreconcilable war" (in Laqueur, *Age of Terrorism*, 68–70).

What makes the Professor particularly modern is his aesthetic appreciation of bombs, reminiscent of Professor Mellerkoff in MacKay's *The Dynamite Ship*. This inventor praises "the beauty" of his device and, when asked if he is pleased with it, replies: "'Satisfied? Yes,' said Mellerkoff, throwing his arms over the cylinder, with a caressing gesture. 'Why should I not be satisfied? It is nearly perfect'" (MacKay 91, 105). But Conrad updates his terrorist from the pastiche of popular Victorian fiction by presenting him as a truly threatening character. Hard-wired and ready to explode at twenty seconds' notice, the Professor is a walking bomb, part of a combined chemical, mechanical, and biological device. His obsession with creating the "perfect detonator" anticipates a key concern of twentieth-century modernity—that of the encroachment of technology over the biological self—encapsulated in the Professor's quest to invent "a detonator that would adjust itself to all conditions of action, and even to unexpected changes of conditions. A variable and yet perfectly precise mechanism. A really intelligent detonator" (*SA* 67). The bomb also has a biological component—the bomber himself—and it is the organic nature of this component that he wants to re-create in this device. The Professor has almost fused himself with the personalized bomb concealed inside his coat and activated by "the principle of the pneumatic instantaneous shutter for a camera lens": "With a swift, disclosing gesture he gave Ossipon a glimpse of an india-rubber tube, resembling a slender brown worm, issuing from the armhole of his waistcoat and plunging into the inner breast pocket of his jacket. . . . 'The detonator is partly mechanical, partly chemical,' he explained, with casual condescension" (*SA* 66). In the Professor's trying to replicate his own physical self in a purely destructive biomechanical form, his experiments, if successful, will lead to the creation of an organic, "intelligent" bomb. This design contrasts with the bourgeois "majesty of inorganic nature; of matter that never dies" (*SA* 14), with which the mansions of Belgravia glow as Verloc walks by. In contrast the dingy Silenus restaurant, where the Professor describes his work to Ossipon, is an atmosphere vivid with new, "smart" technology, where patrons are entertained by a ghostly automatic piano playing popular tunes.

The idea that the metropolis was the site of privatized, irregular warfare was a typically modernist concern, and in 1905 Ford Madox Ford described London as inherently anarchic, "the indecipherable face of a desperate battle field, without ranks, without order, without pity, and with very little discoverable purpose" (Ford 69). Therefore, the assistant commissioner's colonial experience of counterinsurgency is not as far removed from his new London setting as he imagines. In his office, contemplating "the darkness outside," he wonders about "that strange emotional phenomenon called public opinion" (*SA* 102, 99). The Professor thrives on this urban chaos, and the novel closes with him walking through the London crowds, dreaming "images of ruin and destruction"

(*SA* 311). Whereas dynamite novels tend to end either in the reassuring destruction of the terrorist by his own bomb, as in *The Dynamiter* and *Captain Shannon*, or in outright victory for Irish separatists, as happens in *The Dynamite Ship* and *A Modern Dædalus*, Conrad's vision is much less reassuring because, as Heat muses, the true terrorist is an "unreadable" figure, often undetectable and unpredictable. While *The Secret Agent* is a novel that centers on the impossibility of distinguishing between anarchist plots and government counterplots, it is with the "value-free" agent, the Professor, and his vision of political violence that the novel closes (Laqueur, *Age of Terrorism*, 5).

Conclusion

These fictions underline how the demarcation between modernism and popular fiction is not as clear as we might assume. Popular novels and modernism traded on the shocks of political violence. As Conrad wrote to the critic Edward Garnett in 1897, the written word has a subversive and unstable quality: "[T]he illumination, the short and vivid flash" of "words" explodes "like stored powder barrels." Leaving a clue as to the origins of his aesthetic, as expressed in *The Secret Agent*, he added: "An explosion is the most lasting thing in the universe. It leaves disorder, remembrance, room to move, a clear space" (*CL* 1:344). These words anticipate something of the "simplicity" of the Professor's desire to call "madness and despair to the regeneration of the world" (*SA* 311). *The Dynamiter*, on the other hand, is concerned with the complexities and enchantments of urban space and modernity, and for the modern subject, according to the Stevensons, the most fascinating of these attractions is terrorism. The wanderings typical of the *flâneur*, and enacted by bohemian layabouts such as Somerset, Challoner, and Desborough, culminate in political violence. Despite the authors' opening claim to irony, the novel provides a culturally focused examination of terror. As each of these fictions shows, the actual explosions of the Clan na Gael TNT campaign made a lasting literary impact, one in which the imagination of urban chaos was expressed both by a committed modernist writer such as Joseph Conrad and by Robert Louis and Fanny Van de Grift Stevenson, who were equally devoted to the popular aesthetic.

From the City to the Sea:
The Double in Stevenson's "Markheim" and Conrad's "The Secret Sharer"

MARTIN DANAHAY

A COMPARISON of the figure of the double in Robert Louis Stevenson's "Markheim" (1887) and Joseph Conrad's "The Secret Sharer" (1909) underscores the status of Stevenson's short tale as an anomaly in the use of the literary device in the late nineteenth and early twentieth centuries. As I have argued elsewhere, the nineteenth century witnessed the evacuation of ideals of community by what Arnold evocatively termed "the dialogue of the mind with itself."[1] The term *dialogue* in Arnold's formulation raises the possibility of an encounter with a person outside the consciousness of the individual, which is then subverted by the emphasis on the self addressing itself. The very formulation of inner/outer creates a barrier between the individual and the social, and it is this barrier that is explored in nineteenth-century uses of the double, from Victor Frankenstein's creation to Mr. Hyde.

Stories of the double usually end with the social isolation and death of the protagonist. Victor Frankenstein dies alone in a depopulated and icy environment, and Henry Jekyll's suicide takes place in his private laboratory. The social horizon in such stories is narrowed to the double and his other and the fatal isolation of a "dialogue of the mind with itself." The double was thus primarily an antisocial literary device in the nineteenth century. Victor Frankenstein's creation of his "monster" can be read as enacting his own unacknowledged desires to escape the claims of his family and wider society on him. Similarly, Mr. Hyde expresses the repressed antisocial desires of his creator and causes his estrangement from his close circle of male friends. Conrad's use of the double in "The Secret Sharer" is also antisocial in that in his story the protagonist focuses on an encounter with an ambiguous mirror image of himself, isolating himself from his crew. In Stevenson's short story, however, the double acts to reassert the bonds of the community and of the kind of moral judgment that the Conrad story eschews. This is a radically different use of the double.

Stevenson's use of the double is closer to that of James Hogg's *The Private Memoirs and Confessions of a Justified Sinner* (1824) than to *Frankenstein* or "The Secret Sharer." As in Hogg's story of potentially diabolic intervention, Stevenson draws explicitly upon religious belief, although his story, unlike Hogg's, is generally well disposed toward religion. Unlike most other stories of doubles, the central character in Stevenson's story rejoins the community and decides to confess his crime. Stevenson's story thus does not fit easily into one of the master narratives of nineteenth-century literary history: that of the increasing secularization of Victorian society under pressure from advances in science. His story, by contrast, is deeply infused with religious imagery, and it is the religious references that make the double a figure of community and social bonds rather than of isolation.

The narrative of Conrad's *Heart of Darkness* (1899) represents in its purest form the psychological interest of stories of the double as opposed to the more overtly religious approach of "Markheim." *Heart of Darkness* starts out in the Pool of London with Marlow's exclamation that "this also . . . has been one of the dark places of the earth" (*HD* 5). However, the narrative does not explore the urban environment of London as a "heart of darkness," or even that of Brussels, where Marlow receives his first commission, but rather a voyage away from Europe and up a river to the "heart of darkness" in Africa. While the story can clearly be read as implicitly condemning London and Brussels as "hearts of darkness," the main thrust of the narrative is to propel Marlow toward an encounter with Kurtz, or at least the vestiges of Kurtz's life. The sea voyage, as it does in "The Secret Sharer," narrows the horizon to an ambiguous encounter with a violent mirror image of the narrator.

Heart of Darkness, like "The Secret Sharer," tells the story of the protagonist's encounter with a problematic other who represents the potential violence within. Mr. Kurtz can therefore be read as an implicit double for Marlow.[2] Just as the narrator reaches a level of self-awareness, thanks to his double in "The Secret Sharer," Kurtz functions as the nightmare mirror in which Marlow can see his own "heart of darkness" in the potential for violence that lies within each individual. While the story is clearly an indictment of imperialism, it can also be read in purely psychological terms as a journey of self-discovery.[3]

It would have been possible for Conrad to use the phrase "heart of darkness" explicitly about London. Many Victorian commentators used Africa as a metaphor to characterize the East End of London. William Booth in *In Darkest England and the Way Out* explicitly turned the accounts of Stanley's expedition to find Livingstone on their head to suggest that there was a "darkest England" appalling to the "civilized" mind, especially in "our Christian capital" of London (William Booth 9, 11, 13). Booth has social reform in mind, but his narrative dehumanizes the inhabitants of "darkest England" as surely as does the imperialist vocabulary registered by Conrad in *Heart of Darkness*. Conrad, while he may too have been thinking of London in *Heart of Darkness*, did not explicitly map Africa back onto London in the same way as these texts did but rather moved from the city to the sea and used Marlow's journey as a tool with which to understand the violence of imperialism.

Jonathan Arac has suggested that Conrad was an heir to a Romantic sensibility in having an aversion to urban landscapes, preferring a depopulated ocean instead. Arac cites Conrad's Note to *The Secret Agent*, in which he refers to London as "monstrous" and as a "cruel devourer of the world's light" to characterize his experience of the city as "overwhelming shock" (Arac 80). Rather than attempt to represent the "heart of darkness" directly, Arac suggests, Conrad, like Wordsworth, tells stories of individual crisis. Arac's comments help underscore how *The Secret Agent*,

as much as *Heart of Darkness,* is focused more on the individual consciousness than the urban landscape even in a story that is set in London.
In this Conrad prefigures modernist writers such as Woolf, who would
use Clarissa Dalloway's consciousness, for example, as a way to investigate London society rather than use techniques that were more frequently associated with journalism, as I shall suggest in the conclusion.

It may be argued that Conrad had as much interest in analyzing the
urban environment as Stevenson, especially in a text like *The Secret
Agent.* However, while Verloc is supposed to be a "secret agent," he is
actually an inept and lazy parasite on the payroll of a foreign power. Mr.
Verloc has no secrets from the police and represents a threat only to the
most vulnerable member of his family; Inspector Heat is perfectly aware
of Verloc's activities, as he is of those of all the aspiring terrorists. Far
from representing a threat to the social order, as Mr. Hyde does, this
particular "secret" individual succeeds only in destroying his own family
and provoking his wife into killing him. Conrad's story "undermines or
puts in doubt the possibility of moral action" (Fradin 1414) and thus,
unlike "The Secret Sharer," is interested not in using the double to
examine the inner workings of a consciousness that is increasingly isolated from its surroundings or in exploring the social organization of
London but rather in satirizing Verloc and his pretensions as a revolutionary. The only use of *double* in *The Secret Agent* occurs in the frequent
references to Verloc's "double chin," which is a none-too-subtle way of
emphasizing his laziness.

The Secret Agent is therefore above all a satire designed to dramatize
the absurdity of the loose conspiracy of anarchists in London. Mr. Verloc,
like Mr. Hyde, lives in Soho, but they represent two very different ways of
approaching the topic of secrecy. Even Verloc's trade in pornographic
images is shown as seedy and not as a threat to Britain's moral order.
Conrad does not use the figure of the double in this story, nor draw upon
the sea, because the story undermines the possibility of individual action
and subverts the threat represented by Verloc. Unlike Mr. Hyde, who is a
threat to the social order because of his secrecy and potential for violence
and his link through Dr. Jekyll to "respectable" society, Verloc is a pitiable
figure who has no secrets worth keeping.

The idea of secrecy as a potentially socially disruptive force is bound up with the history of individualism and the use of the double. As the interior space of the individual consciousness was created in the romantic and Victorian periods, the relationship between the private life of the individual and social conduct became increasingly problematic. The rise of the detective story can be read as a response to the desire to overcome the inner/outer dichotomy created by individualism. Just as Mr. Utterson decides to become "Mr. Seek" because of "Mr. Hide," the detective examines the traces of the criminal's activities to reconstruct his or her inner existence.

If Conrad had used a double, or if Verloc really had any secrets, then *The Secret Agent* would participate in the same genre as "The Secret Sharer" and "Markheim"; however, the story has very little interest in either the double or the urban environment but instead, as Fradin asserts, is concerned primarily with the impossibility of moral action. By contrast, "The Secret Sharer" demonstrates how an individual, through an encounter with a double, can take direct action even in a morally murky universe. Conrad portrays a self-contained individual who ultimately does not need social or religious values to take decisive action.

The uses of religion in "Markheim" and "The Secret Sharer" index most clearly the different representations of the self as socially constructed or as an atomistic, self-directed unit. Stevenson uses an explicitly religious framework in "Markheim" and in *Jekyll and Hyde*, with the double in each story representing the possibilities of good and evil within a divided consciousness. Stevenson's stories are also embedded in an urban and social context that plays an active role in the plot of both stories. Conrad, by contrast, locates his central characters away from the social in an encounter with doubles that are reflections of their own identities. The encounter with the double leads to self-reflection and self-discovery. This is in keeping with Conrad's own remarks that "we cannot escape from ourselves" and that every novel contains elements of autobiography (Stallman 103).

In Stevenson's short story "Markheim" the city is always present through noises from the street. These noises serve to remind Markheim of his human connections. The noises of people in the street and of clocks in the shop lead to a religious apotheosis in which the double becomes a guardian angel and leads to Markheim's resolve to confess his crime and face punishment. The story thus reasserts the social ties that Markheim severs through his act of violence; while Mr. Hyde is in many ways the antitype of the angelic figure who appears at the end of the story, the revelation of the secret and the breaking down of the laboratory door reassert the bonds of community in much the same way in *Jekyll and Hyde*. Both narratives end with a confession, and even though we do not witness Markheim's ultimate fate, he presumably faces capital punishment. Conrad's stories, by contrast, are more ambiguous in their moral conclusions.

After Markheim has committed murder, he becomes acutely aware of the sound of the clocks in the pawnbroker's shop: "The ticking of many clocks among the curious lumber of the shop, and the faint rushing of the cabs in a near thoroughfare, filled up the interval of silence" (*WRLS* 11:130–31). The story makes insistent connections between the clocks in the shops and the presence of other humans, so that Markheim, even though he is physically alone in the shop with the dead body, is never allowed to forget the existence of a wider human community that would judge his actions and condemn him to death if it were aware of his act. When Markheim forgets his surroundings for a moment he is recalled both by the "small voices" of the clocks and by the sound of a "lad's feet heavily running on the pavement" (*WRLS* 11:134). The connection between the clocks and humans is made explicit when Markheim's murder is compared to that of a repairer of clocks, although Markheim is of course a destroyer of clocks. As a result of the murder "that piece of life had been arrested, as the horologist, with interjected finger, arrests the beating of the clock" (*WRLS* 11:140). The "voices" of the clocks in the shop are by analogy surrogates for all the people that Markheim has not killed but whose presence is carried into the shop by noises from both the street and all the clocks. The clocks in this story are metaphorical human beings who have bodies and voices and thus populate the shop of the pawnbroker even when real people are not present. These virtual human presences produce terror in Markheim at the consequences of his act by reminding him of the laws that will be applied to him.

"Markheim" thus asserts the city as a communal space in which the noise of human activity prevents either complete isolation or the severing of human bonds through murder. Linda Dryden quotes Peter Ackroyd's comments on the importance of noise as part of the experience of London, such as the "low growl" of the city described in *Jekyll and Hyde* (Dryden, *The Modern Gothic*, 107). The noise of the city represents the omnipresent soundscape of human activity in the urban environment. Dr. Jekyll is isolated in his study at the end of *Jekyll and Hyde*, but the breaking down of his door erases the separation between him and the city. Dryden uses terms such as *fraternity* and *community* (Dryden, *The Modern Gothic*, 100) to describe the group of male friends from whom Dr. Jekyll has isolated himself, thanks to his dreadful secret. This male community reasserts its claim on him at the end of the story, so even though Dr. Jekyll dies, the community of men persists. Just as in "Markheim," in *Jekyll and Hyde* the city is connected with noise and the forces of fraternity and community that reassert themselves after the most antisocial act, murder. As Dryden says, "human presence in the city can be reassuring, as well as threatening" (Dryden, *The Modern Gothic*, 88), and in "Markheim" the human presence is reassuring to the reader, promising that social values will be reasserted even in the face of murder.

Thus, while Jekyll/Hyde symbolizes the division of the city into two separate halves, West and East, social bonds persist.[4] Dr. Jekyll's "full statement" of his case is a confession as much as is Markheim's telling the servant girl at the door that he has killed her master. The force of the social exhorts a confession from the murderers in both stories so that even "Mr. Hide" cannot remain in obscurity. Language reveals the connections that the act of murder fails to sever.

Conrad's use of the double is radically different. A major shift in emphasis from Stevenson to Conrad in the use of the double and the city corresponds to the change in context from a religious to a psychoanalytic approach to the double. Barbara Johnson and Marjorie Garber, in "Secret Sharing: Reading Conrad Psychoanalytically," have analyzed the narrative as "an allegory of psychoanalysis" (Johnson and Garber 628).[5] Conrad's double is conducive to such a reading because, like the psychoanalytic project, he seeks to understand human behavior outside of religious and communal relationships. The template for this shift can be found in Freud.

For Freud the double is a reflection of the creation of the ego ideal that does not necessarily disappear with the development from childhood or from so-called primitive to more advanced societies. I am less interested here in the content of Freud's analysis than its reinterpretation of the significance of the double; Freud dismisses the religiously inspired explanation for the double in favor of an explanation that has its origins in the self. The double becomes a reflection solely of individual psychology and loses its connection to communal religious ideas.

In "The Secret Sharer" the narrator moves progressively away from social contact and into the silence and simplified landscape of the sea. Whereas urban noise dominated "Markheim," in "The Secret Sharer" the narrator emphasizes "the great security of the sea as compared with the unrest of the land," where moral questions are reduced to the encounter of the self with a double of itself (*TLS* 96). Even though the "double" may be a murderer, ethical questions are suspended, and the result of the encounter is a strengthened but not redeemed individual.

The sea makes an appearance in both "The Secret Sharer" and "Markheim," but the image registers the profound difference between the narratives. In Stevenson's story the sea serves to reintroduce the human community through the surrogates of the objects in the shop, which seem to be breathing: "The candle stood on the counter, its flame solemnly wagging in a draught; and by that inconsiderable movement the whole room was filled with noiseless bustle and kept heaving like a sea: the tall shadows nodding, the gross blots of darkness swelling and dwindling as with respiration, the faces of the portraits and the china gods changing and wavering like images in water" (*WRLS* 11:134). The sea here is connected with movement and surrogate human presences. The metaphorical sea animates the inanimate objects as if the objects were people themselves, just as the clocks are virtual human beings. Whereas Conrad uses the sea to depopulate the landscape, Stevenson here uses the sea to populate the shop metaphorically with human bustle and reinscribes the city within this space.

The appearance of the sea in "Markheim" also marks an important moment of choice. The vertiginous feeling that Markheim experiences symbolizes a possible cutting of his bonds to the human community; he could potentially ignore his conscience and follow a path closer to Dr. Jekyll's, hiding his violent behavior from society. Markheim has just committed murder, and the imagery of the sea registers his distance from the community around him at this moment. As Juergen Kramer has argued, "the sea is constructed as an antithesis to society" in Stevenson's letters and many of his stories, and in "Markheim" the murder is the negation of social bonds.[6] The sea is constructed similarly in Conrad, but the context of Stevenson's story changes its meaning radically. In Conrad's short story the combination of the sea and the double as "antisocial" forces helps the narrator affirm his own capacity to act as an individual. By contrast the sea in "Markheim" underscores the protagonist's distance from the urban environment and his religious upbringing, both of which are crucial in persuading him to surrender to justice at the end of the story.

When Markheim's double appears, he initially invites him to cut off all human community by not revealing his act. It is clear from the story that it is impossible for Markheim to do this, because he is reminded insistently of the social context in which he is moving, especially that of the city. He is also reminded through his memories of the religious prohibition against murder by both his own memories and the words of the double. Even though Markheim initially believes that his double is "not of the earth and not of God," God makes more appearances in the text as the story progresses (*WRLS* 11:146). Markheim initially fantasizes about escaping "men's observing eyes" and becoming "invisible to all but God" (*WRLS* 11:142). Markheim later asserts that God sees his true self even if others do not, and the story attests to a strong belief in divine justice. "Markheim" makes explicit the more veiled religious references in *Jekyll and Hyde*. Whereas *Jekyll and Hyde* expresses the diabolical side of a binary human nature caught between the twin poles of inner and outer and good and evil, "Markheim" represents the religious and social sides that Dr. Jekyll abjured in his "profound duplicity" of life.[7] Both texts, however, register a social presence that is effaced entirely in Conrad's use of the double.

Conrad's "The Secret Sharer" opens in silence and a profound isolation rather than in an environment full of the noise of human activity. The opening of the story erases all human presence and also flattens out the horizon to eradicate geographical boundaries. The story begins with the description that "there was no sign of human habitation as far as the eye could reach" and that the only moving object is the tug disappearing back up the river. The disappearing tug represents the loss of contact for the narrator with the shore and his life before stepping onto the ship to start his new role as captain of the vessel. The opening of the story does away with all movement and sound to narrow the focus of consciousness to the newly isolated individual. The narrator says that he was "left alone with my ship, anchored at the head of the Gulf of Siam" (*TLS* 91–92). This gives the impression that he is the only human being for miles around and that he is a solitary figure in a depopulated landscape.

As we learn later, the narrator is not truly alone; there is in fact a crew on the ship. However, the narrative continues to erase the human presence to heighten the isolation of the individual; the narrative increases the symbolic isolation of a ship at sea from the human community on the land by reducing the horizon to one man alone on a depopulated deck.[8] The isolation is increased by the further insistence on the absence of all sound from the environment: "At that moment I was alone on her decks. There was not a sound in her—and around us nothing moved, nothing lived, not a canoe on the water, not a bird in the air, not a cloud in the sky" (*TLS* 92). Not only does the opening description deny any human activity; it also makes the sea still and the sky empty of any movement. Partly this is to create a moment of stasis before the beginning of the journey motif, a feature, several commentators have pointed out, that this story shares with *Heart of Darkness*. This description is also intended, however, to pare the narrative down to a question of the psychology of an individual consciousness not defined by communal obligations. The drama that will unfold will not be witnessed by other humans or by God because they have been removed from the equation; this is made explicit by the narrator when he says that his actions will take place "far from all human eyes, with only sky and sea for spectators and for judges" (*TLS* 92). Whereas Markheim has implied judges and spectators in the "voices" of the clocks in the pawnbroker's shop, the narrator in "The Secret Sharer" is able to operate in a social vacuum in which not only are human beings absent, but God also. The social bonds represented by religion in "Markheim" are completely absent in Conrad's story of a double.

The assertion that there are no "human eyes" is not exactly accurate; the narrator is on a ship with other humans, namely, his crew, but they are irrelevant for the purposes of the story. The reference to "judges" also invokes through its absence the world of human laws and religions, both of which could provide the basis for moral condemnation of the events that are to take place. This isolation from judgment has led to a long-standing critical debate on the ethics of the narrator's actions in allowing Leggatt to escape. I am not going to address this set of issues because in the terms of the narrative they are irrelevant. The narrative quite deliberately marginalizes judgments based in communal values. The sea for Conrad is the vehicle for making this isolation and extreme individualism possible.

Conrad makes the isolating effect of the ocean explicit later in the story: "And suddenly I rejoiced in the great security of the sea as compared with the unrest of the land, in my choice of that untempted life presenting no disquieting problems, invested with an elementary moral beauty by the absolute straightforwardness of its appeal and by the singleness of its purpose" (*TLS* 96). A story told about the sea, therefore, in Conrad's view, lends itself to the telling of a story from the point of view of the individual. The so-called unrest and disquieting problems of the land are lost in the narrowing of focus to the solitary individual. Questions of religion and judgment become irrelevant thanks to the ability of the sea to reduce the horizon to its "elements" with none of the social entanglements of the urban environment.

In his letters too Stevenson could describe the sea in terms different from those of Conrad. In contrast to the "security of the sea" above, Stevenson complains about both the sea and being confined to a ship: "And yet the sea is a horrible place, stupefying to the mind and poisonous to the temper; the sea, the motion, the lack of space, the cruel publicity, the villainous tinned foods, the sailors, the captain, the passengers—but you are amply repaid when you sight an island, and drop anchor in a new world" (*SL* 6:216). Whereas Conrad emphasizes the isolation of the ship at the beginning of "The Secret Sharer," with not a single human in sight, in his letter Stevenson makes the ship into a claustrophobic, overcrowded social space from which he is liberated by the sight of an island. As in "Markheim," his emphasis is on the claims of the social world of the ship (the sailors, the captain, the passengers), although their presence is unwelcome rather than comforting.

Conrad's story is the study of a single consciousness, not the ship as a social system. It is no accident that Conrad's text would be congenial to a psychoanalytic reading, because it mimics the effort of psychology as a discipline to sever an understanding of human motivation from a religious and a communal understanding of human behavior and to see such behavior in exclusively secular terms. "The Secret Sharer" dramatizes a human mind splitting itself into two in a "dialogue of the mind with itself," and deciding how to behave without recourse to religious or social values.[9] The story might almost be subtitled "I Am My Own Therapist" in the suggestion that the narrator helps himself through a crisis. I am suggesting, therefore, that these two stories be seen in the context of the development of psychoanalysis as a discipline and that Conrad's text, with its emphasis on existential experiences, is the most congenial to a psychoanalytic approach.[10]

This difference can be seen most vividly in the way the stories end. Markheim addresses the maid at the door and sets in motion the process of trial and judgment that will lead to his own death. By contrast, the ending of "The Secret Sharer" emphasizes the solitude of the narrator: "Already the ship was drawing ahead. And I was alone with her. Nothing! no one in the world should stand now between us, throwing a shadow on the way of silent knowledge and mute affection, the perfect communion of a seaman with his first command" (TLS 143). The ideal of perfect communion of the self with itself is realized in this conclusion. Once again, the narrator is not really alone, because the ship has a crew; the crew as a group of human beings in this narrative is conflated with the physical presence of the ship, and the ship itself is turned into an extension of the narrator's consciousness. The landscape is reduced to one human consciousness in this way. The narrative envisions an ideal state in which the individual can act and have his wishes executed without interference from moral issues. There has been much discussion of the morality of Conrad's story and much anxiety over the justice of the narrator's shielding a murderer. However, the narrative works to make judgments based on religious or social values irrelevant. The ideal in the story is the individual who reaches within himself for the courage to take an action and the right to make these actions in isolation from other considerations. One odd consequence of this is that the ship becomes a surrogate presence, returning the captain's affection and carrying on a silent communion as if it were alive. This communion, a word that originally had a religious meaning, refers to the captain as the autocratic ruler of his own private world. Instead of *communion* representing a religious and social act, here it stands for a mind in total control of its own universe.

For this reason "The Secret Sharer" is a much more frequently studied text than is "Markheim." In a post-Freudian perspective the aims of Conrad's story dovetail with those of psychoanalysis and provide rich material for an analysis of the individual psyche. "Markheim" by contrast has to be understood within the contexts of the social and the religious and is thus more overtly welded to its social and historical context. The interlacing of the social and religious is underscored in "Markheim" by a crucial passage in which the sounds of the city prompt memories of the past:

> Presently, on the other side, the notes of a piano were wakened to the music of a hymn, and the voices of many children took up the air and words. How stately, how comfortable was the melody! How fresh the youthful voices! Markheim gave ear to it smilingly, as he sorted out the keys; and his mind was thronged with answerable ideas and images: church-going children, and the pealing of the high organ; children afield, bathers by the brookside, ramblers on the brambly common, kite-flyers in the windy and cloud-navigated sky; and then, at another cadence of the hymn, back again to church, and the somnolence of summer Sundays, and the high genteel voice of the parson (which he smiled a little to recall) and the painted Jacobean tombs, and the dim lettering of the Ten Commandments in the chancel. (*WRLS* 11:144–45)

To contemporary readers this passage may seem overly idealized and romanticized, but it is a crucial index of the interpenetration of the religious and social in the text. Memories of childhood and of nature dovetail with church sermons and lead to the Ten Commandments and of course the prohibition against murder. These memories illuminate a path of rectitude leading Markheim the sinner back into God's presence. Instead of insisting on the isolation and silence of the narrator's situation, "Markheim" makes the urban environment into a crucial protagonist in the unfolding drama. It is precisely because he can hear other human voices, not only the surrogate voices of the clocks, that Markheim is redeemed at the end of the story.

The uses of doubles by Stevenson and Conrad thus represent fundamentally different ways of understanding the city. Stevenson sees the urban environment as a network of social bonds that are threatened by antisocial forces but are resilient enough to detect and neutralize the threat. For Conrad the city is populated by atomistic individuals whose attempts at radical action are subverted by their own ineptitude. The city is unshaken by Verloc's conspiracy, and he was in any case under police surveillance throughout. Rather than address London as social system, Conrad sees issues in existential and psychoanalytic terms, paralleling the development as a discipline that addressed individual psychological issues.[11]

An alternative view of the city is represented by sociology and texts such as Jack London's *People of the Abyss*. London's title is reminiscent of descriptions of East London as a "hell" or a "darkest London" in earlier accounts of the city. In contrast to the movement from the city to the sea that I have sketched above, Jack London went from the sea to the city. To explain his presence in the East End, he posed as an American sailor who was seeking employment on land. Unlike Marlow, who sails from London to the heart of darkness in Africa, Jack London goes from the Pool of London to the abyss of poverty and crime in the East End. His text is closer to Henry Mayhew's *London Labour and the London Poor* or George Orwell's later *Down and Out in Paris and London* than to either Stevenson's or Conrad's texts. The city as a social system can perhaps be better understood by journalism or sociology and can chart a course from the sea to the city rather than from the city to the sea.

NOTES

1. See Martin A. Danahay, *A Community of One: Masculine Autobiography and Autonomy in Nineteenth-Century Britain* (Albany: State University of New York Press, 1993).

2. Dryden links Dr. Jekyll and Mr. Kurtz in terms of their desires (Dryden, *The Modern Gothic,* 85), underlining the connection between Mr. Hyde and the heart of darkness within individuals in Conrad's story. Gekoski's argument that Kurtz is the "incarnation of evil" would link him to the diabolical Mr. Hyde.

3. Simmons has commented on the "self-consciousness" of the story, which would

suggest that Conrad is making encounters with the self the center of the plot (Simmons 210). Guerard in one of the earliest studies of the story termed it a "journey within" (Guerard 14).

4. Dryden notes that *Jekyll and Hyde* is "linked to the social and physical aspects of the city" through its dualism (Dryden, *The Modern Gothic*, 83).

5. See also Dussinger on the story as a "psychological study."

6. Juergen Kramer, "The Sea as Culturally Constructed Space," unpublished paper delivered at "RLS 2006: Transatlantic Stevenson," Saranac Lake, New York, July 19, 2006.

7. Linehan remarks perceptively that a residual "Scotch Presbyterianism" informs *Jekyll and Hyde* and the language of "the diabolic in man" (*JH* Linehan ed., 207).

8. Tymieniecka has argued that the sea in Conrad's story is a symbol of the unconscious, which suggests that the story is an encounter with displaced images of the self (Tymieniecka 67).

9. Kim has extended the solipsistic implications of a "dialogue of the mind with itself" to implicate the narrator in narcissism.

10. See Brown on the narrator as an existential hero.

11. Dryden refers to the "ominous darkness" of the city at the beginning of the narrative, which is not dispelled at the end of *Heart of Darkness* (Dryden, *The Modern Gothic*, 94).

"Affairs in Different Places":
Symbolic Geography in Stevenson and Conrad

JANE V. RAGO

> The prehistoric man was cursing us, praying to us, welcoming
> us—who could tell? We were cut off from the comprehension of
> our surroundings; . . . [t]he earth seemed unearthly.
>
> (*Heart of Darkness* 35–36)

*I*N 1894 Rider Haggard proclaimed, "[S]oon, Africa will have no secrets, and then where will we turn for a space of fancy?" (quoted in McClintock 236). Haggard here articulates the core of the imperial project as it is represented in late-nineteenth-century adventure novels: a space of fancy to be illuminated by the imaginations of intrepid British authors. The fantastical space of Africa relies upon the idea that it is a place of secrets to be dissected and illuminated by the penetrating knowledge of the imperial author qua colonial explorer. Narrative representations of this knowledge filled scientific and ethnographic as well as literary texts. Adventure novels became increasingly popular at the end of the nineteenth century. Novels such as Haggard's *She* (1887), Henty's *Dash for Khartoum* (1892), and H. G. Wells's *Island of Dr. Moreau* (1896) helped to feed a seemingly insatiable Western audience with fantastic tales of the "far off." The same insatiable audience also relished tales of the "gloom" of inner London, represented not only in fiction, such as Gissing's *The Nether World* (1889), but also in journalism—W. T. Stead's *Maiden Tribute of Modern Babylon*

(1885), for example—and in urban ethnography, exemplified by Charles Booth's *Life and Labour of the London Poor* (1892). Both the secret place of Africa and the secret place of inner London are represented as dark spaces that need the penetrating gaze of the authorial explorer to map out and make sense of them.

Darkness and secrecy in the late Victorian imperial adventure tale symbiotically mirror the narratives of degeneration and atavism in the heart of London. Anne McClintock uses the term "anachronistic space" as a trope that gained full authoritative force by the end of the nineteenth century, in which "colonized people—*like women and the working class in the metropolis*—do not inhabit history proper but exist in a permanently anterior time within the geographic space of the modern empire as anachronistic humans, atavistic" (McClintock 30, emphasis added). The space of the far-off empire is here linked with the inner space of the metropolis through the anachronistic people who inhabit these spaces. Evolutionary theory provides a culturally viable way to link such seemingly disparate geographies via narratives that mapped place onto body in an aggressive and melodramatic language.

These productions of meaning emerge in a symbolic geography. A shared set of words and metaphors holds larger complex, and often obscured, cultural assumptions about space and time that repeatedly appear across disciplines and genres. These meanings necessarily emerge through representations of the people who inhabit the dark spaces of the empire. Symbolic geography borrows from scientific and pseudoscientific discourse, yet it emerges most prevalently in fictional narratives at the end of the century. Critical examinations of these works tend to occlude the primary, perhaps even constitutive, role that evolutionary theory plays in representing race, class, and gender within these fantastical and dark places. Evolutionary theory itself transgressed the boundary of science, becoming shaped by people across disciplines into an explanatory paradigm for many, and often contradictory, social phenomena.

With the popularization of Darwinian theory, Britain's national narrative was shaped around the image of the evolutionary family of man. The family offered an indispensable metaphor for national identity. The merging racial evolutionary schema within the family of man provided scientific racism with both gendered and racial images through which national identity and progress are represented in adventure narratives. These narratives focus on the healthy propagation of a national race in the face of anxiety about "going native." Yet the family of man metaphor here assumes an ironic twist: women, nearly absent from these stories, are replaced by a self-perpetuating mode of reproduction through travel, adventure, and science that renders the family entirely homosocial. The family of man metaphor allows a hierarchy of value to be placed on people by classifying scientific data that conflate people, space, and time. At the apex of the scale is the middle-class white Euro-male, and the rest of the family is placed somewhere below in a nebulous understanding of anterior time and anachronistic space. The family of man schema is understood both as the domestic body politic of England and also as the global metaphor of imperial domination with England as the paternalistic parent. This metaphor retells a common myth of the normative middle class through its critique of the differentiated Other. However, in cases in which this metaphor is used domestically as well as abroad, the family of man invokes scientific authority to make class a matter of biology.

Robert Louis Stevenson's group of short stories *The Suicide Club* was published in 1878. These are the stories of Prince Florizel, a prince from Bohemia who passes as a native and seeks out adventures in the unknown urban space of London. He falls in with the Suicide Club, an example of the omnipresent "gentleman's club" of late Victorian London—evocative of closed doors, ritualized secrecy, and nighttime atrocities. This secret space is *not* Booth's space of London's East End nor the choking streets of Dickensian urban squalor. This is the space of the over-evolved: the decadent, the dissipated, the ennui-ridden, enervated gentleman. The middle-class critique of the decadence and vice found in the aristocracy had been familiar in English literature for a century. Stevenson subtly rewrites the story, however, by relying upon geographical causation and evolution. The symbolic geography here is wedded to a biologic discourse entrenched in the assumption that the very space that these men inhabit has led to their biological obsolescence. They are no longer fit for society and therefore have no place in the family of man.

In Joseph Conrad's *Heart of Darkness*, Marlow's narrative, offered in the darkness of the Thames, tells of the darkness of the river that flows into the very heart of "uncomprehended" space in Africa. The tale narrates Marlow's struggle to remain Marlow. What is threatening, and a central generic theme in these adventure novels, is the danger that the narrator faces in going native, in becoming something other than what he originally was: a British man. It is a well-known tale that Conrad himself, as a boy, was seized with a desire to fill in the unknown spaces in the maps of Africa. Subsequently, he traveled; later still, he narrated these acts of exploration. It is only by entering these spaces that one can illuminate with the light of science, and yet it is the mutability and the instability of the narrator that threatens the entire race of British subjects. In a fantasy space without women, what is reproducible is the self, the "I" that must constantly be reiterated "in a panicked imitation of its own naturalized ideation" (Butler 46).

Evolutionary theory profoundly affected perceptions of time and space, invigorating geography with a heightened semiotic ability to shape identity. Stevenson and Conrad's representations of space use a symbolic geography that is less concerned with an actual physical place than with the imaginary mindscape that produces these secret places. These places are represented as dark so that the story of illuminating knowledge may be told again and again: it is a seemingly endless story, redefining and delineating strict boundaries of selfhood that must constantly be reiterated to ensure a privileged position on the nebulous scale of evolution. This reiteration of illumination was deployed in almost any manner to enable an entire nation's definition of what, indeed, these secret places of Africa and urban London actually are—or at least what they can offer to a beleaguered England's sense of itself.

Referring to the British "race," Edwin Ray Lankester wrote in 1880: "We are as a race more unfortunate than our ruined cousins—the degenerate Ascidians. . . . To us has been given the power to *know the causes of things*, and by the use of this power, it is possible for us to control our destinies" (Lankester 24, emphasis added). Degeneration is an implicit threat, and knowledge is the antidote. Significantly, it is *specialized* knowledge that has the potential to save all of England. The rise of the professional in the nineteenth century and the power of science to explain all social phenomena solidified an elite and homosocial network of knowledge. Lankester writes: "The full and earnest cultivation of

Science—the Knowledge of Causes—is that which we have to look to for the protection of our race" (Lankester 24). Novelists such as Stevenson and Conrad employ this specialized "Knowledge of Causes" in their work, detailing and interpreting dark, secret places in order to reaffirm the authorial "I" that reassures Victorian readers.

In the language of evolutionary theory, racial and national identities become inextricable from geographic specificity. One year after Lankester published his cautionary essay *Degeneration: A Chapter in Darwinism*, Oxford and Cambridge officially recognized geography as a science for the first time. Space is thus imbued with scientific import. Its secrets must be investigated, dissected, and taxonomized to reveal truth about people within a particular space.

Common tropes that cut across fiction and nonfiction narratives pose an interesting phenomenon of shared paradigms—the imagery and the rhetoric signify, to the culturally encoded reader, an entire subtext in just a few phrases and catchwords. The shared epistemology of differing discourses "suggests ... that both scientists and novelists belonged to a linguistic as well as 'class' community" (Mighall 181). I see this as a dialectical process of larger cultural productions of meaning and signification that originates from popular conceptions of evolutionary theory. Evolutionary theory enraptured the British public by offering a story of origins, a story that was widely interpreted across all layers of social strata. Evolutionary theory also provided the paradigm that enabled the solidification of science as authoritative and powerful through all layers of social strata. The professional, with his specialized knowledge, knows the causes of things. This privileged information is accessible only to those within the professional circle. Frank Mort writes that from mid-century on, the manner in which experts closed ranks around the urban problem produced a "[p]rofessional masculinity [that] was a mixture of scientific, hard-edged expertise ... and an ideology of dedication to public service. This male identity was forged through the new intellectual knowledges which endowed the experts with a caste-like mode of cohesion" (Mort 51). By the end of the century, the castelike mode of cohesion is exemplified by the homosocial world in Conrad's and Stevenson's texts. The narrators of the stories assume the privileged position of the scientist-qua-explorer, reiterating their own male identities while also using the paradigm of degeneration theory to grant their adventures the authority of science. These stories seek to know the causes of things and to illuminate them to the British public.

In the last two decades of the nineteenth century the problem of the urban poor reached a crisis. The middle of the century saw numerous sanitary reports on the East End, and it was increasingly assumed that moral reform would naturally emerge from healthier bodies. These reports are part of the long ascent of medical influence in how best to solve the "problem of the poor" in Victorian England. Public focus on the East End was set into motion by the Contagious Diseases Acts of 1864, 1866, and 1869. Reform rhetoric constructed a repertoire of sexual and racial knowledge around themes of ill health and immorality. The growing hegemony of state medicine written into public regulation bore witness to a substantial shift in the focus of the sanitary movement. Midcentury doctors used their representations of the poor to insist that medics rather than moralists had greater claim to authority on social and environmental issues. This shift from the social to the biological effected two changes. First, it solidified the homosocial authority of the male professional via the related acts of exploring spaces and keeping secrets. Second, the increased power of the medics to make policy on social issues, such as the urban poor, made class a matter of degeneration by the end of the century, crucially rooted in a symbolic geography.

Mapping Social Ills: Disease and Poverty in the East End

In February 1832 a cholera epidemic broke out in London. Because of inept sanitary systems and contaminated water, it devastated the East End in particular. Many doctors studied the patterns of how the disease moved, mapping the hardest hit areas over street maps that demonstrated a direct correlation between the disease and poverty. The overcrowded conditions of particular areas of the East End, the cesspools, and the proximity of the slaughterhouses to these areas all highlighted the spread of the disease. This first epidemic is key in understanding later reform movements that focus on the East End. The visualized correlation between disease and poverty marks a paradigm shift wherein social ills (heretofore primarily in the domain of theology and morality) were imbued with a sense of the scientific. A few reformers who believed in the need for scientific government intervention to cure social ills virulently tried to educate Parliament about the correlations between poverty and mortality rates from cholera. Although these few reformers initially met with much resistance, they presented a case that increasingly gained authority. In the 1850s the belief in science as a cure for the social problems of East End London was quite common; by the 1880s this biological approach to the darkest heart of London assumed the status of "common sense." The reform debates then were not between science and theology but between science and science.

Edwin Chadwick was one of the pioneers of sanitation and public health in England. After the 1832 cholera epidemic he began mapping the trajectories of epidemics in London. When Chadwick became secretary of the new Poor Law Commissioners in 1832, he immediately asked for detailed reports from the districts with the heaviest claims for relief: Stepney, Bethnal Green, and Whitechapel. That all of these are in the heart of the East End furthered the public conception of East End as an area of filth, contagion, and pestilence.

Many in the propertied classes were familiar with East End London as a fictional concept, as a dark space full of poverty, rookeries, and disease. Dickens's early work *Sketches by Boz* (1836) describes the East End as a reservoir of dirt and drunkenness, while *Oliver Twist* (1838) portrays life in seedy Whitechapel. Nonetheless, members of Parliament and upperclass gentlemen alike were shocked to learn of "the unemptied cesspools and privies; open sewers; stinking slaughterhouses; and the . . . nauseating burial grounds, where decomposing bodies were inadequately interred" (quoted in Palmer 53). In 1847 Dr. Hector Gavin appealed for sanitary reform in *Sanitary Ramblings: Being Sketches and Illustrations of Bethnal Green.* This book was one of the first to provide scientific statistics and hard numbers to enhance the already familiar descriptions of deplorable conditions. What his unambiguous numbers and statistical calculations perpetuated was the notion that science could not only locate the source of the problem but also provide the solution to the problem. According to Frank Mort, "the logic which twinned poverty and immorality with contagion was made through a specific language— the discourse of early social medicine—and was circulated at key institutional sites within the central and local state" (Mort 16). The intersections between science and government intervention grew as public debate usually centered in one of these two institutions, each self-referentially deferring to the other.

Within the sanitary reports on the East End it was assumed that moral reform would naturally emerge from healthier bodies. The growing hegemony of state medicine written into public regulation bore witness to a substantial shift in the focus in the sanitary movement. This relationship between doctors and politicians was symbiotic in that the doctors as well were looking toward government to solve these ills. The authority of one backed up and helped to solidify the authority of the other. Many of the medical supporters of public health legislation had a history of involvement in hospitals and in sanitary work among the poor. Their biographies, according to Mort, attest to the "professional and class alliance which fed into the politics of mid-Victorian reform" (Mort 72). The medical circle used the already established authority of the government to bolster their authority by making matters of health intrinsically linked to matters of the state via both practice and rhetoric. This alliance was made possible and smooth by the already existing structures of the male homosocial cadre.

As Mort argues, the links among science, the government, and reform have their roots in the 1700s with the concern over prisons, reform, and criminality. The writings of John Locke, to name only one example, clearly demonstrate the already established links in public discourse among disease, morality, and class. With the rise of the medical profession in the nineteenth century, these links became more concretized and specific, building upon a previously established structure and helping not only to shape public perception of the urban poor but also to solidify the professionalization of scientific medicine itself. Mort writes that the "medic's own desire for status and authority found *form* in narratives of *reform*" (Mort 33, emphasis in the original). Furthermore, the new medical theories relied upon geography for meaning. Public discourse about the root of the social ills of the East End helped lead to the myth that the area itself was somehow endemically diseased, that the people of East End must be cured or else all of London would suffer.

From the early 1850s on, however, there was a gradual move away from insistence on the interrelated nature of all social, political, and economic problems and a shift toward specialization. Specialization leads to professionalization, and the ranks of the experts closed (Heyck 21). The unsuitable and the untrained are the rest of the family in the family of man: women, children, the laboring class, the urban poor, and those from underdeveloped countries. In imperial and colonial rhetoric the "natives" are depicted as childlike, thus needing the paternal guidance of the British male. The ordering of the professions relied upon exclusivity and secrecy—themes that echo throughout multigeneric and homosocial writings at the close of the nineteenth century and that are highlighted in both Conrad's and Stevenson's texts. Legislation worked in tandem with the medics to perpetuate the concept of separate apparatuses and spheres of activity with distinctive forms of knowledge and expertise. Social problems could only be cured via painstaking scientific observation. The National Association for the Promotion of Social Science, founded in 1865, "typified this approach" (Mort 64). The genesis of social science in this epoch underlies the move both to combine knowledge, evinced by the enormous medico-legal influence in Parliament, and also to separate knowledge into taxonomies of expertise, as seen by the formation of increasingly distinct scientific and medical fields: sexuality, criminality, prostitution, and, ultimately, degeneration theories.

Evolutionary Theory, Degeneration, and National Identity

Although evolutionary theory had been expressed before the nineteenth century, Charles Darwin popularized and vastly expanded the concept. Darwinian theory introduced the ideas of struggle, competition, and heredity into the concept of the mutable organism. The logical coherence of evolution relies on the steady progression of time along a perceived line. Degeneration, then, is the necessary subtext that reinforces this progressive ideology through its sense of deviation from this timeline. This deviation implies either a backward movement through time (anachronism, atavism) or a monstrous bodily morph according to one's environment (adaptation). The result was widespread and varied interpretations of this new science and an immense cultural power to rewrite social and political issues, such as nationality, gender, class, and race, into and onto the body.

This firmly roots the metaphysical in the sheer physicality of the human body. Science explains all social interactions. And since this particular brand of science relies so much on space and time, the body becomes at once over-determined and fluid, unfixed. Within this fluid materiality of the body, race, class, and gender form a triumvirate of highly contested notions of who, or what, a body is. Kelly Hurley calls this mutability of the body the "abhuman," in that "the abhuman subject is a not-quite-human subject, characterized by its morphic variability, continually in danger of becoming not-itself, becoming other" (Hurley 3–4).

The metaphorical representations of the dark places signify this perpetual danger of the body becoming not-itself, either through anachronism or adaptation. Conrad's narrator reiterates the danger he felt of becoming something other the longer he stayed in the dark place of the Congo. As Marlow hikes through the African jungle, he muses to himself: "I remembered the old doctor—'It would be interesting for science to watch the mental changes of individuals on the spot.' I felt I was becoming scientifically interesting" (HD 20). This sentiment clearly shows the link between science and identity—the paradigm of Enlightenment selfhood—"I think, therefore I am" is replaced with a much more biologically based idea of self: "I evolve, therefore I am." In fact, one could argue that the horror of Conrad's text is precisely the monstrous morphing of Kurtz from a promising businessman who can get more ivory than other traders to a hybrid native. Monstrous in his mutability, he is neither native nor colonizer. He defies the mapping and taxonomization that colonial domination fundamentally relied upon. His adaptation is so terrifying precisely because it is so incomplete. Marlow's experience belies a sense of surviving what is often a fatal disease. He is a survivor, but he is marked by the traces left in his body—he is a degenerate self. Within this text the body—always mutable—is perceived as threatening, at any moment able to betray the self, the ego, that inhabits the body. Adaptation threatens to undo these carefully wrought boundaries, the mapping, of these secret places. Within this biologist rhetoric the body always threatens to undo itself, and the ensuing contagion and chaos is staved off by representational means: maps, narratives, and symbolic geography.

Late Victorian maps encapsulate disparate time, with London in real

time and Africa in "prehistoric" time. Marlow, traveling on the river
through evolutionary time, posits something altogether different from
metaphysical time, effectively understood in one of the most famous
articulations of time, Henri Bergson's notion of duration. In a classic
metaphor of time as a river that flows inexorably along, Bergson writes of
"our own personality in its flowing through time—our self which
endures" (Bergson 14). Evolutionary time threatens the stability of
Bergsonian selfhood and offers quite a different sense of time. The self is
not a separate entity from space/time, but directly shaped and made and
identified by, with, and through space/time. *Where* one lives on the earth
determines *when* one lives, which signifies one's evolutionary status.
Implicit, then, is the notion that one can help the unevolved evolve,
which in turn intimates that the unevolved can help one devolve or go
native or degenerate. Marlow's river of time justifies colonial domination
in that the more evolved can enlighten the less evolved—the ultimate
manipulation of time. Yet the danger therein lies in the acceptance that
time itself is pliable. If one can increase the flow, so one can also reverse
the flow. The white Euro-male self is destabilized. In this context it fails
to have the stolid stability of the Bergsonian self who endures while flowing through time (Bergson 69). Marlow's secret is how close he came to
being "incomprehensible" to himself. This must be kept a secret because
scientific authority relies upon the premise that the scientist himself is a
stable and fixed point.

If evolutionary theory helped to shape cultural understandings of
imperial and colonial spaces, its counterpart, degeneration theory, helped
to shape cultural understandings of the urban landscape and its inhabits
at the very center of England. Many critics have observed that by the
1880s degeneration theory was so widely circulated across different areas
of society that it ceased to have any sort of coherence at all. Stephen
Arata claims: "Like its better-documented counterpart, 'progress,' 'degeneration' was a term no late-Victorian thinker could do without" (Arata,
Fictions of Loss, 2). Furthermore, he claims, degeneration became a
species of common-sense knowledge, naturalized into cultural discourse,
which obscured its status as a material theory. The open semiotic of
degeneration became a catch phrase in the multifaceted and often competing discourses on the urban poor as well as in the "native problem" that
was widely argued both domestically and abroad.

Based on the idea of survival of the fittest, the question of *who* will survive in a noxious and degenerate London plagued social theorists. The teeming humanity of inner London was increasingly represented as an urban race of degenerates. This fluid idea of race alludes back to Lamarckian ideas of how the environment produces and affects race. The influence of degeneration theory in urban narratives helped to shape the very understanding of London; what the city could be, what the city hid, and who the city produced were all posited as potentially threatening, obscured from view, and dangerous to the average British subject in the 1880s and 1890s. Julian Wolfreys writes that "urbanization disturbs the assumptions about identity, progress, and narrative that shaped the bourgeois text, so those who can read the city and reconstruct coherent stories are the new heroes" (Wolfreys 98). Indeed, there were prolific examples of these new heroes and their reconstructed stories in the form of the urban ethnographic study. These studies were part sensation and part scientific, and all addressed the problems of the East End, exemplified by Charles Booth's ten-volume *Life and Labour of the People of London*, published in 1895.

Booth's famous maps of the economic classes of late Victorian London identify eight classes of people, assigning each class its most prevalent position according to geographical demarcations. Table three, "Numerical Tables of Classes," has in its left column the names of physical spaces in London, while the following columns show the numerical proportion of each class within that section. The visual logic of these charts, graphs, and taxonomies tabulates people and their space as mutually constitutive. Booth's use of these ostensibly objective tools signifies to his readers that his narrative is scientific: his text is not social theory but scientific fact. Furthermore, these facts refer to the causal relationship between people and the spaces they inhabit. What began in the midcentury reform movement as a hierarchy of the poor, from those who deserve help to those who are beyond help, here assumes a more fixed, biological tenor. I use the term *biological* because hitherto social issues, such as poverty, are here rewritten as scientific issues. Class and race are conflated into a mutually constitutive biopolitical identity, one that relies upon geography for meaning. Booth writes of the lowest class, "[T]he children are street arabs" (Charles Booth 34–35). This narrative conflates people with their physical location and also assumes a racialized notion of class by invoking the term *arab*, a word that derives its meaning from association with a specific region of the world, obviously not London. They have degenerated into atavistic beings: the abject poor and the primitive man are equalized and assume the same space in time within the hierarchical family of man.

The evolutionary conception of anachronistic space provides an ideological schema, a shared language, through which imperial rhetoric and domestic rhetoric signify the same troubling aspects of degeneration for the middle class. Within this symbolic geography Booth simultaneously assumes the authority of a scientist (able to dissect and view dark spaces), a novelist (revealing these secrets to rapt readers), and an imperialist (as urban explorer, going native in order to achieve cultural, economic, and intellectual gain). He writes: "East London lay hidden from view behind a curtain on which were painted terrible pictures. . . . This curtain we have tried to lift" (Charles Booth 173). His narrative is understood by middle-class readers as well as by many polymath Victorians, who, whether in disagreement (that is, Huxley the scientist condemning H. G. Wells the novelist as "ridiculous") or in agreement, all use the same language, the same generic paradigm of meaning making.

The dark space of Stevenson's urban gentleman's club is cast in a similarly ritualized manner of meaning making as is the dark space of Conrad's Africa. The shared paradigmatic language is firmly entrenched in popular assumptions and conceptions of degeneration theories. Assuming the role of the intrepid explorer who is ostensibly out to help the unfortunate natives of urban club-land, Prince Florizel must bring light into the dark crannies and places of the club. The first sentence of the "Story of the Young Man with the Cream Tarts" is: "During his residence in London, the accomplished Prince Florizel of Bohemia gained the affection of all classes by the seduction of his manner and by a well-considered generosity" (*WRLS* 3:11). Immediately, we learn that the prince has the ability to move through classes and is thus positioned as an expert, or one who is perceived as existing outside of class. After penetrating the private space of the club, Prince Florizel then narrates what he has seen. He reconstructs a story about this unknown space in the same manner as the urban ethnographer. Like Charles Booth, Prince Florizel embarks on an elaborate adventure. Disguised as a native of

London, he gains access to this exclusive club. Unlike Booth's narrative, however, Prince Florizel's narrative locates the site of degeneration within the upper classes in the privileged spaces of London. Both narratives conflate people and space in a biological discourse of degeneration and serve as cautionary and illuminating tales for a "normative" British public by locating degeneration in the upper and the lower classes, positioning the middle class as the highest echelon of evolution.

Like Marlow, Prince Florizel attempts to rescue a young man who seems to have gone native by joining a club full of overevolved and dissipated English men. Yet instead of the "prehistoric men" that Marlow encounters, this narrator observes, "As in all other places of resort, one type predominated: people in the prime of youth, with every show of intelligence and sensibility in their appearance, but with little promise of strength or the quality that makes success" (*WRLS* 3:34). The true darkness of the club, then, is the prevalence of degeneration in London. The lower classes are in teeming dens of atavism, while the upper classes are marked by enervation and ennui. In 1880 Lankester had defined degeneration as "a gradual change of the structure in which the organism becomes adapted to *less* varied and *less* complex conditions of life. . . . In Degeneration, there is *suppression* of form, corresponding to the cessation of work" (Lankester 6, emphasis in the original). What is striking here is that Lankester explicitly links degeneration with cessation of work. This sentiment is at odds with other notions of degeneration that specifically locate degeneration in the working classes, such as Charles Booth's racialized schema of the urban poor. The shocking threat is that degeneration is endemic, not entirely confined to the East End, as Booth believed.

In the first short story in *The Suicide Club*, "Story of the Young Man with the Cream Tarts," Prince Florizel penetrates the secret space of the gentleman's club and is thus privileged to know the men there and their various reasons for wanting to commit suicide—several citing boredom or loss of finances or hinting at "disgraceful actions" from which they can hope for no redemption. Yet one particular suicide-seeker (referred to as the "remarkable suicide") stands out for two reasons. First, he is granted a voice, in that he is one of the only members of the club who actually articulates to us, the reader, why he has joined such a club. Second, his statement directly attests to the prevalence of evolutionary theory in popular discourse. It is understood that the reader will know who and what the "remarkable suicide" is referring to: "[A] fourth professed that he would never have joined the club, if he had not been induced to believe in Mr. Darwin. 'I could not bear,' said this remarkable suicide, 'to be descended from an ape'" (*WRLS* 3:36).

In Victorian iconography, the ritual recurrence of the monkey figure is eloquent of a crisis in value and hence anxiety at possible boundary breakdowns—the uncivilized spreading into the civilized, the conflation of dark places: inner Africa and inner London. Anne McClintock observes that "monkeys were seen as allied with the dangerous classes: the 'apelike' wandering poor, the hungry Irish, Jews, prostitutes, impoverished black people, the ragged working class, criminals, the insane, and female miners and servants, who were collectively seen to inhabit the threshold of racial degeneration" (McClintock 216). The monkey in London occupies anachronistic space, condensing time and space into an embodied metaphor of evolutionary theory. Here, however, the monkey does not represent the lower classes. Instead, the reference to the monkey serves as an indicator of degeneration. The monkey does not represent the white Euro-male's barbarous past as much as it represents the threat that one can overevolve into a degenerate form. Lankester writes:

> The traditional history of mankind furnishes us with notable examples of degeneration. High states of civilization have decayed and given place to low and degenerate states. At one time it was a favorite doctrine that the savage races of mankind were degenerate descendants of the higher and civilized races . . . , [and] there is no doubt that many savage races as we at present see them are actually degenerate and are descended from ancestors possessed of a relatively elaborate civilization. (Lankester 15)

The remarkable suicide finds death preferable to believing in his fragile and fluid position in the hierarchy of the family of man. The pessimism of descent and the optimism of origins are here embodied in a direct metaphor of degeneration as the new original sin: the horror of origins, an atavistic dark, tainted past that hints at racial blurring within the highest echelons of London society. In this paradigm, identity and ideas of selfhood are not static, and the anxious narratives of race belie the quest of the author as explorer to establish a coherent and authoritative identity located on the apex of the evolutionary timeline.

Stevenson's story relies entirely upon secrets. Prince Florizel and his sidekick, Colonel Geraldine, assume elaborate disguises as Theophilus Goodall and Major Hammersmith, respectively; the young man with the cream tarts withholds his name and never fully explains his silly joke; and the Suicide Club itself relies on secrecy for its very existence, in part because to be a member of the club one has to commit murder. In this story, however, there are good secrets and bad secrets. The Suicide Club is represented as a den of degenerates, with "little decency among the members of the club" (*WRLS* 3:35). The existence of the club relies on secrecy and exclusivity, as we witness through the prince's attempts to gain access to the inner sanctum of the club. After Prince Florizel meets with the president and engages in a ritual of coded language, the president acknowledges that "'some of the club's formalities require to be fulfilled in private.' With these words he opened the door of a small closet, into which he shut the Colonel" (*WRLS* 3:31–32). While the Colonel is locked in a closet, the prince gains access to the inner sanctum of the club.

According to the logic of the club, then, illumination and opening its secrets to the public will necessarily destroy it—and this is exactly what Prince Florizel does. However, the prince also relies heavily upon secrets, not simply with his disguise, but also for his own redemption. Like Kurtz, the prince becomes unsure of himself. In order to gain access to the club, he has to become "one of them." In other words, he "goes native" and threatens to degenerate into "a man more naturally hideous, . . . ravaged by disease and ruinous excitements" (*WRLS* 3:35). The Colonel saves Prince Florizel, unlike Marlow, who was unable to save Kurtz (due to Marlow's own identity crisis). The Colonel remains a stable identity because he was not privy to the club: he did not become a member. He saves the prince through an arrangement with a "celebrated detective," and he reassures the prince that "[s]ecrecy has been promised and paid for" (*WRLS* 3:54). The secrecy that has been promised is that the prince will emerge from his adventures untainted by scandal and thus untainted by degeneration. He will retain his status as an expert explorer and continue to have more adventures in the following two short stories of *The Suicide Club*. Stevenson's story relies on not revealing how close the narrator comes to losing his selfhood, and this mirrors *Heart of Darkness*. Marlow too redeems himself through the use of a secret: he lies to Kurtz's fiancée. Both narratives uphold the perceived normativity of domestic England. They work to maintain the high status on the evolutionary scale of the European middle-class professional through the narration of these dark places within and without the empire. The homosocial world of the club mirrors the homosocial world of the explorer, both reiterating their respective places in the family of man.

At the end of the nineteenth century the unmapped darkness of the far off places of the empire and the dark places of the city streets obsessed the imagination of England. Daniel Pick claims that late Victorian England was "powerfully invested with the sense of imperial mission; what was 'strained' was exactly the viability of the ideology of a cohesive and unified ruling race" (Pick 184). It is significant that Pick uses the term "ruling race" instead of "ruling class." Race becomes entangled in notions of national identity and relies upon gender, class, and geographical space to grant it meaning. The family of man metaphor realigns cultural understandings of time and space in such a way as to posit England as the apex of history.

In 1890 World Standard Time was implemented. Dividing the world into twenty-four distinct time zones, it was agreed upon (although with much conflict) that Greenwich, England, would stand as ground zero: the place of absolute time, effectively making England the center of the world. This geography of the world relies upon the notion of time as a determinant for spatial representations. Maps of the world represented unknown spaces, unknown because of their precarious placement in the historical timeline of evolution. The conflation of space with time illustrates the enormous impact that evolutionary theory had on cultural understandings and narrative representations of geographical space as comprised of different times, that is, historical moments. The infamous "blank spaces" on the map (that apparently inspired Marlow and the young Conrad) offered a space to be filled by the imagination of those inhabiting the center of the world and the epicenter of history itself: imperial England (*HD* 8). The symbolic geography that serves to tell the stories of exploration to the furthest reaches of the empire and the inner sanctum of the interior obscure the familial in a metaphor of the family of man. This obfuscation perpetuates a continual reiteration and illumination into the dark places of the British Empire that are, indeed, *everywhere*.

Beyond Freud and Jung:
The Analysis of Evil in *Heart of Darkness* and *Dr. Jekyll and Mr. Hyde*

NANCY BUNGE

$\int$IGMUND FREUD and his rebellious student Carl Jung frequently disagree, but both see artists as unwitting vehicles and even victims of unconscious forces. Robert Louis Stevenson's *Strange Case of Dr. Jekyll and Mr. Hyde* and Joseph Conrad's *Heart of Darkness* add a new dimension to this discussion by showing that literary artists not only write out of the unconscious but also create works that reveal an astonishingly sophisticated understanding of it. Even before Freud articulated the view, Conrad's work presents the Freudian notion that the evil lurking in human nature inevitably surfaces when society's constraints disappear. Stevenson's novel characterizes evil as something that develops when a human being fails to face and embrace traits that conflict with his or her self-image, a notion that later played a central role in Jung's psychology.

Not surprisingly, critics have produced several Freudian readings of *Heart of Darkness*, for Conrad's novel embodies many concepts that Freud later developed, especially in *Civilization and Its Discontents*, wherein

Freud argues that sexual and aggressive drives provide the fundamental energy for human behavior and need sublimating for human society to persist. Social norms transmute the sexual desire threatening the community into a generalized brotherly love that unites it. Socially induced guilt brings about this magical transformation by turning the other dangerous human impulse, aggression, inward. As a result, when social mores weaken, people attack each other: if "the mental counter-forces which ordinarily inhibit it [aggression] are out of action, it . . . reveals man as a savage beast to whom consideration towards his own kind is something alien" (Freud, *Civilization*, 69). Because of civilization's restraints, its denizens never achieve happiness. Freud argues: "primitive man was better off in knowing no restrictions of instinct" (Freud, *Civilization*, 73).

In *Heart of Darkness*, Europeans go to Africa, eluding their culture's inhibitions, but some struggle to preserve European norms. Marlow encounters an accountant who maintains propriety and cleanliness while bemoaning the chaos around him: "'When one has got to make correct entries one comes to hate those savages—hate them to the death'" (*HD* 19). The station manager excels at nothing except maintaining regularity: "He originated nothing, he could keep the routine going—that's all. But he was great" (*HD* 2). Freud declares organization and cleanliness hallmarks of civilization, and reasonably so: "The benefits of order are incontestable. It enables men to use space and time to the best advantage, while conserving their psychical forces" (Freud, *Civilization*, 46).

As Marlow moves further into the African wilderness, conventional systems fall away, along with brotherly love. Although sometimes claiming a desire to redeem the Africans, most Europeans seek easy profit and fall into abusive behavior, working the Africans mercilessly, sometimes even beating them. Kurtz has apparently descended into barbarism, for heads on pikes surround his home. Even though the wilderness has him firmly in its grip, Kurtz maintains the illusion of civility and control: "'My Intended, my ivory, my station, my river, my——' everything belonged to him. It made me hold my breath in expectation of hearing the wilderness burst into a prodigious peal of laughter that would shake the fixed stars in their places" (*HD* 48). As he dies, Kurtz seems to face what Marlow knows about him and make an honest assessment of what he has become, declaring, "The horror!" Marlow believes this comment "had the appalling face of a glimpsed truth—the strange commingling of desire and hate" or, as Freud names them, sex and aggression (*HD* 70). After visiting the African wilderness, the falsity of civilized life strikes Marlow: "I found myself . . . resenting the sight of people hurrying through the streets to filch a little money from each other, to devour their infamous cookery, to gulp their unwholesome beer, to dream their insignificant and silly dreams" (*HD* 70). For Freud and Conrad, human evil comes with human life; culture simply helps people evade awareness of the unlovely urges that motivate them.

Stevenson's *Strange Case of Dr. Jekyll and Mr. Hyde* has also received Freudian analyses, with, for example, Jekyll portrayed as the ego, Utterson as the superego, and Hyde as the id (*JH* xxviii–xxix). But in Freud's scheme the id remains unconscious, while Jekyll knows about Hyde. Moreover, according to Freud, this repression results from shame at perverse desires that dominate childhood, but as Jekyll explains in the confession left behind after his death, he had only mild character flaws when young: "[T]he worst of my faults was a certain impatient gaiety of disposition, such as has made the happiness of many" (*JH* 58). Jekyll hid this "gaiety" not because of its perversity but because it conflicted with the impressive demeanor he liked to present to the world: "I found it hard to reconcile with my imperious desire to carry my head high, and wear a more than commonly grave countenance before the public" (*JH* 58). So, out of pride, Jekyll *consciously* hid his weaknesses, despite their slight nature, and as a result became alienated from himself: "[W]hen I reached years of reflection, . . . I stood already committed to a profound duplicity of life" (*JH* 58). Early in the novel, Utterson validates this analysis, recalling that Harry Jekyll "was wild when . . . young," and guesses that Jekyll's willingness to align himself with Hyde grows from an attempt to hide "the ghost of some old sin, the cancer of some concealed disgrace" (*JH* 19).

In Jungian terms, Jekyll disowns his shadow, which Jung defines as "everything that the subject refuses to acknowledge about himself and yet is always thrusting itself upon him directly or indirectly" (Jung, *Collected Works*, 9i:284–85). Jung believes the shadow often reveals itself in dreams and finds it significant that "the British author Robert Louis Stevenson had spent years looking for a story that would fit his 'strong sense of man's double being' when the plot of *Jekyll and Hyde* was suddenly revealed to him in a dream" (Jung, *Man and His Symbols*, 25). Jung argues that the more passionately one consciously embraces a flattering self-image, or what he calls a persona, the more virulently one's disowned character traits grow in the unconscious.

One may suppress traits society admires, so one's shadow does not necessarily consist of conventionally undesirable characteristics. Thus, Jung would agree with Jekyll's assertion that the two sides of his character have become so estranged that both misrepresent him: "I was no more myself when I laid aside restraint and plunged in shame, than when I laboured, in the eye of day, at the furtherance of knowledge or the relief of sorrow and suffering" (*JH* 58). Jekyll is the shadow of Hyde as much as Hyde is the shadow of Jekyll. If one repudiates one's shadow, according to Jung, one feels intense hostility toward anyone who reminds one of it. Hence, it makes complete psychological sense that the corrupt Hyde abuses an innocent young girl and beats Sir Danvers Carew to death after seeing Carew's face that "seemed to breathe such an innocent and old-world kindness of disposition, yet with something high too, as of a well-founded self-content" (*JH* 24).

Following this murder, Jekyll attempts to shut down the part of his nature tied to Hyde. After he appears to succeed, he becomes more arrogant: "I smiled, comparing myself with other men, comparing my active goodwill with the lazy cruelty of their neglect" (*JH* 69). Soon, as Jung could have warned him, Jekyll discovers that Hyde has become so powerful he can now take over, even though Jekyll has stopped using drugs.

Utterson, the lawyer whose perspective governs the story, offers Jekyll the only solution that Jung believes will work, confession: "'Jekyll,' said Utterson, 'you know me: I am a man to be trusted. Make a clean breast of this in confidence; and I make no doubt I can get you out of it'" (*JH* 22). Jung agrees that sharing flaws heals, for "privacy prolongs my isolation and the damage is only partially mended. But through confession I throw myself into the arms of humanity again, free at last from the burden of moral exile" (Jung, *Collected Works*, 16:59). Presumably because Hyde understands that confession would end his life, Jekyll arranges it so that Hyde cannot destroy the confession he leaves behind: "Should the throes of change take me in the act of writing it, Hyde will tear it in pieces" (*JH*

73). For Jekyll to confide in Utterson makes good sense, for Utterson has no difficulty owning his own faults: "Few men could read the rolls of their life with less apprehension; yet he was humbled to the dust by the many ill things he had done, and raised up again into a sober and fearful gratitude by the many that he had come so near to doing, yet avoided" (*JH* 19–20). This willingness to admit his shortcomings gives Utterson "an approved tolerance for others" (*JH* 7). Jung argues that this kind of humility best qualifies one to have good relationships: "A human relationship is not based on differentiation and perfection, for these only emphasize the differences or call forth the exact opposite; it is based, rather, on imperfection, on what is weak, helpless and in need of support" (Jung, *The Undiscovered Self*, 116–17).

And so, Conrad's novel presents the essentially Freudian view that, at bottom, lust and aggression motivate all human beings. The civilized manage to give these impulses socially acceptable disguises, which primitive life rips away and exposes. Stevenson's novel complements Jung's more benign view that the modern passion for control has separated people from the unconscious and each other. This breech can be healed by precisely the tolerance and compassion Conrad and Freud present as illusory.

Not surprisingly, considering their fascination with the problem of defining human nature, Conrad and Stevenson shared Jung and Freud's interest in "primitive peoples," or those unshaped by Western civilization. Stevenson's characterization of primitive peoples coordinates as closely with Jung's as the views implicit in *Heart of Darkness* resemble Freud's. While Freud saw primitive peoples as happy but uncivilized because they lived out the urges more cultivated people repress, Jung suggests that those who, like Conrad and Freud, associate "primitive cultures" with unbridled evil passions do not recognize that participants in those cultures often enjoy psychic integration that repression makes difficult for denizens of modern culture. In Jung's scheme, the unconscious contains beneficial as well as destructive impulses, so he argues that dreams restore some psychological richness to those contaminated by Western culture:

Primitive man was much more governed by his instincts than are his "rational" modern descendants, who have learned to "control" themselves. In this civilizing process, we have increasingly divided our consciousness from the deeper instinctive strata of the human psyche. . . . Fortunately, we have not lost these basic instinctive strata; they remain part of the unconscious, even though they may express themselves only in the form of dream images. These instinctive phenomena . . . play a vital part in what I have called the compensating function of dreams. (Jung, *Man and His Symbols*, 36–37)

In order to avoid facing the unconscious, Jung believes that most modern people split themselves, much as Jekyll did: "What we call civilized consciousness has steadily separated itself from the basic instincts. But these instincts have not disappeared. They have merely lost their contact with our consciousness and are thus forced to assert themselves in an indirect fashion" (Jung, *Man and His Symbols*, 72). As a result, Jung sees primitive cultures at much greater risk from psychic damage by the intrusion of "civilized" people than vice versa: "Anthropologists have often described what happens to a primitive society when its spiritual values are exposed to the impact of modern civilization. Its people lose the meaning of their lives, their social organization disintegrates, and they themselves morally decay." Indeed, the kind of splitting that results in Hyde's evil behavior, Jung asserts, happens much more frequently in so-called civilized societies than in "primitive" ones: "In earlier ages, as instinctive concepts welled up in the mind of man, his conscious mind could no doubt integrate them into a coherent psychic pattern" (Jung, *Man and His Symbols*, 84).

Similarly, Stevenson's *The Ebb-Tide* opens with: "Throughout the island world of the Pacific, scattered men of many European races and from almost every grade of society carry activity and disseminate disease" (*WRLS* 18:3). The novel's protagonist, Herrick, feels ashamed of himself when he encounters the sublime decency of the natives: "They were kindly, cheery, childish souls. . . . It was thus a cutting reproof to compare the islanders and the whites abroad the *Farrallone*. Shame ran in Herrick's blood to remember what employment he was on, and to see these poor souls—even Sally Day, the child of cannibals, in all likelihood a cannibal himself—so faithful to what they knew of good" (*WRLS*

18:48). Thus, Stevenson joins Jung in suggesting that "primitive peoples" have an innate sense of goodness that civilization often undermines.

It would not surprise or embarrass Jung and Freud to discover that Stevenson and Conrad had anticipated the core of their psychologies, for they agreed that compelling art, like dreams, grows from and reflects the unconscious. They would probably also assent to this analysis since both linked their writing and its impact to their ability to access dimensions of the human psyche that lie deeper than reason. Stevenson explains that "Brownies" inhabiting his unconscious deserve the credit for the literature he has written: "And for the Little People, what shall I say they are but just my Brownies, God bless them! who do one-half my work for me while I am fast asleep, and in all human likelihood, do the rest for me as well, when I am wide awake and fondly suppose I do it for myself" (*WRLS* 12:246). Stevenson sees such fundamental incompatibility between the world his "Brownies" construct and his outward life that he fears they have done everything for him, allowing him to pretend to originality and insight beyond his capacities: "For myself—what I call I, my conscious ego, . . . the man with the conscience and the variable bank-account, the man with the hat and the boots, and the privilege of voting and not carrying his candidate at the general elections—I am sometimes tempted to suppose he is no story-teller at all" (*WRLS* 12:246).

Stevenson suggests that dreams, and by implication, literary works, although factually false, reveal important truths often set aside in order to function effectively in the world. As a result, he credits his "Brownies" with a moral sense profounder than Bunyan's: "[S]ometimes I cannot but suppose my Brownies have been aping Bunyan, and yet in no case with what would possibly be called a moral in a tract; never with the ethical narrowness; conveying hints instead of life's larger limitations and that sort of sense which we seem to perceive in the arabesque of time and space" (*WRLS* 12:249).

Conrad shares Stevenson's sense that his work has sources beyond the reach of conventional self-awareness. Like Stevenson, he suggests that the idealism of dreams gives them a reality that transcends that of actual experience, for mankind's "most positive achievements are born from dreams and visions followed loyally to an unknown destination" (*NLL* 190). But while Stevenson admits that his "Brownies" "have no prejudice against the supernatural" (*WRLS* 12:249), Conrad reports that if he ever attempted to "put the strain of the Supernatural" on his imagination, "it would fail deplorably and exhibit an unlovely gap." But then he would never make the attempt "because all my moral and intellectual being is penetrated by an invincible conviction that whatever falls under the dominion of our senses must be in nature and, however exceptional, cannot differ in its essence from all the other effects of the visible and tangible world of which we are a self-conscious part." This commitment to reality does not limit Conrad, for he believes "the world of the living contains enough marvels and mysteries as it is; marvels and mysteries acting upon our emotions and intelligence in ways so inexplicable that it would almost justify the conception of life as an enchanted state."[1] So, while Stevenson links art to dreams and even suggests a tie to the supernatural, Conrad ties it to real life but still argues that art manifests a deeper reality than the physical surface of daily existence: "[A]rt itself may be defined as a single-minded attempt to render the highest kind of justice to the visible universe, by bringing to light the truth, manifold and one, underlying its every aspect" (*NNTOS* vii).

Conrad's deeper truth has the same source as Stevenson's: the artist's willingness to explore and articulate personal depths most people ignore: "The artist descends within himself, and in that lonely region of stress and strife, if he be deserving and fortunate, he finds the terms of his appeal. His appeal is made . . . to that part of our nature which, because of the warlike conditions of existence, is necessarily kept out of sight within the more resisting and hard qualities" (*NNTOS* vi–vii).

Both Conrad and Stevenson believe that if they successfully fulfill their roles as artists, their work, no matter how fancifully constructed, exposes a reality beyond convention that both they and their readers understand intuitively captures significant truths. Despite this agreement, Conrad, like Freud, sees writing as a fundamentally narcissistic exercise in which the artist creates a world out of his or her own experiences and needs: "In truth every novelist must begin by creating for himself a world, great or little, in which he can honestly believe. This world cannot be made otherwise than in his own image" (*NLL* 6). Freud adds: "The writer softens the character of his egotistic day-dreams by altering and disguising it, and he bribes us by the purely formal—that is, aesthetic—yield of pleasure which he offers us in the presentation of his phantasies" (Freud, *On Creativity*, 54). Conrad, unlike Stevenson and Jung but, again, like Freud, waxes ironic at any suggestion of spirituality or religion: "[T]o believe that these manifestations, which the author evidently takes for modern miracles, will stay our tottering faith; to believe that the new psychology has, only the other day, discovered man to be a 'spiritual mystery,' is really carrying humility towards that universal provider, Science, too far" (*NLL* 69). When Freud describes religion as "the universal obsessional neurosis of humanity," it would probably not offend Conrad (Freud, *The Future of an Illusion*, 77–78).

Stevenson claims that his unconscious, his "Brownies," leads him into a moral dimension totally incompatible with Freud's amoral stance but completely consistent with Jung's notion that the unconscious can help human beings discover absolute values. As Jung puts it: "General conceptions of a spiritual nature are indispensable constituents of psychic life" (Jung, *Collected Works*, 8:356). This is exactly what Stevenson discovers when he looks within himself and finds that his "Brownies" have an even wiser and broader moral sense than that shaping Bunyan's *Pilgrim's Progress*. Because exemplary behavior has universal attraction, Jung believed all human beings arrive on the planet with a love of the hero myth hardwired into their psyche: "The hero figure is a typical image, an archetype, which has existed since time immemorial" (Jung, *Collected Works*, 18:252). Stevenson agrees, arguing that this myth often explains the power of literature: "Sacrifice and death and unmerited suffering humbly supported, touch in us the vein of the poetic. We love to think of them, we long to try them, we are humbly hopeful that we may prove heroes also" (*WRLS* 4:267).

By relying solely on their own minds and hearts, Stevenson and Conrad produced not only two short novels that generations of readers have enjoyed but also fictions that offer astonishingly accurate anticipations of the two major psychological theories that would dominate the twentieth century. This suggests that Jung and Freud were right: unconscious forces do inspire artists to create, although Jung and Freud failed to acknowledge that the best writers not only submit to the power of those forces; they intuitively understand their dynamic and render them compellingly to their audiences. But there is a crucial difference between psychologists and novelists: psychologists believe they report the truth, a conviction that led Freud and Jung into conflict with one another. Stevenson and Conrad, on the other hand, knew they wrote fiction heavily shaped by their biases.

Conrad argued that individual temperament determines the nature of one's unconscious as well as the kind of literature that emerges from it:

> Fiction—if it at all aspires to be art—appeals to temperament. And in truth it must be, like painting, like music, like all art, the appeal of one temperament to all the other innumerable temperaments whose subtle and resistless power endows passing events with their true meaning, and creates the moral, the emotional atmosphere of the place and time. Such an appeal to be effective must be an impression conveyed through the senses; and, in fact, it cannot be made in any other way, because temperament, whether individual or collective, is not amenable to persuasion. (*NNTOS* ix–x)

So the writer's goal is to communicate as specific a sense as possible of the version of reality he or she apprehends: "By the power of the written word to make you hear, to make you feel—it is, before all, to make you *see*." If the writer does this job well, the work opens the reader's mind, if only for a moment: "If I succeed, you shall find there according to your deserts: encouragement, consolation, fear, charm—all you demand—and, perhaps, also that glimpse of truth for which you have forgotten to ask" (*NNTOS* x). Art evokes intensity and passion because it conveys one truth, but life has far too much richness and the artist too much awareness of the fundamental subjectivity of his or her vision for any artist to claim to render the truth.

Stevenson also asserts that the successful work of art grows from the author's loyalty to his or her distinctive point of view: "Man is imperfect; yet, in his literature, he must express himself and his own views and preferences; for to do anything else is to do a far more perilous thing than to risk being immoral; it is to be sure of being untrue" (*WRLS* 4:410). Even the "Little People" or "Brownies" Stevenson credits with his creativity "are near connections of the dreamer's" (*WRLS* 4:245). Like Conrad,

Stevenson believes literature has value not because it delineates the truth but because "there is probably no point of view possible to a sane man but contains some truth and, in the true connection, might be profitable to the race" (*WRLS* 4:410). The "Brownies" notwithstanding, "the health or disease of the writer's mind or momentary humour forms not only the leading feature of his work, but is, at bottom, the only thing he can communicate to others. In all works of art, widely speaking, it is first of all the author's attitude that is narrated, though in the attitude there be implied a whole experience and a theory of life" (*WRLS* 4:407). The difference in Conrad's and Stevenson's temperaments reveals itself when they both go live among non-Western peoples. For the two authors not only shared Freud's and Jung's fascination with tribal peoples unshaped by the Euro-British culture but from an early age they also both wanted to experience these cultures for themselves. The gulf between their dispositions reveals itself in the results when they fulfilled these early wishes.

When a boy, Conrad proclaimed his determination to go to Africa, a place he believed distinguished by mystery:

> It was in 1868, when nine years old or thereabouts, that while looking at a map of Africa of the time and putting my finger on the blank space then representing the unsolved mystery of that continent, I said to myself with absolute assurance and an amazing audacity which are no longer in my character now:
>
> "When I grow up I shall *go there.*" (*Personal Record* 13)

When Conrad did go to Africa, neither the rapacious Europeans nor the "black savages" he encountered there appealed to him; as he wrote his aunt: "Everything here is repellent to me. Men and things, but men above all" (*CL* 1:62). *Heart of Darkness*, the book that grew from this trip, reflects the misery of his experience and the pessimistic view of human nature that Conrad brought home. Gerard Jean-Aubry argues that, in fact, Conrad's experiences simply validated the perspective he dragged with him to Africa: "It is not altogether correct to say, as John Galsworthy does, that 'that lingering Congo fever which dogged his health fastened a deep, fitful gloom over his spirit.' This gloom was the very basis of his character; he had breathed it since he was born" (Jean-Aubry 176).

Stevenson dreamt of escape to a warmer place, the South Seas, and when he finally arrived there, he found it even better than he'd hoped. He explains why: "I had gained a competency of strength; I had made friends; I had learned new interests; the time of my voyages had passed like days in fairyland. . . . If more days are granted me, they shall be passed where I have found life most pleasant and man most interesting" (*Dreams of Elsewhere* 280). While Africa's blankness drew Conrad, Stevenson anticipated that the people in the South Seas would behave in much the same way that people in the Scottish Highlands conducted themselves before the imposition of "alien authority" (*Dreams of Elsewhere* 285). Stevenson argues that because he used his past experience to understand and communicate with his new neighbors, they treated him well: "The native was no longer ashamed, his sense of kinship grew warmer, and his lips were opened. It is this sense of kinship that the traveller must rouse and share" (*Dreams of Elsewhere* 287). So, although, like Conrad, Stevenson sought relief from conventional British society, Conrad saw only blankness, and then evil, in this new world, while Stevenson used his imagination and his earlier experiences to transform it into a welcoming, comfortable place.

It makes sense that even though Conrad and Stevenson both aspire to write the truth, and both write out of the deeper realities presented by the unconscious, they produce entirely different kinds of work that reflect the differences in their temperaments. Moreover, they go beyond simply presenting the same views of human nature as those of Jung and Freud in *Jekyll and Hyde* and *Heart of Darkness*: they engage the readers in these points of view. Certainly the compelling plots of their novels go a long way toward pulling in their audiences, but the language used by both authors also helps set a tone appropriate to the works' ideas. The dense, melodic, dramatic, tortured language of *Heart of Darkness* gives an ominous sense of humanity run amok, as in this passage:

> There were moments when one's past came back to one, as it will sometimes when you have not a moment to spare to yourself; but it came in the shape of an unrestful and noisy dream remembered with wonder amongst the overwhelming realities of this strange world of plants and water and silence. And this stillness of life did not in the least resemble a peace. It was the stillness of an implaca-

ble force brooding over an inscrutable intention. It looked at you
with a vengeful aspect. (*HD* 34)

No one mastered incantation better than Kurtz, the most corrupt person
in the jungle. Here is Marlow's report on how it felt to read Kurtz's writing: "The peroration was magnificent, though difficult to remember, you
know. It gave me the notion of an exotic Immensity ruled by an august
Benevolence. It made me tingle with enthusiasm. This was the
unbounded power of eloquence—of words—of burning noble worlds.
There were no practical hints to interrupt the magic current of phrases"
(*HD* 50). The language of both Marlow and Kurtz gives the sense of a
cultivated surface that cannot completely hide the destructive forces
lurking within both men—and all other human beings.

Conrad's ornate eloquence contrasts sharply with the ordinary language Stevenson uses to describe extraordinary events. Here is how Jekyll
summarizes his transformation: "I was slowly losing hold of my original
and better self, and becoming slowly incorporated with my second and
worse" (*JH* 66). This direct language also coordinates with the perspective
of Stevenson's tale, for it warns against the danger of pretense and for
accepting one's humanity, flaws and all. In order to capture this spirit, the
teller of the tale must do the same. Generally, Stevenson feels simplicity
best serves the novelist: "Let him bear in mind that his novel is . . . a simplification of some side or point of life, to stand or fall by its significant
simplicity. For although, in great men, working upon great motives, what
we observe and admire is often their complexity, yet underneath appearances the truth remains unchanged: that simplification was their method,
and that simplicity is their excellence" (*WRLS* 12:221–22).

That Conrad and Stevenson rendered their distinctive perspectives
not through abstract pronouncements but by means of stories that join
intellectual insight to emotional and aesthetic appeal verifies their total
engagement in the works they created and helps explain why these novels
have endured for over a century. As Stevenson points out, the variety of
faculties that must collaborate to produce good writing explains both its
rarity and its power:

We begin to see now what an intricate affair is any perfect passage;
how many faculties, whether of taste or pure reason, must be held

upon the stretch to make it; and why, when it is made, it should afford us so complete a pleasure. From the arrangement of according letters, which is altogether arabesque and sensual, up to the architecture of the elegant and pregnant sentence, which is a vigorous act of pure intellect, there is scarce a faculty in man but has been exercised. We need not wonder, then, if perfect sentences are rare, and perfect pages rarer. (*WRLS* 4:450)

Artists apparently understand something that Freud and Jung have overlooked: one's disposition toward a view does not verify it. Stevenson and Conrad knew that their expositions and analyses of human nature, although profound and moving, were fictions shaped by their respective temperaments and experiences, as well as whatever impulses emerged from their unconscious. Jung and Freud would probably have profited from a touch of the same humility, for their conclusions rested on limited experience, which they apparently analyzed in terms of their prejudices. Historian of science Frank Sulloway explains Freud's failures precisely in these terms: "Time and time again, Freud saw in his patients what psychoanalytic theory led him to look for and then to interpret the way he did; and when the theory changed, so did the clinical findings" (Sulloway 498). While Stevenson's and Conrad's novels continue to move people, whatever validity Freud's and Jung's theories can claim today depends upon how successfully their insights coordinate with the conclusions of modern researchers—most of whom agree that Freud and Jung were, at best, visionaries, not scientists or truth-sayers. Virtually anyone who has read these four authors would agree that Stevenson and Conrad present the insights they shared with Jung and Freud much more compellingly than did the psychologists, perhaps because their roles as fiction writers freed them from the burden of objectivity, allowing them to draw on all their capacities when they wrote. As a result, readers not only understand their ideas, but they see and feel them as well.

That Stevenson's explanation of evil matches Jung's analysis of human nature and Conrad's coordinates with Freud's suggests that although Jung and Freud do an excellent job of delineating the characteristics appropriate to their respective views of human nature, instead of disputing with each other they would have done well to accept that one's perspective inevitably shapes what one considers true and that although no person can completely embrace works that reflect and embody fundamentally different temperaments from one's own, anyone can profit from resting in another perspective for a time.

NOTE

1. Unless otherwise noted, the Conrad references in this paragraph are from the "Author's Note," *The Shadow-Line* (London: Dent, 1920), ix–x, reprinted in *Heart of Darkness*, Kimbrough edition (New York: Norton, 1988), 223.

Pleasant Spectres and Malformed Shades: Stevenson, Conrad, and Spiritualism

STEPHEN DONOVAN

[M]ost of us walk very contentedly in the little lit circle of their own reason, and have to be reminded of what lies without by specious and clamant exceptions—earthquakes, eruptions of Vesuvius, banjos floating in mid-air at a *séance*, and the like....

> R. L. Stevenson, *Virginibus Puerisque* (*WRLS* 2:21–22)

The so-called sailors' yarn proper is never concerned with the supernatural. A sailors' folk lore is to me an inconceivable thing.

> Joseph Conrad to John Livingston Lowes,
> November 29, 1921 (*CL* 7:385)

*A*CCORDING TO a small volume titled *The Strange Case of the Ghosts of the Robert Louis Stevenson House* (1988), there is a dark lady who walks abroad at night in Stevenson's house in Monterey (Bergez et al.). The owners of the Stevenson House Museum in Edinburgh go a step further and claim that the author himself still paces the corridors of 17 Heriot Row.[1] Academic readers, one suspects, will be more embarrassed than charmed by these nuggets of information. Anyone who believes that the paranormal can be a friend to literary reputation should try persuading Henry James scholars that the Master's specter is haunting Lamb House or telling Joyceans that a ghostly "Sunny Jim" is to be seen atop the battlements of a martello tower outside Dublin. Like the supernatural more broadly, spiritualism seems to belong to a discourse that is wholly incompatible with serious literary analysis.

At the same time, ghostly apparitions of dead writers function as spectacular embodiments (so to speak) of the operations of literary posterity. The unquiet spirit of Monterey, for example, is all too symptomatic of Stevenson's indeterminate status: on the one hand it chimes with the sentimental image of Stevenson as a romantic "personality" given currency by numerous popular biographies, and on the other it exemplifies the ease with which "Stevenson" has been appropriated by a touristic sensibility, whether the kitsch Scottishness of shortbread tins or the modern heritage industry proper, both of which regard ghosts as handy endorsements of Hibernian authenticity. The "black lady" of Monterey offers too a farcical reminder of that persistent tendency of considering Stevenson solely as a writer of the fabulous and the fantastic, a reductive and dated reading, to be sure, and one that Stevenson scholars have done much to rectify. By contrast, and in keeping with his assured place in the modernist pantheon, Joseph Conrad seems largely to have escaped such attention. In a 1932 pamphlet titled *Did Joseph Conrad Return as a Spirit?* Jessie Conrad briskly denied that her husband had been in contact with an array of spiritualist believers, ranging from Arthur Conan Doyle and Helen Crane (niece of Stephen Crane) to Lord Northcliffe's former private secretary, Hennen Swaffer, and an unidentified musician named Van Reuter. It is hard to imagine the current owners of Pent Cottage ever claiming that a ghostly master mariner is rattling around their home, and readers of a recent article by John Chambers in the news sheet *Conrad Today* about purported spirit "conversations" with Conrad can be forgiven for thinking themselves the victims of an elaborate joke.

These cultural stakes in the relation of spiritualism to literary production provide the starting point for the following essay. Stevenson's and Conrad's treatments of this subject constitute significant responses to one of late Victorian Britain's most publicized and controversial popular movements. More than simply evidence of their differing conceptions of the margins of human psychology, the two men's responses tell us much about the antithetical ways in which they envisaged both the imagination and writing itself during an era of secularization and literary growth. For his part, Stevenson regarded artistic representation as the portal to another, invisible realm, one capable of satisfying what he elsewhere called the "phantom aspirations" of the common reader (*WRLS* 4:342). For this reason, and notwithstanding his ready criticism and debunking of unorthodox beliefs, he remained generally sympathetic toward supernaturalist beliefs such as spiritualism, seeing them as sincere if misguided attempts to restore a dimension of wonder to the prosaic materiality of everyday life.

This fundamentally democratic perspective contrasts starkly with Conrad's own patrician view of literary art as being essentially the reverse: a means of combating the commodification and mystification that, as he saw it, had come to saturate popular experience. In his manifesto-like preface to *The Nigger of the "Narcissus,"* for example, he defines the modern writer as seeking to "reveal the substance" of "a passing phase of life," an ambition that might be paraphrased as a desire to offer a corrective to the human tendency of mistaking appearance for reality (*NNTOS* xiv). Small wonder, then, that Conrad's fiction should repeatedly cast as sheer fraud or self-delusion a philosophy whose fundamental premise is that there is not less but more to the phenomenal world than meets the eye. As the paired quotations at the start of this essay remind us, Stevenson's and Conrad's views on spiritualism and the supernatural comprise two irreconcilable conceptions of artistic truth, one open to "what lies without" human knowledge, the other opposed to the foolish pursuit of such properly "inconceivable thing[s]."

What Lies Without

Spiritualism, an array of practices and beliefs that includes séances, Ouija-board communication, and sensational epiphenomena such as apparitions, ectoplasm, table rapping, and object levitations, today finds itself relegated to a despised middle ground of crankery somewhere between established religion and psychoanalysis. Only a reckless controversialist would dare suggest that the Madjegore messages might be considered cases of mediumship or that word association as a clinical practice has anything in common with automatic writing. But in Stevenson's day, when hypnosis was principally known through the performance entertainment of mesmerism and when models of the conscious and unconscious mind still lay in the future, spiritualism could attract serious attention precisely because of its liminal status and the not unreasonable supposition that behind the palpable fakery of some of its practitioners lay a genuinely new dimension of human experience. Indeed, no less a person than Prime Minister William Gladstone declared psychic research to be "the most important work which is being done in the world—by far the most important."[2] As the name of one of its most active advocates, the Society for Psychical Research, suggests, late-nineteenth-century spiritualism could, for a time, at least, plausibly claim to be an alternative mode of scientific enquiry. Thus, Janet Oppenheim concludes her standard history of the movement: "The attempt to enunciate [general scientific laws], to locate the common denominators of the universe, to find the ever-elusive 'basic building block' or 'ultimate substance' of nature—these aspirations inspired spiritualists and psychical researchers, just as they inspired scientists who criticized spiritualism and psychical research" (Oppenheim 396).

It is within this historical nexus that we need to locate Stevenson's writerly engagements with the supernatural. Despite having been roundly pilloried as "folly and worse" (Browning 854) by Robert Browning in his satirical poem "Mr. Sludge, 'The Medium'" (1864), spiritualism seems to have presented itself as a realm of creative and expressive possibilities to the writer whom Elaine Showalter has memorably called "the fin de siècle laureate of the double life" (Showalter 67). From his celebrated evocation of "the playmate that never was seen / . . . a picture you never could draw" in "The Unseen Playmate" (*WRLS* 8:49) to his description of fictional-factual personages as "pleasant specters" in "Memoirs of an Islet" (*WRLS* 12:95) and, above all, his account of the "Little People" who supply authors with storylines in "A Chapter on Dreams" (*WRLS* 12:238), Stevenson's writing provides ample evidence of his lifelong fascination with the imaginative power of the supernatural, whether taking the form of an intense childhood memory or an entire system of folkloric belief. Like the possibility of reanimation, which Oliver Buckton has characterized as a "vital source of narrative energy and interest" (Buckton 37) in Stevenson's fiction, spiritualism and paranormal phenomena appeared to him less as relics of a benighted era of superstition than as popular attempts to conceptualize marginal and mysterious mental phenomena in terms of explicable causes and effects.

As might be expected, given his progressive political views and cultural ecumenism, Stevenson himself was a highly appealing figure for spiritualist practitioners. The Beinecke Collection at Yale University contains an affidavit dated "5 min to 11 on the 30th July 1889" in which

Charles Baxter attests to the fact that he had been angrily reading *The Wrong Box* on the very day that Fanny, by Stevenson's own account, had had a vision of their friend in a bad temper. In July 1892 Stevenson sent a detailed analysis of his own schizophrenic delusions during a bout of fever to another spiritualist friend, Frederic Myers, who published the letter in the *Proceedings of the Society for Psychical Research* and subsequently reprinted it in his 1903 study *Human Personality and Its Survival of Bodily Death* in order to illustrate what he called "supraliminal duality" (Myers 1:301). Significantly, as Furnas notes, Stevenson also submitted a draft of *Dr. Jekyll and Mr. Hyde* to Myers (Furnas 278).

Stevensonian sightings and paranormal communications multiplied briskly after his death. In 1895 the spiritualist and crusading journalist W. T. Stead devoted two articles of his journal *Borderland* to an author he approvingly described as "first and foremost a Borderlander" ("Man of Dreams" 13), "a conflation of real and cosmic geographies that was further underscored by photographs of the Pentland Hills captioned 'Stevenson's Poetic Nursery'" (Cargill 15). On March 9, 1898, David Murray startled readers of the *London Morning* with an account of how Stevenson had appeared to him in a dream in order to dictate a verse for a poem that he (Murray) had been struggling to finish. Like that other Scottish Victorian icon David Livingstone, Stevenson became a regular feature of spiritualist séances on both sides of the Atlantic during the twentieth century. The Edinburgh journalist J. W. Herries devoted a chapter of his 1937 memoir, *I Came, I Saw*, to Stevenson's putative appearance at a séance twenty years earlier, and in his handbook *Intention and Survival* the Canadian psychic investigator T. Glen Hamilton analyzed five hundred communications alleged to have passed between Stevenson and a Scottish medium known as "Elizabeth M."[3] Although the Stevensonian apparitions and dialogues in these transcripts and spiritualist memoirs are often unintentionally comic or bizarre, they are not without interest for the literary historian as well-documented case studies for an alternative reception history of Stevenson, as early examples of nonacademic textual exegesis, and as popular versions of psychobiography.[4]

From his earliest years Stevenson had been attracted by the possibility of acting as a medium to the invisible world, an ambition he was ultimately to realize in the vocation of writer. Late in life, Mary and Craig

Balfour recalled how their cousin regularly "undertook to make his younger cousins 'see ghosts'; they were shut, each in his turn and alone, in a dark room, where the specters were produced by a magic-lantern worked by threads passing out under the door. Louis, upon the landing outside, vastly enjoyed the fun; the small boy within submitted to it—with a difference" (Terry 17). Stevenson's adult interest in spiritualism is likewise a matter of record. From 1869 to 1870 he served as the secretary of Edinburgh's newly founded Psychological Society, a forum for spiritualists of which his cousin Bob was also a member and later vice-president.[5] According to David Gow, editor of the paranormal journal *Light* at that time, the society was more social than academic in character, comprising a group of "medical men, artists, students and others" under the presidency of Dr. Gavin Clark, house surgeon at the Royal Maternity Hospital, where some of its meetings were held (Herries 286).

Although the extent of Stevenson's activities in the society is unknown, their timing is significant. These were the years in which he began to travel overseas, to experiment with drugs, and to question the authority of Christianity; spiritualism might be described as a synthesis of all three. And even though he would later voice his scorn for spiritualist frauds in both Europe and Samoa—in likening Uma Tarleton's sleight of hand to "that Blavatsky business in the papers" (*WRLS* 15:45) the narrator of "The Beach of Falesá" recalls Helena Blavatsky's humiliating exposure as a cheat in 1884—what exercised Stevenson most about such charlatans was their signal failure to provide honest emotional or aesthetic satisfaction, let alone value for money. In turn, the mediumship practiced by the Whistler sect of the Pacific island of Anaa, he noted acidly in *In the South Seas*, was not merely "very dreary, very silly, and very European" but also medically irresponsible: one unfortunate client had died after being prescribed immersion in scalding water (*WRLS* 16:236).

It goes without saying that there is no shortage of Stevenson texts that lend themselves to reexamination in terms of late Victorian theories of the paranormal. From domestic shockers such as *Dr. Jekyll and Mr. Hyde* to tales of Polynesian folklore such as "The Isle of Voices" in *An Island Night's Entertainment*, the margins of the knowable are repeatedly figured as a core preoccupation of Stevenson's narratives. And, to be sure, this broad range of supernaturally inspired fiction has already been prof-

itably analyzed in relation to Victorian medical discourse, sexual legislation, psychoanalytic theories of the uncanny, colonial ideology, and the
emergence of anthropology as a discrete field of knowledge. From this
perspective, the particular significance of spiritualism derives from its
unusually systematic and inclusive character. Stead, for example, sought
to use *Borderland* as a means of integrating spiritualism with the historical archive on witchery and ghosts, the rituals of the Roman Catholic
Church, the latest discoveries in what we now know as neuropsychology,
and the new forms of collective and individual consciousness being
encouraged by photography, long-distance travel, and telegraphy. As
Roger Luckhurst observes: "Stead's apparently diverse interests in mass
democracy, spirits and phantasms, an Empire-wide penny post, telepathy,
imperial federation, new technology, astral travel, and popular science
were less the result of individual foible than of a wider *episteme*, a network
of knowledges in which forms of the occult promised to make revelatory
connections across the territory of late Victorian modernity, rather than a
consolatory exit from it" (Luckhurst 125).

   With customary forthrightness, Stead argued in an extended commentary upon *Dr. Jekyll and Mr. Hyde* that Stevenson had deployed the
resources of literature in order to reveal the tale as "a foreshadowing of
the most startling scientific discovery which will probably be fully established early in the twentieth century, viz., that the disintegration of personality is not merely possible but is of constant occurrence" (Stead,
"Man of Dreams," 17). As enthusiasts such as Stead recognized, attempts
to rationalize the supernatural through spiritualism were for Stevenson a
form of materialism, scientific as well as social, that promised to retain
the numinous elements of superstition and religious belief even as they
anatomized and recorded the precise operations of human consciousness.

   The short story "Markheim" nicely illustrates the way in which
Stevenson's interest in spiritualism contributed to his unique social
vision. First published in *Unwin's Christmas Annual* in 1886, the story is
ostensibly a cautionary tale in the style of Poe or Hoffman. Stevenson's
protagonist bloodily murders an antiques dealer for money only to find
himself unable to flee from the scene of the crime. After conversing with
a diabolic apparition who bears an uncanny resemblance to himself,
Markheim is sickened at the realization of what he has become and turns

himself in to the police. For all its hokey supernaturalism and melodrama, the tale's narrative logic is firmly grounded in the material universe: Markheim has resorted to murder in order to finance his gambler's
addiction to the stock market, and even during his initial shock at the
violence of the crime he is described as "fear[ing] the laws of nature, lest,
in their callous and immutable procedure, they should preserve some
damning evidence of his crime" (*WRLS* 11:143).

And it is here that spiritualism's unique perspective can be discerned.
When the scales fall from Markheim's eyes, it is in a moment of revelation
that is as much physical as it is moral. Now suddenly aware of shadowy
"presences" moving all around him, he is gripped by what Stevenson calls
"a slavish, superstitious terror, some scission in the continuity of man's
experience, some wilful illegality of nature . . . [by which] the solid walls
might become transparent and reveal his doings like those of bees in a
glass hive" (*WRLS* 11:142, 143). Since the supernatural encounter is strictly
related as a phenomenon of consciousness, these words serve as an accurate description of the tale itself, which, in exposing the duality of consciousness, addresses not only a common theme in spiritualist writings,
such as Stead's article "Has Man Two Minds or One?" which appeared in
Borderland in October 1893, but also Stevenson's own forays into the
darker recesses of human identity in *Dr. Jekyll and Mr. Hyde.* If spiritualist
ideas did indeed shape Stevenson's literary investigations into the "double
life," it was surely in this fashion: as an apparatus for integrating scientific
thought and the creative imagination into a "higher" moral materialism.

Inconceivable Things

In his memoir *Joseph Conrad: Times Remembered* John Conrad describes
how a family friend, Arthur Marwood, once told his father about a
nearby haunted house that no horse would pass at midnight. According
to John Conrad, his father was so amused by Marwood's apparent belief
in the tale that on their way home he made a point of taking the family
on a detour past the house in question:

> We harnessed the pony and set off along the lane at the foot of
> Cobb Hill, timing our departure so as to arrive at the drive

entrance to the house at midnight. We approached the gate in bright moonlight and the pony became more and more nervous and finally stopped about twenty-five or thirty yards short of the gate across the entrance. After several attempts to drive past JC got down and tried to lead the animal past but it reared up and nearly deposited my mother and me in the roadway. My father tried persuasion but Jenny was not going to pass that entrance for anyone and at last JC gave way to my mother's entreaties and turned round to drive home by our usual route. (John Conrad 74)

One would like to imagine Conrad as having somehow staged this "supernatural" incident for the benefit of his youngest son, but the more likely explanation is that he was genuinely frustrated in an attempt to explode a local superstitition. What seems to have affronted him most, however, is less the superstition's existence—tales of haunted houses must have been commonplace in rural Kent a hundred years ago—than the fact that the legend should have been accorded any credence by Marwood, an intellectual and a literary man. For Conrad, ghost stories and superstitions belonged to a facile and debased mode of representation, and his desire to drive a horse and cart literally through such silliness aptly symbolizes his broader literary ambition of providing an alternative to the popular cultural narratives now being peddled, as he frequently complained, to audiences of credulous women and young boys.

While Conrad's recorded opinions on the supernatural are invariably inflected with his trademark irony, he singled out spiritualism for particular attention. In a letter of April 1922 he told the novelist and journalist Edmund Chandler, "[Y]ou haunt [our house]!" before quipping that this was a "phenomenon not of spiritism but of affectionate memory" (*CL* 7:444). In a manuscript passage in *The Secret Agent*, cut from the version serialized by *Ridgway's Magazine*, he openly mocked the belief in bodily existence after death: "Mr. Verloc exhaled a deep sigh of death. If it is true that the spirit carries the reflection of the earthly shape into the other world and seeks there the old associates of its earthly life the spiritual part of Mr. Verloc appearing suddenly in the Elysian fields must have astonished the shade of the late Baron Stott-Warthenheim, its appreciative patron, by its air of vexation and fatigue" (*SA* 404).

Such prejudices, as one would expect, also extended to the way that Conrad's own works were read. Despite the fact that he had himself described *The Shadow-Line* as having "a sort of spiritual meaning" (*CL* 5:458) and an "experience transposed into spiritual terms" (*CL* 6:37), he could not conceal his vexation at the *Daily News* critic who discussed the novella in terms of the supernatural: "Imagine he reviews . . . Shadow-Line from a *Ghost Story* point of view!! Would you believe it? Is it stupidity or perversity, or what?" (*CL* 6:51, Conrad's emphasis). More than simply expressing a different intellectual perspective, Conrad's comments betray the class-cultural premise that can be discerned in the *Nation*'s praise for his novella, on precisely contrary grounds, as being "as far removed as possible from a vulgar occultism" (Sherry 307). In his 1920 Author's Note to *The Shadow-Line*, he defiantly spelled out the implications of this stance:

> The world of the living contains enough marvels and mysteries as it is;—marvels and mysteries acting upon our emotions and intelligence in ways so inexplicable that it would almost justify the conception of life as an enchanted state. No, I am too firm in my consciousness of the marvellous to be ever fascinated by the mere supernatural, which (take it any way you like) is but a manufactured article, the fabrication of minds insensitive to the intimate delicacies of our relation to the dead and to the living, in their countless multitudes; a desecration of our tenderest memories; an outrage on our dignity. (*Shadow-Line* vii–viii)

Even so, Conrad would have been hard-pressed to deny the affinities between his own profession and that of the spirit-conjuror or medium. In an important early review of Conrad's writing in 1898, Edward Garnett praised the artist's ability to dissolve "this light-of-day, solid world of matter-of-fact appearances" by offering "a glimpse of a mysterious world behind the apparent" and declared appreciatively: "The blank solid wall of the familiar . . . has melted away before this artist" (Sherry 104, 106). And these sentiments were echoed by Conrad the following year when he tried to convey to Ted Sanderson the peculiarity of writing fiction for a living:

It is strange. The unreality of it seems to enter one's real life, penetrate into the bones, makes the very heart beats pulsate illusions through the arteries. One's will becomes the slave of hallucinations, responds only to shadowy impulses, waits on imagination alone. A strange state, a trying experience, a kind of fiery trial of untruthfulness. . . . But I shall soon come out of my land of mist peopled by shadows, and we shall meet again for another midnight communion—as though we too also had been ghosts, shadows. I question however whether the most desolate Shade that ever haunted this earth of ours carried in its misty form a heart as heavy as mine is—sometimes. (*CL* 2:205–6)

On the face of it, Conrad's explicit references to the writer as a magician appear to suggest that he, like Stevenson, fancied himself as a latter-day Prospero, gifted with the power of breathing life into the creatures of his imagination. "All creative art is magic, is evocation of the unseen," he declared in his essay "Henry James" (*NNL* 13), and in his memoir *A Personal Record* he confessed to desiring "to hold the magic wand giving that command over laughter and tears which is declared to be the highest achievement of imaginative literature" (*Personal Record* xviiii–xix). Writing to Sidney Colvin in July 1919, Conrad again praised his correspondent in similar terms: "You are the most quietly effective of magicians. The masterly, slightly amused, serenity with which you evoke all these distinguished, glorious shades of the first article, by (as it were) a mere turn of the hand (a wonderful turn of the hand it is, too) is a joy to the discriminating reader" (*CL* 6:447).

However, it would be a mistake to place Conrad among the ranks of those modern artists for whom the prospect of summoning spirits and communicating with the dead exerted a special fascination, such as Pablo Picasso, whose interest in séances and automatic writing found expression in the "cultural cryptography" of his Cubist phase (Staller 213–14), or the avant-gardists of the early Bauhaus, whose theories of color and form were deeply indebted to pseudoscientific New Age works such as C. W. Leadbeater's *Man Visible and Invisible* and the theosophist axiom "God geometrizes," coined by Helena Blavatsky. Nor should he be included among those modernist writers such as Rainer Maria Rilke, Hilda

Doolittle, W. B. Yeats, and Thomas Mann whose interest in spiritualism as a mode of literary inspiration has recently been documented by Helen Sword. On the contrary, Conrad never wavered in his professed contempt for the idea that spiritualism might in any way be related to the writerly project that he defined in the preface to *The Nigger of the "Narcissus"* as the attempt "to render the highest kind of justice to the visible universe" (*NNTOS* xi). His reference to "my land of mist" in his letter to Sanderson—an allusion to Coleridge's *Rime of the Ancient Mariner*—is strictly humorous, precisely the reverse of the naïve faith in such a realm's possibility that inspired Arthur Conan Doyle's spiritualist propaganda novel *The Land of Mist*. Indeed, Conrad often uses ghosts as metaphors for inferior writing, as when he pronounced Henry James's fictional creations as immeasurably superior to "the Shades of the contemporary fiction . . . , the more or less malformed shades" (*CL* 2:174).

Far from being artistic magic, spiritualism was for Conrad a willful mistaking of illusion for reality, one in which spectators and in some cases even practitioners, believed themselves to be engaged in something truly otherworldly. When an American theosophist named Claude Bragdon, presumably emboldened by Conrad's own treatment of the fourth dimension in *The Inheritors*, sent him a copy of an esoteric work titled *Four-Dimensional Vistas*, Conrad replied politely by declaring himself to be "singularly inapt to embrace metaphysical speculation" and confided disingenuously: "[T]o tell you the truth I never trouble my head about the Fourth Dimension" (*CL* 7:123). However, in a review of another work titled *Existence after Death Implied by Science*, whose purview ranged from telepathy and mediumship to dreams and X-rays, Conrad was less restrained, openly ridiculing the bogus logic with which its author, Jasper Hunt, had sought to prop up his claims. The truth of spiritualism, he explained satirically, was evident from the enduring popularity of the circulating libraries upon which authors like Hunt were dependent: "What would become of us if the circulating libraries ceased to exist? It is a horrid and almost indelicate supposition, but let us be brave and face the truth. . . . Their spirit shall survive. I declare this from inward conviction, and also from scientific information received lately. For observe: the circulating libraries are human institutions, . . . and, being human, . . . they are spiritual" (*NNL* 66–67). In suggesting that any man possessed of sufficient capital and moved by "his own commercial spirit" might evoke the "specter" of the circulating libraries, Conrad added his voice to those critics who accused spiritualism of being little more than a financial fraud (*NNL* 67). As he asked sardonically of an Italian medium who had been discredited with the help of John Maskelyne in the mid-1890s: "Can you imagine anything more squalid than an Immortality at the beck and call of Eusapia Palladino? That woman lives on the top floor of a Neapolitan house, and gets our poor, pitiful, august dead . . . to beat tambourines in a corner and protrude shadowy limbs through a curtain" (*NNL* 69).[6]

Inspired by both the runaway success of the first "Pepper's ghost" illusion of 1863 and spiritualism's own growing popularity, professional magicians of the late Victorian period made stage "ghosts" a central feature of their elaborate theatrical shows. This historical overlap between illusionism and supernatural belief has an interesting sidelight in the present context. Despite the protestations of the magicians themselves, many convinced spiritualists stubbornly refused to believe in the fakery of stage apparitions, claiming instead that the performers were in fact eliciting the participation of the spirits without realizing it.[7]

It is of some significance, then, that the stage magicians whom Conrad most admired, men like John Maskelyne, had made their names as creative artists by showing how convincing spiritualistic "phenomena" could be reproduced upon demand. Indeed, Conrad's description of himself to Edmund Gosse as "[no] magician evoker of the past either in its spirit or its form" suggests that it was primarily in this capacity, as a summoner of man-made "ghosts," that he envisaged the professional magician (*CL* 3:224). When in *The Rescue* Tom Lingard questions Jörgenson "much as a magician would interrogate an evoked shade" and gives directions "as one would make use of some marvellous automaton" (*Rescue* 279), we may well be hearing a specific reference to the stage show of one of spiritualism's best known debunkers, John Maskelyne, whose automaton illusion "Psycho" was being trumpeted as "more popular than ever" (Steinmeyer 110) when Conrad first visited London in 1878.[8]

Certainly the intersection of spirit-raising with performance magic is reiterated throughout Conrad's fiction. In *Lord Jim* Jewel's irrational fantasies about her lover's secret past prompt Marlow to reflect that "the spirits evoked by our fears and our unrest have ever to vouch for each other's constancy before the forlorn magicians that we are" (*LJ* 315). In *Chance*, Marlow disparages his own memory as a "mausoleum of proper names . . . inanimate, awaiting the magic touch—and not very prompt in arising when called," and, in a highly elaborate metaphor, describes the former convict de Barral as an "awful ghost" who has been produced "automatically" by the British prison system (*Chance*, ed. Ray, 69, 245). In *The Arrow of Gold* too Dominic Cervoni is likened to "a magician at the end of a successful incantation that had called out a shadow" (*Arrow* 128). The consummate artistry displayed by this kind of magician recalls Conrad's famous definition of art in the preface to *The Nigger of the "Narcissus"* as "a single-minded attempt to render the highest kind of justice to the visible universe" (*NNTOS* xi): a challenge, among other things, to symbolism's cult of the spiritual and ideal of writing as, in Arthur Symons's words, "a literature in which the visible world is no longer a reality, and the unseen world no longer a dream" (quoted in *CL* 6:211n).

It is fitting, therefore, that Conrad should have tackled the subject of spiritualism in his very first literary effort. "The Black Mate," a slight tale originally written for a fiction competition in *Tit-Bits* magazine in 1886 and eventually published in *London Magazine* in 1908, concerns the deception of a spiritualist captain by an ingenious crew member who pretends to have seen a ghost.[9] In rather obvious fashion, this comic plot device enables Conrad to score easy points against what he saw as the credulousness of spiritualism's enthusiasts and the cupidity of what his narrator calls "fraudulent mediums" ("Black Mate" 92). At the same time, Captain Johns's irrational belief in spiritualism, a subject with which he is obsessed to the point of monomania, is presented as synecdochic of a more profound unreasonableness. That this humorless martinet adheres to a policy of hiring only dark-haired men, on the principle that gray hair signifies infirmity or feebleness, is accordingly offered as a corollary to the naïve faith in the "evidence" of the visual sense by which Johns feels authorized to declare sagely of ghosts: "Why, they have been photographed! What more proof do you want?" ("Black Mate" 89).[10] Appropriately, then, Johns ends up deceiving himself on both counts by retaining a crew member whose hair has gone white in the belief that the sailor has witnessed a ghostly apparition when in fact he has simply run out of hair dye.

Had Conrad's engagement with spiritualism remained limited to mockery of its more absurd aspects, the topic would have only marginal significance for critics today. And yet what is striking about his fictional treatment of the supernatural, and of spiritualism in particular, is its evident overdetermination. "The Black Mate" may be of doubtful literary merit, but Conrad's first attempt at fiction is noteworthy in its thematizing of spiritualism as a form of ideological blindness, something that was to emerge as a central theme in all his major works. To some extent, the overdetermination of spiritualism in Conrad's fiction can be traced to the complex of political meanings that attached to spiritualism at the time. For example, Captain John's scheme to help the police through mediumistic communication with the dead, a proposal Conrad ironically describes as a kind of "weird utilitarianism" ("Black Mate" 102), gestures toward the espousal of spiritualism by prominent liberals and social campaigners such as Annie Besant, Robert Owen, and William Gladstone. Indeed, Johns's references to "Professor Cranks" and "that newspaper fellow . . . who had a girl-ghost visitor" allude specifically to two of the most prominent liberals in the spiritualist movement: William Crookes, president of the Society for Psychical Research and a distinguished physicist and chemist, and Stead, whose spirit "conversations" with his late colleague Julia Ames were published as *Letters from Julia* in 1898.

Conrad further developed this view of spiritualism as a form of psychological sublimation or projection of the believer's own desires in his 1914 tale "The Planter of Malata." The famous philosopher Professor Moorsom, a spiritualist fellow traveler, is presented as a "man ready to be amused by the side of the grave" and as an intimate of prominent spiritualists, including "a very famous author . . . [whose] ghost is a girl" and "a very great man of science" who is also "friendly" with a girl ghost (*WT* 45, 67)—allusions, respectively, to spiritualism's popularity among novelists such as Marie Corelli and to the interest shown in the subject by scientists such as the naturalist Alfred Wallace and the Harvard psychologist William James. Moorsom himself makes a little joke at the anthropomorphizing tendencies of investigators into spiritualist phenomena:

"A ghost here!" exclaimed the amused professor. "Then our whole conception of the psychology of ghosts must be revised. This island has been uninhabited probably since the dawn of ages. How did a ghost come here? By air or water? And why did it leave its native haunts? Was it from misanthropy? Was he expelled from some community of spirits? . . . "

"Let us investigate the matter, Renouard," proposed the professor half in earnest. "We may make some interesting discoveries as to the state of primitive minds, at any rate." (*WT* 69–70)

As events turn out, however, what supernatural fantasies tell Conrad's readers most about is the disordered state of "civilized" minds. The sternly rationalistic silk planter Renouard remarks drily to Moorsom's spiritualist sister, "Those plantation boys of mine see ghosts too," yet he proves unable to save himself from mental collapse under the strain of concealing the death of an employee from the dead man's fiancée, with whom he has fallen in love (*WT* 67). Appropriately, then, Renouard's psychic conflict between desire and suppression finds expression in a series of disturbing dreams and the growing belief that he is living on "an island haunted by the ghost of a white man" (*WT* 84).

The hostility toward spiritualism discernible in Conrad's fiction seems to have been accentuated by its appeal for women, in particular what Alex Owen characterizes as its license "to infringe culturally imposed limits" (Owen 11). The skeptical protagonist of "The Black Mate" refers sneeringly to "ladyish" apparitions ("Black Mate" 110), and spiritualism's feminizing aspect is again evoked in "The Planter of Malata" when Conrad's narrator mentions the London fad for conversing with "girl" ghosts (*WT* 67) and when Renouard feels himself sliding into a deathly state after the Moorsom women's arrival in pursuit of their own phantom. Conrad makes the association most explicit in *Under Western Eyes*, in which he portrays Russia as a breeding ground for millenarianism and philosophical crankery of every stripe. A belief in the "spiritual superiority" of women is thus described as having emerged from the pages of Peter Ivanovitch's autobiography "like a white figure from a dark confused sea," while his revolutionary coconspirator Eleanor de S—— is figured as a "supernaturalist" who untiringly restates her opinion that political discontent must be "spiritualized" in order to prevail (*UWE* 121, 222, 221). Indeed, the novel might be described as a record of Razumov's fatal absorption into this hallucinatory world of self-delusion. The unheroic protagonist of Conrad's tragedy declares himself unwilling "to turn into a dilettante spiritualist" or to "spend my time in spiritual ecstasies or sublime meditations upon the gospel of feminism," but he fails to shake off the feeling that he is being pursued by the "phantom" of the fellow student who has told him, ominously, "They can kill my body, but they cannot exile my soul from this world" (*UWE* 58, 225, 226).

Conclusion

The representation of spiritualism in Conrad's and Stevenson's fiction and prose not only attests to the diversity of the cultural and philosophical issues raised by this movement during their lifetimes, it throws into relief the two men's very different conceptions of their own literary projects. In addition to its more obvious target, Conrad's burlesque of spiritualism in "The Black Mate" can be understood as offering an oblique commentary upon the popularity of ghost stories among readers of popular magazines, an audience to whose debased tastes he felt that Stevenson's tales of romantic adventure and the supernatural had pandered. Struggling to finish *The Rescue*, a novel originally conceived along Stevensonian lines as "a kind of glorified book for boys," Conrad could thus complain of feeling like "the ghost of a blonde and sentimental woman, haunting romantic ruins" (*CL* 1:289, 392). Seen in this light, spiritualist fakery embodies the kind of artistic staginess which Stevenson had celebrated as "Skeltery" in his famous essay "A Penny Plain, Twopence Coloured."

At the same time, what scholars have come to acknowledge as Conrad's hidden debt to Stevenson is perhaps nowhere more apparent than in his treatment of spiritualism and the supernatural. Such a reevaluation becomes possible when Conrad's oft-quoted disavowal of the "airy R. L. Stevenson who considered his art a prostitute and the artist as no better than one" (*CL* 2:371) is set alongside his more generous valuation of his predecessor in a letter to Sidney Colvin in 1919:

I regret only that I may appear in my admiration of the South Sea
Vol: as not appreciative of RLS as a "creator". Indeed my dear
Colvin it is on that very ground that I admire the book. The islands
may sink and the Pacific evaporate and even the terrestrial globe
fly to pieces; but as long as one copy of the *South Seas* exists the
King of Apamama will live, for R.L.S. has breathed his humanity
into that "weird and ominous" figure. . . . (*CL* 6:447)

That Conrad is here offering not merely flattery but a more sincere gesture of filiation is borne out by the otherwise mystifying presence of
Tahitian plantation workers in "The Planter of Malata," whose description as members of a "'ghost-ridden race" (*WT* 70) evokes Stevenson's
well-known account of Polynesian ghost folklore in the "Death" and
"Graveyard Stories" chapters of *In the South Seas*. Like the narrator of
"Karain," whose professed skepticism toward Malay superstition is belied
by his fleeting glimpses of an invisible phantasmagoria of "homeless
ghosts" (*TU* 48) and "gasping voices" (*TU* 54), Conrad can be seen to follow Stevenson in drawing upon the "weird and ominous" resources of
spiritualism and psychical research to present his own peculiar vision of
the power of human imagination and its subordination to unconscious
desires and fears.

NOTES

1. Stevenson House Museum website, http://www.stevenson-house.co.uk/rls.htm
(accessed July 1, 2004).

2. Http://www.survivalafterdeath.org.uk/researchers/gladstone.htm (accessed
December 3, 2008).

3. For transcripts of the communications, see http://www.survivalafterdeath.org.uk/
books/hamilton/contents.htm (accessed December 3, 2008).

4. "Of the four hundred and seventy transmissions analysed, eight were found to
have been based on material taken from Stevenson poems in 'In Scots'; fifty on material found in various other poems in the *Underwoods* collection; sixty on excerpts
found in *A Child's Garden of Verses*; twelve dealt with brief extracts from the essay
'Thomas Stevenson'; two were lifted from 'A Humble Remonstrance'; two had to do
with 'The Manse'; two with 'A Penny Plain'; one mentioned *The Merry Men*; four
related to events recorded in *The Amateur Immigrant* [*sic*]; fourteen found their basic
material in *Treasure Island*; twenty-two showed certain sections of the essay 'A Gossip
on Romance' to be their source; twenty-five and twenty-two respectively were

founded on brief selections taken from the dedication to *Underwoods*, and the preface note to *Underwoods*; a number gave the names of Stevenson's leading novels; and the remainder, referring to innumerable phases of the author's life, from childhood to his last days, were largely biographical" (Hamilton 256–57).

5. William F. Alexander to Edward J. Beinecke, June 18, 1940, Beinecke Collection, Yale University.

6. Maskelyne's detection of Palladino's trickery is recorded in a manuscript letter to Dr. Ellison dated November 23, 1909, and now held by the New York Public Library.

7. Recognizing good publicity when he saw it, Maskelyne eventually gave up arguing the point.

8. A perennial favorite, "Psycho" was relaunched by Maskelyne in 1885 and 1910. Conrad describes automata in some detail in both *The Secret Agent* and *Victory*.

9. For a reconstruction of the likely circumstances of Conrad's composition of the text, see Carabine

10. On Conrad's hostility towards photography more broadly, see Donovan, *Joseph Conrad and Popular Culture*, 27–32.

Bibliography

Primary Sources

MANUSCRIPTS

Pratt, Rev. G. London Missionary Society Archives Notebook #163. School of Oriental and African Studies, University of London.
Turner, Reverend Mr. "Ethnology of Polynesia." London Missionary Society Archives, School of Oriental and African Studies, University of London.
Turner, Dr. George. "Notes on Dr. [George] Turner's Voyage in 1876." HM 2398. Huntington Manuscript and Rare Book Library. San Marino, Calif.

WORKS OF CONRAD

Conrad, Joseph. *Almayer's Folly and Tales of Unrest*. London: Dent, 1947.
———. *The Arrow of Gold: A Story Between Two Notes*. London: T. Fisher Unwin, 1919.
———. "The Black Mate," in *Tales of Hearsay*, 85–120. London: Dent, 1955.
———. *Chance: A Tale in Two Parts*. London: Methuen, 1913.
———. *Chance: A Tale in Two Parts*. Ed. Martin Ray. Oxford: Oxford University Press, 2002.
———. *Collected Letters*. 7 vols. Vols. 1–5 ed. Frederick R. Karl and Laurence Davies. Vol. 6 ed. Laurence Davies, Frederick R. Karl, and Owen Knowles. Vol. 7 ed. Laurence Davies and J. H. Stape. Cambridge: Cambridge University Press, 1983–2005.
———. *Heart of Darkness: An Authoritative Text: Backgrounds and Sources, Criticism*. 3rd ed. Ed. Robert Kimbrough. New York: Norton, 1988.
———. *Heart of Darkness: An Authoritative Text: Backgrounds and Sources, Criticism*. 4th ed. Ed. Paul Armstrong. New York: Norton, 2006.
———. *Lord Jim: A Tale*. London: Dent, 1923.
———. *Last Essays*. London: Dent & Sons, 1955.
———. *Notes on Life and Letters*. Ed. J. H. Stape with Andrew Busza. Cambridge: Cambridge University Press, 2004.
———. *The Nigger of the "Narcissus" and Typhoon and Other Stories*. London: Dent, 1950.
———. *The Nigger of the "Narcissus," Typhoon, Amy Foster, Falk and Other Stories*.

London: Dent, 1978.

———. *An Outcast of the Islands*. London: Dent, 1949.

———. *A Personal Record*. London: Dent, 1946.

———. *The Rescue: A Romance of the Shallows*. London: Dent, 1949.

———. *The Secret Agent*. Cambridge Edition of the Works of Joseph Conrad. Ed.
Bruce Harkness and Sid Reid. Cambridge: Cambridge University Press, 1990.

———. *A Set of Six*. London: Dent, 1946.

———. *The Shadow-Line*. Ed. Jeremy Hawthorn. Oxford: Oxford University Press,
2003.

———. *'Twixt Land and Sea: Three Tales*. London: Dent, 1923.

———. *Under Western Eyes*. London: Dent, 1947.

———. *Victory: An Island Tale*. London: Dent, 1946.

———. *Within the Tides*. London: Dent, 1950.

———. "Youth" (1898), in *Youth: A Narrative, Heart of Darkness and The End of the
Tether*. London: Dent, 1982.

WORKS OF STEVENSON

Stevenson, Robert Louis. *Dreams of Elsewhere: Selected Travel Writings of Robert Louis
Stevenson*. Ed. June Skinner Sawyers. Glasgow: Neil Wilson, 2002.

———. *Dr. Jekyll and Mr. Hyde and Other Stories*. London: Penguin, 1987.

———. *The Ebb-Tide: A Trio and Quartette* (1894). Ed. Peter Hinchcliffe and
Catherine Kerrigan. Edinburgh: Edinburgh University Press, 1995.

———. "The Ebb-Tide," in *Dr. Jekyll and Mr. Hyde and Other Stories*. London:
Penguin, 1987.

———. *In the South Seas*. Ed. Neil Rennie. London: Penguin, 1998.

———. *Island Landfalls*. Ed. Jenni Calder. Edinburgh: Canongate Classics, 1987.

———. *The Letters of Robert Louis Stevenson*. Ed. Bradford A. Booth and Ernest
Mayhew. 8 vols. New Haven: Yale University Press, 1994–95.

———. *Memories and Portraits*. London: Chatto & Windus, 1891.

———. "Missions in the South Seas." Sydney: State Library of New South Wales,
AS25/19. Published with slight variation in *The Life of Robert Louis Stevenson*
2:193–95. Ed. Graham Balfour. London: Methuen, 1901.

———. *The Prose Writings of Robert Louis Stevenson*. Ed. Roger George Swearingen.
Hamden, CT: Archon Books, 1980.

———. *Strange Case of Dr. Jekyll and Mr. Hyde*. Ed. Katherine Linehan. New York:
Norton, 2003.

———. *Strange Case of Dr. Jekyll and Mr. Hyde*. Ed. Richard Dury. Edinburgh:
University of Edinburgh Press, 2004.

———. *The Thistle Edition of the Works of Robert Louis Stevenson*. 25 vols. New York:
Charles Scribner's Sons, 1924.

———. *Travels in Hawaii*. Ed. A. Grove Day. Honolulu: Hawaii University Press,
1973.

———. *Treasure Island*. Tusitala Edition. London: William Heinemann, 1923.

———. *Treasure Island*. Ed. Nicholas McGuinn. Cambridge: Cambridge University
Press, 1995.

————. *Treasure Island*. Ed. Wendy Katz. Edinburgh: Edinburgh University Press, 1998.
————. *The Works of Robert Louis Stevenson*. Vailima Edition. 26 vols. New York: Charles Scribner's Sons, 1921.

WORKS OF OTHER AUTHORS

Ballantyne, R. M. *The Coral Island*. New York: Garland, 1977.
Bythe, Harry. "The Accusing Shadow," in *Victorian Detective Stories*, 301–41. Ed. Michael Cox. Oxford: Oxford University Press, 1992.
Brontë, Charlotte. *Villette*. Harmondsworth, UK: Penguin, 1979.
Browning, Robert. "Mr. Sludge, 'The Medium,'" in *Robert Browning: The Poems*, 1:821–60. Ed. John Pettigrew. New Haven: Yale University Press, 1981.
Collins, Wilkie. *No Name*. Harmondsworth, UK: Penguin, 1994.
Dickens, Charles. *Great Expectations*. Harmondsworth, UK: Penguin, 1965.
Doyle, Arthur Conan. *The Land of Mist*. New York: George H. Doran, 1926.
Fawcett, E. Douglas. *Hartmann the Anarchist; or, the Doom of the Great City*. London: Edward Arnold, 1893.
Ford, Ford Madox. *The Soul of London: A Survey of a Modern City*. London: Everyman, 1995.
Joyce, James. *Ulysses*. Ed. Declan Kiberd. Harmondsworth, UK: Penguin, 1992.
MacKay, Donald. *The Dynamite Ship*. London: Page, Pratt, and Turner, 1888.
Maginn, J. D. *Fitzgerald the Fenian*. Vol. 2. London: Chapman and Hall, 1889.
Melville, Herman. *Typee: A Peep at Polynesian Life*. New York: Penguin, 1996.
Poe, Edgar Allen. *Poems and Tales*. Ed. Patrick F. Quinn. New York: Library of America, 1984.

BIOGRAPHIES

Conrad, John. *Joseph Conrad: Times Remembered*. Cambridge: Cambridge University Press, 1981.
Furnas, J. C. *Voyage to Windward: The Life of Robert Louis Stevenson*. New York: William Sloane Associates, 1951.
Gray, William. *Robert Louis Stevenson: A Literary Life*. London: Palgrave, 2004.
Hammond, J. R. *A Robert Louis Stevenson Chronology*. Basingstoke, UK: Macmillan, 1997.
Karl, Frederick R. *Joseph Conrad: The Three Lives*. London: Faber and Faber, 1979.
McLynn, Frank. *Robert Louis Stevenson: A Biography*. London: Hutchinson, 1993.
Terry, R. C. *Robert Louis Stevenson: Interviews and Recollections*. Iowa City: University of Iowa Press, 1996.
Watts, Cedric. *Joseph Conrad: A Literary Life*. London: Macmillan, 1989.

Secondary Sources

Achebe, Chinua. "An Image of Africa: Racism in Conrad's *Heart of Darkness*." *The Massachusetts Review* 18 (1977): 782–94.

Agnew, John, and Stuart Corbridge. *Mastering Space: Hegemony, Territory, and International Political Economy*. London: Routledge, 1995.

Ambrosini, Richard. *Conrad's Fiction as Critical Discourse*. Cambridge: Cambridge University Press, 1991.

———. "R. L. Stevenson and the Ethical Value of Writing for the Market." *Journal of Stevenson Studies* 1 (2004): 24–41.

Anderson, Robert. *Sidelights on the Home Rule Movement*. London: John Murray, 1906.

Arac, Jonathan. "Romanticism, the Self, and the City: *The Secret Agent* and Literary History." *Boundary* 29, no.1 (Autumn 1980): 75–90.

Arata, Stephen D. *Fictions of Loss in the Victorian Fin de Siècle*. Cambridge: Cambridge University Press, 1996.

———. "The Sedulous Ape: Atavism, Professionalism, and Stevenson's *Jekyll and Hyde*." *Criticism* 37 (Spring 1995): 233–59.

Archer, William. "Robert Louis Stevenson: His Style and His Thought." *Times* (London), November 1885, 581–91. Reprinted in Maixner, 160–69.

Arens, W. *The Man-Eating Myth: Anthropology and Anthropophagy*. New York: Oxford University Press, 1979.

Arnett Melchiori, B. *Terrorism in the Late Victorian Novel*. London: Croom Helm, 1985.

Ash, Beth Sharon. *Writing in Between: Modernity and Psychosocial Dilemma in the Novels of Joseph Conrad*. New York: Macmillan, 1999.

Banton, Michael. *Racial Theories*. Cambridge: Cambridge University Press, 1987.

Barnett, Louise K. "'The Whole Circle of the Horizon': The Circumscribed Universe of 'The Secret Sharer.'" *Studies in the Humanities* 8, no. 2 (March 1981): 5–9.

Barthes, Roland. *Le Neutre*. Cours au collège de France (1977–78). Paris: Seuil, 1977–78.

Baudrillard, Jean. *The Spirit of Terrorism*. London: Verso, 2002.

Beales, Derek. *From Castlereagh to Gladstone, 1815–1885*. London: Sphere Books, 1969.

Benjamin, Walter. *Charles Baudelaire: A Lyric Poet in the Era of High Capitalism*. Trans. Harry Zohn. London: Verso, 1997.

Bergez, John B., Allen Iliff, and Randall A. Reinsteadt. *The Strange Case of the Ghosts of the Robert Louis Stevenson House*. Carmel, CA: Ghost Town Publications, 1988.

Bergson, Henri. *An Introduction to Metaphysics*. London, 1903.

Berman, Marshall. *All That Is Solid Melts into Air: The Experience of Modernity*. London: Ferguson, 1988.

Bhabha, Homi. *The Location of Culture*. New York: Routledge, 1994.

Blouet, Brian W. *Geopolitics and Globalization in the Twentieth Century*. London: Reaktion Books, 2001.

Bongie, Chris. "Exotic Nostalgia: Conrad and the New Imperialism." *Macropolitics of Nineteenth-Century Literature: Nationalism, Exoticism, Imperialism*, 268–85. Ed. Jonathan Arac and Harriet Ritvo. Durham: Duke University Press, 1995.

Booth, Charles. *Life and Labour of the People in London*. London, 1895.

Booth, Howard J., and Nigel Rigby. *Modernism and Empire*. Manchester: Manchester University Press, 2000.

Booth, William. *In Darkest England and the Way Out*. London: International Headquarters of the Salvation Army, 1890.

Borges, Jorge-Luis. *Selected Non-Fictions*. Ed. Eliot Weinberger. Trans. Esther Allen, Suzanne Jill Levine, and Eliot Weinberger. New York: Viking, 1999.

"Bourdin's Antecedents." *Times* (London), February 17, 1894, 5.

Brantlinger, Patrick. *Bread and Circuses: Theories of Mass Culture as Social Decay*. Ithaca, NY: Cornell University Press, 1983.

———. *Rule of Darkness: British Literature and Imperialism, 1830–1914*. Ithaca, NY: Cornell University Press, 1988.

———. "Victorians and Africans: The Genealogy of the Myth of the Dark Continent." *Critical Inquiry* 12 (Autumn 1985): 166–203.

Brooks, Peter. *Reading for the Plot: Design and Intention in Narrative*. Cambridge: Harvard University Press, 1992.

Brown, P. L. "'The Secret Sharer' and the Existential Hero." *Conradiana* 3, no. 3 (1971): 22–30.

Buckton, Oliver S. "Reanimating Stevenson's Corpus." *Robert Louis Stevenson Reconsidered: New Critical Perspectives*, 37–67. Ed. William B. Jones, Jr. Jefferson, NC: McFarland, 2003.

Butler, Judith. *Bodies That Matter: On the Discursive Limits of Sex*. New York: Routledge, 1993.

Camaroff, Jean, and John Camaroff. *Of Revelation and Revolution: Christianity, Colonialism, and Consciousness in South Africa*, vol. 1. Chicago: University of Chicago Press, 1991.

Carabine, Keith. "'The Black Mate': June–July 1886; January 1908." *The Conradian* 13, no. 2 (December 1988): 128–48.

Cargill, Alexander. "The Man of Letters." *Borderland* 2, no. 7 (January 1895): 12–16.

Cesaire, Aime. "Discourse on Colonialism," in *Colonial Discourse and Postcolonial Theory: A Reader*, 172–80. Ed. Patrick Williams and Laura Chrisman. London: Harvester Wheatsheaf, 1993.

Chalmers, Rev. J. "Explorations of South-Eastern New Guinea." *Proceedings of the Royal Geographical Society and Monthly Record of Geography*, no. 9 (February 1887): 600–608 (Read at evening meeting, January 17, 1887).

Chambers, John. "Channeling Joseph Conrad." *Conrad Today: Publication of the Joseph Conrad Society of America* 30, no. 1 (Spring 2005): 3–6.

Clifford, James. *The Predicament of Culture: Twentieth-Century Ethnography, Literature, and Art*. Cambridge: Harvard University Press, 1988.

Compagnon, Antoine. *Il demone della teoria: Letteratura e senso comune*. Turin: Einaudi, 2000. Originally published as *Le démon de la théorie: Littérature et sens commun*. Paris: Seuil, 1988.

Conrad, Jessie. *Did Joseph Conrad Return as a Spirit?* Webster Groves, MO: International Mark Twain Society, 1932.

Crawford, Robert. *Devolving English Literature*. Oxford: Clarendon Press, 1992.

Curtis, L. Perry. *Jack the Ripper and the London Press*. New Haven: Yale University Press, 2001.

Daly, Nicholas. *Modernism, Romance, and the "Fin de Siècle": Popular Fiction and British Culture, 1880–1914*. Cambridge: Cambridge University Press, 1999.

De Bord, Guy. *The Society of the Spectacle*. Trans. Donald Nicholson-Smith. New York: Zone Books, 1999.

DeKoven, Marianne. *Rich and Strange: Gender, History, Modernism*. Princeton: Princeton University Press, 1991.

Deleuze, Gilles. *Foucault*. Paris: Minuit, 2004.

———. *Mille Plateaux*. Paris: Minuit, 1980.

Deleuze, Gilles, and Felix Guattari. *Anti-Oedipus: Capitalism and Schizophrenia*. London: Athlone Press, 1984.

Derrida, Jacques. *On Cosmopolitanism and Forgiveness*. London: Routledge, 2001.

Devoy, John. *Recollections of an Irish Rebel*. New York: Charles P. Young, 1929. Reprint, Shannon: Irish Universities Press, 1968.

———. Untitled article. *Illustrated London News*, June 7, 1884, 542.

Dimock, Wai Chee. "A Theory of Resonance." *PMLA* 112 (1997): 1060–71.

Doane, Janice, and Devon Hodges. "Demonic Disturbances of Sexual Identity: The Strange Case of Dr. Jekyll and Mr/s. Hyde." *Novel* 23, no. 1 (Fall 1989): 63–74.

Donovan, Stephen. "Gorgeous Eloquence: Conrad and Shadowgraphy," in *Conrad and the Performing Arts*. Ed. Richard J. Hand and Katherine Baxter. Farnham, VT: Ashgate, 2009, 97–110.

———. *Joseph Conrad and Popular Culture*. Basingstoke, UK: Palgrave, 2005.

———. "That Newspaper Fellow—What's His Name: Joseph Conrad on W. T. Stead." *NewsStead: A Journal of History and Literature* 17 (Fall 2000): 3–10

Dryden, Linda. *Joseph Conrad and the Imperial Romance*. Basingstoke, UK: Macmillan, 2000.

———. *The Modern Gothic and Literary Doubles: Stevenson, Wilde and Wells*. London: Palgrave Macmillan, 2003.

Dussinger, Gloria R. "'The Secret Sharer': Conrad's Psychological Study." *Texas Studies in Literature and Language* 10 (1969): 599–608.

"The Dynamite Party." *Times* (London), April 24, 1886, 8.

Eigner, Edwin. *Robert Louis Stevenson and Romantic Tradition*. Princeton, NJ: Princeton University Press, 1966.

Elbert, Monika. "The 'Dialectic of Desire' in '*Twixt Land and Sea*." *The Conradian* 17, (Spring 1993): 123–46.

Emmett, Paul J. "Conrad's Secrets: Narrative, Suppression, and Dream Distortion in 'The Secret Sharer.'" *Journal of Evolutionary Psychology* 25, no. 3 (August 2004): 154–69.

Epstein, Hugh. "*Victory*'s Marionettes: Conrad's Revisitation of Stevenson," in *Conrad, James, and Other Relations*, vol. 6, *Eastern and Western Perspectives*, 189–216. Ed. Keith Carabine and Owen Knowles, with Paul Armstrong. Boulder, CO: Social Science Monographs, and Lublin: Marie Curie-Sklodowska University, 1988.

Erdinast-Vulcan, Daphna. "The Failure of Textuality," in *Joseph Conrad*, 247–69. Ed. and intro. by Andrew Michael Roberts. Longman Critical Readers Series. London: Longman, 1998.

"The Explosive Substances Bill." *Times* (London), April 10, 1883, 10.

Fanon, Franz. *The Wretched of the Earth*. New York: Grove, Widenfeld, 1963.

Fernando, Lloyd. "Other Worlds, Other Seas, the Imperial Theme in British Fiction." *Victorian Studies* 20 (Spring 1977): 299–309.

Firchow, Peter Edgerly. *Envisioning Africa: Racism and Imperialism in Conrad's* Heart of Darkness. Lexington: University Press of Kentucky, 2000.

Fowler, Alastair. *Kinds of Literature: An Introduction to the Theory of Genres and Modes*. Oxford: Clarendon Press, 1982.

Fradin, Joseph L. "Anarchist, Detective and Saint: The Possibilities of Action in *The Secret Agent*." *PMLA* 83, no. 5 (October 1968): 1414–22.

Fraustino, Daniel V. "The Not So Strange Case of Dr. Jekyll and Mr. Hyde." *Journal of Evolutionary Pyschology* 5 (August 1984): 205–29.

Freud, Sigmund. *Civilization and Its Discontents*. Trans. and ed. James Strachey. New York: Norton, 1961.

———. *On Creativity and the Unconscious*. Ed. Benjamin Nelson. New York: Harper & Brothers, 1958.

———. *The Future of an Illusion*. Trans. W. D. Robson-Scott. Garden City, NY: Doubleday, 1953.

Gaughan, Richard T. "Mr. Hyde and Mr. Seek: Utterson's Antidote." *Journal of Narrative Technique* 17 (Spring 1987): 184–97.

Geduld, Harry M. *The Definitive Dr. Jekyll and Mr. Hyde Companion*. New York: Garland, 1983.

Gekoski, R. A. "Kurtz as the Incarnation of Evil," in *Readings on* Heart of Darkness, 80–86. Ed. Clarice Swisher. San Diego: Greenhaven Press, 1999.

Gilman, Susan, and Forrest G. Robinson, eds. *Mark Twain's Pudd'nhead Wilson: Race, Conflict, and Culture*. Durham: Duke University Press, 1990.

Gilmour, Peter. "Robert Louis Stevenson: Forms of Evasion," in *Robert Louis Stevenson*, 188–201. Ed. Andrew Noble. Totowa, NJ: Barnes & Noble, 1983.

Ginzburg, Carlo. *Nessuna isola è un'isola: Quattro sguardi sulla letteratura inglese*. Milano: Feltrinelli, 2000.

Goh, Robbie B. H. "(M)Othering the Nation: Guilt, Sexuality and the Commercial State in Coleridge's Gothic Poetry." *Journal of Narrative Theory* 33, no. 3 (2003): 270–91.

Golby, J. M. *Culture and Society in Britain, 1850–1890*. Oxford: Oxford University Press / The Open University, 1986.

Graver, Lawrence. *Conrad's Short Fiction*. Berkeley: University of California Press, 1969.

Green, Martin. *Dreams of Adventure, Deeds of Empire*. London: Routledge & Kegan Paul, 1980.

Griffith, John W. *Joseph Conrad and the Anthropological Dilemma: "Bewildered Traveller."* Oxford: Clarendon Press, 1995.

Gross, John. *The Rise and Fall of the Man of Letters: Aspects of English Literary Life Since 1800*. Chicago: Ivan R. Dee, 1992.

Guerard, Albert J. *Conrad the Novelist*. Cambridge: Harvard University Press, 1958.

Hamilton, T. Glen. *Intention and Survival: Psychical Research Studies and the Bearing of Intentional Actions by Trance Personalities on the Problem of Human Survival.* Toronto: Macmillan, 1942.

Hammond, J. R. *A Robert Louis Stevenson Chronology.* Basingstoke, UK: Macmillan, 1997.

Hampson, Robert. *Cross-Cultural Encounters in Joseph Conrad's Malay Fiction.* London: Palgrave, 2000.

———. *Joseph Conrad: Betrayal and Identity.* Basingstoke, UK: Macmillan, 1992.

The Heart of the Empire: Discussions of the Problems of Modern City Life in England, with an Essay on Imperialism. London: T. Fisher Unwin, 1901.

Heidegger, Martin. *Being and Time.* Albany: State University of New York Press, 1996.

Heise, Ursula K. *Chronoschisms: Time, Narrative, and Postmodernism.* Cambridge: Cambridge University Press, 1997.

Herries, James W. *I Came, I Saw.* Edinburgh: Oliver & Boyd, 1937.

Heyck, T. W. *The Transformation of Intellectual Life in Victorian England.* New York: St. Martin's Press, 1982.

Hobsbawm, Eric. *The Age of Empire, 1875–1914.* New York: Vintage Books, 1989.

Hunter, Allan. *Joseph Conrad and the Ethics of Darwinism: The Challenges of Science.* London: Croom Helm, 1983.

Hurley, Kelly. *The Gothic Body: Sexuality, Materialism, and Degeneration at the Fin de Siècle.* Cambridge: Cambridge University Press, 1996.

"Irish Agitation in New York." *Times* (London), April 12, 1884, 11.

Jameson, Fredric. *The Political Unconscious: Narrative as Socially Symbolic Act.* Ithaca, NY: Cornell University Press, 1981.

———. *Postmodernism: or, the Cultural Logic of Late Capitalism.* Durham: Duke University Press, 1991.

JanMohamed, Abdul. "The Economy of Manichean Allegory: The Function of Racial Difference in Colonialist Literature," in *Race, Writing, and Difference,* 78–106. Ed. Henry Louis Gates. Chicago: Chicago University Press, 1986.

Jean-Aubry, Gerard. *The Sea-Dreamer.* Trans. Helen Sebba. North Haven, CT: Archon Books, 1967.

Johnson, Barbara, and Marjorie Garber. "Secret Sharing: Reading Conrad Psychoanalytically." *College English* 49, no. 6 (October 1987): 628–47.

Johnson, Captain Charles. *A General History of the Robberies and Murders of the Most Notorious Pyrates. . . .* London: Printed for C. Rivington, J. Lacy, and J. Stone, 1724. Reprint, London: J. M. Dent, 1972.

Jung, Carl. *The Collected Works of C. G. Jung.* New York: Bollingen Foundation, 1964.

———. *Man and His Symbols.* Ed. Marie-Luise von Franz. New York: Dell, 1964.

———. *The Undiscovered Self.* Trans. R. F. C. Hull. New York: New American Library, 1958.

Kaplan, Carola M., Peter Lancelot Mallios, and Andrea White, eds. *Conrad in the Twenty-First Century.* London: Routledge, 2005.

Kaplan, Carola, Peter Mallios and Andrea White. *Conrad in the Twenty-First Century: Contemporary Approaches and Perspectives.* London: Routledge, 2004.

Kaplan, Justin. *Mr. Clemens and Mark Twain.* New York: Simon & Schuster, 1966.

Karl, Frederick. *Joseph Conrad: The Three Lives.* New York: Farrar, Straus & Giroux, 1979.

Kiely, Robert. *Robert Louis Stevenson and the Fiction of Adventure.* Cambridge: Harvard University Press, 1965.

Kim, Jong-Seok. "Narcissus and the Double in Conrad's 'The Secret Sharer.'" *Journal of English Language and Literature* 44, no. 4 (Winter 1998): 927–46.

Kreitzer, Larry. "R. L. Stevenson's *Strange Case of Dr. Jekyll and Mr. Hyde* and Romans 7:14–15: Images of the Moral Duality of Human Nature." *Literature and Theology,* June 1992, 125–44.

Lankester, Edwin Ray. *Degeneration: A Chapter in Darwinism.* London: Macmillan, 1880.

Laqueur, Walter. *The Age of Terrorism.* London: Weidenfeld and Nicholson, 1987.

———, ed. *The Terrorism Reader.* London: Wildwood House, 1979.

Latouche, Peter. *Anarchy! An Authentic Exposition of the Methods of Anarchists and the Aims of Anarchism.* London: Everett, 1908.

Le Caron, Henri [Thomas Beach]. *Twenty-Five Years in the Secret Service.* 1893. Reprint, Wakefield, UK: EP Publishing, 1974.

Ledger, Sally, and Roger Luckhurst, eds. *The Fin de Siècle: A Reader in Cultural History, c. 1880–1900.* Oxford: Oxford University Press, 2000.

Linehan, Katherine. "Sex, Secrecy, and Self-Alienation," in *Strange Case of Dr. Jekyll and Mr. Hyde,* 204–13. New York: Norton, 2003.

Luckhurst, Roger. "W. T. Stead's Occult Economies," in *Culture and Science in the Nineteenth-Century Media,* 125–35. Ed. Louise Henson et al. Aldershot: Ashgate, 2004.

Maixner, Paul, ed. *Robert Louis Stevenson: The Critical Heritage.* London: Routledge and Kegan Paul, 1981.

Malinowski, Bronislaw. *A Diary in the Strict Sense of the Term.* New York: Harcourt, Brace & World, 1967.

Manlove, Colin. "'Closer Than an Eye': The Interconnection of Stevenson's *Dr. Jekyll and Mr. Hyde.*" *Studies in Scottish Literature* 23 (1988): 87–103.

Maude, H. E. "Baiteke and Binoka of Abemama: Arbiters of Change in the Gilbert Islands," in *Pacific Island Portraits.* Ed. J. W. Davidson and Deryk Scarr. Canberra: Australian National University Press, 1970.

McClintock, Anne. *Imperial Leather: Race, Gender, and Sexuality in the Colonial Conquest.* New York: Routledge, 1995.

McClure, John A. *Kipling and Conrad: The Colonial Fiction.* Cambridge: Harvard University Press, 1981.

McLynn, Frank. *Robert Louis Stevenson: A Biography.* London: Hutchinson, 1993.

Menikoff, Barry. *Narrating Scotland: The Imagination of Robert Louis Stevenson.* Columbia: University of South Carolina Press, 2005.

Merritt, Travis R. "Taste, Opinion, and Theory in the Rise of Victorian Prose Stylism," in *The Art of Victorian Prose.* Ed. George Levine and William Madden. New York: Oxford University Press, 1968.

Michie, Helena, and Ronald Thomas, eds. *Nineteenth-Century Geographies: The Transformation of Space from the Victorian Age to the American Century.* New Brunswick, NJ: Rutgers University Press, 2002.

Mighall, Robert. *A Geography of Victorian Gothic Fiction: Mapping History's Nightmares*. Oxford: Oxford University Press, 1991.

Miller, Karl. *Doubles: Studies in Literary History*. Oxford: Oxford University Press, 1985.

Miyoshi, Masao. "Mr. Jekyll and the Emergence of Mr. Hyde." *College English* 27 (March 1966): 470–80.

Moore, Gene M., ed. *Conrad's Cities: Essays for Hans van Marle*. Amsterdam: Rodopi, 1992.

Mort, Frank. *Dangerous Sexualities: Medico-Moral Politics in England since 1830*. London: Routledge, 1987.

Myers, Frederic W. H. *Human Personality and Its Survival of Bodily Death*. 2 vols. London: Longman, 1903.

Ngugi, Wa Thiong'o. *Decolonising the Mind: The Politics of Language in African Literature*. London: James Currey, 1986.

Obeyeseker, Gananath. "Narrative of the Self: Chevalier Peter Dillon's Fijian Cannibal Adventures," in *Body Trade: Captivity, Cannibalism, and Colonialism in the Pacific*, 69–111. Ed. Barbara Creed and Jeanette Hoorn. New York: Routledge, 2001.

Oppenheim, Janet. *The Other World: Spiritualism and Psychical Research in England, 1850–1914*. Cambridge: Cambridge University Press, 1985.

Owen, Alex. *The Darkened Room: Women, Power, and Spiritualism in Late Victorian England*. London: Virago Press, 1989.

Palmer, Alan. *The East End: Four Centuries of London Life*. New Brunswick, NJ: Rutgers University Press, 2000.

Parker, Geoffrey. *Western Geopolitical Thought in the Twentieth Century*. London: Croom Helm, 1985.

Peck, John. *Maritime Fiction: Sailors and the Sea in British and American Novels, 1719–1917*. Houndmills, UK: Palgrave, 2001.

Pick, Daniel. *Faces of Degeneration: A European Disorder, c. 1848–1919*. Cambridge: Cambridge University Press, 1989.

"A Press Organ of the Dynamite Party." *Times* (London), March 24, 1884, 8.

Price, Blanche A., ed. *The Ideal Reader: Selected Essays of Jacques Rivière*. London: Harvill Press, 1960.

Priestly, J. B. *The English Novel*. London: Ernest Benn, 1931.

Proust, Marcel. *À la recherche du temps perdu*. Paris: Gallimard (La Pléiade), 1954.

Quiller-Couch, Sir Arthur. *Adventures in Criticism*. London: Cassell, 1896.

Raban, Jonathan. Introduction to *The Oxford Book of the Sea*, 1–34. Oxford: Oxford University Press, 1992.

Raleigh, Sir Walter A. *Robert Louis Stevenson*. London: Arnold, 1895.

Rankin, Nicholas. *Dead Man's Chest*. London: Faber, 1987.

Reid, Julia. *Robert Louis Stevenson, Science and the Fin de Siecle*. Basingstoke: Palgrave Macmillan, 2006.

Richetti, John, et al., eds. *Columbia History of the British Novel*. New York: Columbia University Press, 1994.

Rivière, Jacques. *Le roman d'aventure*. Paris: Editions des Syrtes, 2000.

Rossetti, Carlo. "B. Malinowski: The Sociology of Modern Problems in Africa and the Colonial Situation." *Cahiers d'Etudes Africaines* 10 (1985): 477–503.

Said, Edward. *Culture and Imperialism*. New York: Knopf, 1993.

Sandison, Alan. *Robert Louis Stevenson and the Appearance of Modernism*. London: Macmillan, 1996.

Sartre, Jean-Paul. *Being and Nothingness: An Essay on Phenomenological Ontology*. Trans. Hazel E. Barnes. London: Methuen, 1969.

Sedgwick, Eve Kosofsky. *The Coherence of Gothic Conventions*. New York: Methuen, 1980.

Sherry, Norman, ed. *Conrad: The Critical Heritage*. London: Routledge and Kegan Paul, 1973.

Showalter, Elaine. "Dr. Jekyll's Closet," in *The Haunted Mind: The Supernatural in Victorian Literature*, 67–88. Ed. Elton E. Smith and Robert Haas. Lanham, MD: Scarecrow Press, 1999.

Simmons, J. L. "The Dual Morality in Conrad's 'The Secret Sharer,'" *Studies in Short Fiction* 2 (1965): 209–20.

Simpson, Brian. *Cannibalism and the Common Law*. Chicago: Chicago University Press, 1985.

Singer, Ben. *Melodrama and Modernity: Early Sensational Cinema and Its Contexts*. New York: Columbia University Press, 2001.

Smith, Vanessa. *Literary Culture and the Pacific: Nineteenth-Century Textual Encounters*. Cambridge: Cambridge University Press, 1998.

"Spain." *The Torch*, December 18, 1894, 5.

Spengemann, William. *The Forms of Autobiography: Episodes in the History of a Literary Genre*. New Haven: Yale University Press, 1980.

Staller, Natasha. *A Sum of Destructions: Picasso's Cultures and the Creation of Cubism*. New Haven: Yale University Press, 2001.

Stallman, R. W. "Conrad and 'The Secret Sharer,'" in *Conrad's "Secret Sharer" and the Critics*, 94–109. Belmont: Wadsworth Publishing, 1962.

Stampfl, Barry. "Marlow's Rhetoric of (Self-) Deception in *Heart of Darkness*." *Modern Fiction Studies* 37 (Summer 1991): 183–96.

Staten, Henry. "Conrad's Mortal Word." *Critical Inquiry* 12 (Summer 1986): 720–40.

Stead, W. T. "Has Man Two Minds or One?" *Borderland: A Quarterly Review and Index* 1, no. 2 (October 1893): 170–73.

———. *Letters from Julia; or, Light from the Borderland*. London: Grant Richards, 1898.

———. "The Man of Dreams." *Borderland: A Quarterly Review and Index* 2, no. 7 (January 1895): 13, 17–24.

Stedman Jones, Gareth. *Outcast London: A Study in the Relationship between Classes in Victorian Society*. New York: Pantheon Books, 1971.

Steinmeyer, Jim. *Hiding the Elephant: How Magicians Invented the Impossible and Learned to Disappear*. Berkeley, CA: Carroll and Graf, 2004.

Stevenson, Margaret. *From Saranac to the Marquesas and Beyond*. Ed. Marie Clothilde Balfour. New York: Scribner's, 1906.

Stocking, George W., Jr. *After Tylor: British Social Anthropology, 1888–1951*. Madison: University of Wisconsin Press, 1995.

———. *Victorian Anthropology*. New York: Free Press, 1987.

Sulloway, Frank. *Freud, Biologist of the Mind*. New York: Basic Books, 1979.

Sword, Helen. *Ghostwriting Modernism*. Ithaca, NY: Cornell University Press, 2002.

Tanner, Tony. Introduction to *The Oxford Book of Sea Stories*. Oxford: Oxford University Press, 1994.

Terry, R. C. *Robert Louis Stevenson: Interviews and Recollections*. Iowa City: University of Iowa Press, 1996.

Thorburn, David. *Conrad's Romanticism*. New Haven: Yale University Press, 1974.

"Trial of the Walsall Anarchists." *Times* (London), April 5, 1892, 8.

Tymieniecka, Anna-Teresa. "Ego Formation and the Land/Sea Metaphor in Conrad's 'Secret Sharer,'" in *Poetics of the Elements in the Human Condition: The Sea*, 67–76. Dordrecht: Reidel, 1985.

"UN Condemns DR Congo Cannibalism." BBC News, Wednesday, January 15, 2003, http://news.bbc.co.uk/2/hi/africa/2661365.stm.

Veeder, William, and Gordon Hirsch, eds. *Dr. Jekyll and Mr. Hyde after One Hundred Years*. Chicago: University of Chicago Press, 1988.

Walkowitz, Judith. *City of Dreadful Delight*. Chicago: University of Chicago Press, 1992.

Watts, Cedric T. "*The Ebb-Tide* and *Victory*." *Conradiana* 28, no. 2 (1986): 133–37.

———. *Joseph Conrad: A Literary Life*. London: MacMillan, 1989.

———, ed. *Joseph Conrad's Letters to R. B. Cunninghame Graham*. Cambridge: Cambridge University Press, 1969.

———. "The Narrative Enigma of Conrad's 'A Smile of Fortune.'" *Conradiana* 17, no. 2 (1985): 131–36.

Watts, Cedric T., and Laurence Davies. *Cunninghame Graham: A Critical Biography*. Cambridge: Cambridge University Press, 1979.

Weber, Max. *Essays in Sociology*. Ed. and trans. H. H. Gerth and C. Wright Mills. London: Routledge, 1948.

Wells, H. G. *Experiment in Autobiography*. London: Victor Gollancz, 1934.

White, Andrea. *Joseph Conrad and the Adventure Tradition: Constructing and Deconstructing the Imperial Subject*. Cambridge: Cambridge University Press, 1993.

Wilde, Oscar. *The Picture of Dorian Gray*. Ed. D. L. Lawler. London: Norton, 1988.

Williams, Anne. *Art of Darkness: A Poetics of Gothic*. Chicago: University of Chicago Press, 1995.

Wolfreys, Julian. *Writing London: The Trace of the Urban Text from Blake to Dickens*. New York: St. Martin's Press, 1987.

Yelton, Donald C. *Mimesis and Metaphor: An Inquiry into the Genesis and Scope of Conrad's Symbolic Imagery*. The Hague: Mouton, 1967.

Young, Robert. *Colonial Desire: Hybridity in Theory, Culture, and Race*. London: Routledge, 1999.

———. *White Mythologies: Writing History and the West*. London: Routledge, 1990.

Contributors

Richard Ambrosini, professor of English literature at the University of Roma Tre, has written two books on Joseph Conrad, *Conrad's Fiction as Critical Discourse* (Cambridge University Press, 1991) and *Introduzione a Conrad* (Laterza, 1991), and one on R. L. Stevenson, *R. L. Stevenson: La poetica del romanzo* (Bulzoni, 2001). He has translated and edited, among other novels, *An Outcast of the Islands* (Garzanti, 1994), *Treasure Island* (Garzanti, 1996), and *The Secret Agent* (Frassinelli, 1996). He has also written a book on the teaching of English poetry, *Il piacere della poesia inglese* (Cuem, 2000); has coedited, with Piero Boitani, *Ulisse: Archeologia dell'uomo moderno* (Bulzoni, 1998); and has published essays on a variety of subjects, including Chaucer, Shakespeare, William Cowper, Coleridge, and Canadian literature. He is currently working on Rudyard Kipling.

Stephen Arata is Richard A. and Sara Page Mayo Distinguished Teaching Professor in the Department of English at the University of Virginia. His publications include *Fictions of Loss in the Victorian Fin de Siècle* (Cambridge University Press, 1996) and essays in periodicals such as *Victorian Studies, Criticism, Victorian Institutes Journal,* and *ELT.* He also contributed the essay on the Victorian fin de siècle for the new *Cambridge History of English Literature* (forthcoming). He has edited William Morris's *News from Nowhere* (2002) and George Gissing's *New Grub Street* (2007) for the Broadview Literary Texts series and the Norton Critical Edition of *The Time Machine* (2008). He is currently writing a book on reading practices in the nineteenth century.

Monica Bungaro has been a lecturer in English literature, mainly in postcolonial theory and literature, at the University of Birmingham since 2001. She has researched in the field of Anglophone African and Caribbean literatures for the past seven years and has published articles and book chapters on transcultural writers, African fiction, Black British women writers, and postcolonial pedagogy. Among her recent publications are "Women's Histories in West Africa" (2005) in *A Historical Companion to Postcolonial Literatures in English* (Edinburgh University Press, 2005) and "Feminist Fiction: Recent Subversions of a Gender-Biased Script" in *Body, Sexuality, and Gender: Versions and Subversions in African Literatures 1,* ed. Flora Veit-Wild and Dirk Naguschewski (Rodopi, 2005). Her forthcoming book is titled *Images of Women in Recent African Fiction in English* (Peter Lang).

Nancy Bunge is a professor at Michigan State University, where she won the 2005 Fintz Award for excellence in teaching the arts and humanities. In 2003–4, she was a visiting scholar at the Harvard Divinity School. Her most recent book is *Master Class: Lessons from Leading Writers* (University of Iowa Press, 2005). She is also the interviewer and editor of *Finding the Words: Conversations with Writers Who Teach* (Swallow Press, 1985), the editor of *Conversations with Clarence Major* (University Press of Mississippi, 2002) and the author of *Nathaniel Hawthorne: A Study of the Short Fiction* (Macmillan, 1993). She has held senior Fulbright lectureships at the University of Vienna, the University of Siegen in Germany, and the University of Ghent and the Free University of Brussels in Belgium.

Ann C. Colley is a professor of English at the State University College of New York at Buffalo. She is the author of several books: *Tennyson and Madness* (University of Georgia Press, 1983), *The Search for Synthesis in Literature and Art* (University of Georgia Press, 1990), *Edward Lear and the Critics* (Camden, 1993), *Nostalgia and Recollection in Victorian Culture* (Macmillan, 1998), and *Robert Louis Stevenson and the Colonial Imagination* (Ashgate, 2004). She has also written articles on Stevenson that have appeared in *The Journal of Victorian Literature and Culture* (Cambridge University Press) and, most recently, in *Studies in English Literature*. She is also a guest editor of a special edition of the *Journal of Stevenson Studies*.

Martin Danahay is a professor of English at Brock University, Canada. His most recent publication is *Gender at Work in Victorian Culture: Literature, Art and Masculinity* (Ashgate Publishing, 2005). He is currently working on a book on Robert Louis Stevenson's *Strange Case of Dr. Jekyll and Mr. Hyde*.

Laurence Davies is a senior research fellow in English literature at the University of Glasgow. With Cedric Watts he is the coauthor of *Cunninghame Graham: A Critical Biography* (Cambridge University Press, 2008). He is general editor of *The Collected Letters of Joseph Conrad* (Cambridge University Press, 1983–2007), and in various combinations has worked on the edition with J. H. Stape, Gene M. Moore, Owen Knowles, and the late Frederick R. Karl. Volumes 8 and 9, the last in the series, appeared toward the end of 2007. Davies also works on speculative fiction, literature and science, millenarianism, and the literatures of the Celtic nations. He has held fellowships from the National Endowment for the Humanities, the National Endowment for the Arts, and the Woodrow Wilson Endowment.

Stephen Donovan is a lecturer in English literature at Uppsala University, Sweden. His work has appeared in *Journal of Modern Literature*, *The Conradian*, *James Joyce Quarterly*, and *Conradiana*. He is the author of *Joseph Conrad and Popular Culture* (Palgrave, 2005).

Linda Dryden is a reader in literature and culture at Edinburgh Napier University. She has published a monograph on Conrad, *Joseph Conrad and the Imperial Romance* (Palgrave, 1999) and numerous articles in journals such as *The Conradian*, *Conradiana*,

L'Epoque Conradienne, and *Notes & Queries*. She has also written on Stevenson in her monograph *The Modern Gothic and Literary Doubles: Stevenson, Wilde, and Wells* (Palgrave, 2003). She is coeditor of the *Journal of Stevenson Studies* and of a double issue of *Conradiana* on Conrad and serialization, to be published in 2009, and she has contributed essays to the latest Norton edition of *Heart of Darkness* and to *Joseph Conrad's Heart of Darkness*, ed. D. C. R A. Goonetilleke (Routledge, 2007).

Robbie B. H. Goh is head of the Department of English Language and Literature, National University of Singapore. He teaches critical theory and gothic literature and has published essays on Stevenson, Kipling, Coleridge, Angela Carter, Clive Barker, and other authors in *Gothic Studies, Journal of Narrative Theory, Ariel*, and other journals and edited volumes. He also writes on postcolonial studies and Asian cultures, with recent publications including *Sparks of Grace: The Story of Methodism in Asia* (Methodist Church in Singapore, 2003), *Asian Diasporas: Cultures, Identities, Representations* (coedited with Shawn Wong; Hong Kong University Press, 2004), and *Theorizing the Southeast Asian City as Text* (coedited with Brenda Yeoh; World Scientific, 2003).

Robert Hampson is a professor of modern literature and head of the Department of English at Royal Holloway, University of London. He is the author of *Joseph Conrad: Betrayal and Identity* (St. Martin's, 1992) and *Cross-Cultural Encounters in Joseph Conrad's Malay Fiction* (Palgrave, 2000). He is coeditor of *Conrad and Theory* (with Andrew Gibson), *New British Poetries: The Scope of the Possible* (with Peter Barry), *Ford Madox Ford: A Reappraisal* (with Tony Davenport), and *Ford Madox Ford's Modernity* (with Max Saunders). He has edited a number of works by Conrad—*Heart of Darkness, Victory*, and *Nostromo*—and works by Kipling and Haggard (*Something of Myself, In Black and White, Soldiers Three*, and *King Solomon's Mines*). He has also written on Pound and Joyce.

Nathalie Jaëck is a lecturer in Bordeaux University, France. Her PhD thesis is "Types and Archetypes in Arthur Conan Doyle's Sherlock Holmes Stories," and she currently works on fiction of the end of the nineteenth century. She has written several articles on Doyle, Stevenson, Dickens, and Conrad.

Eric Massie, FRSA, was born in the northeast of Scotland and educated at the University of Aberdeen. He carried out research at Oxford, Yale, and the University of Virginia and was awarded a PhD by the University of Stirling. He teaches British and American literature of the nineteenth and twentieth centuries and has additional research interests in literary history. He was founding editor of the *Journal of Stevenson Studies* and has published on Stevenson, Conrad, and the Scottish romantic James Hogg. He is currently on secondment as an adviser on tertiary education policy and funding.

Deaglán Ó'Donghaile is an Irish Research Council for the Humanities and Social Sciences Postdoctoral Research Fellow based at the Department of English, National

University of Ireland, Maynooth. In 2006 he was named Bruce Harkness Young Conrad Scholar of the Year by the Joseph Conrad Society of America in recognition of his essay "Conrad, the Stevensons, and the Imagination of Urban Chaos." He is currently working on a book monograph examining terrorism in modernism and popular fiction.

Jane V. Rago is a visiting professor at Armstrong Atlantic State University and also a doctoral candidate at West Virginia University. Her dissertation, "Dissecting the Angel of the House: Reform, Eugenics, and the New Woman in Late Victorian London," explores the impact of evolutionary theory on political movements at the end of the nineteenth century.

Andrea White teaches literature and critical theory at California State University, Dominguez Hills, where she is a professor of English and coordinator of graduate studies. She is the author of *Joseph Conrad and the Adventure Tradition* (Cambridge University Press, 1993) and coeditor of *Conrad in the 21st Century* (Routledge, 2005). She has also written articles for various journals and collections such as *The Cambridge Companion to Conrad* and *Approaches to Teaching "The Secret Sharer" and Heart of Darkness*, and has presented at local and international conferences. She is currently a trustee of the Joseph Conrad Society of America, having just served as its president for two years.

Index

writers, 233–234. *See also specific writers*
Moipu, Chief, 120–121
Molokai, 93
money, social relations of, 147
Montaigne, Michel de, 103, 118
morality/immorality, 195, 197
Mort, Frank, 194, 196–197
"Mr. Sludge, 'The Medium'" (Browning), 226
Murray, David, 227
Myers, F. W. H., 25, 227

narratives
  of doubling, 54, 176–177. *See also* duality
  exclusions, 144
  and human positionings, 138, 220
  juxtaposition of, 10
  popular forms of, 18
  transitory technique, 41–46, 192–193
narrators, 46, 63 *See also* narratives
Nation, 232
national identity, 191, 194, 198–207
nationalism, 127. *See also* imperialism
National Association for the Promotion of Social Science, 198
natives, 23, 26–27, 36, 94. *See also* primitivism; savagery/savage
Nechaev, Sergei, 172
Nesbit, Edith, 59
Nether World, The (Gissing), 190
New Age works, 233
New Arabian Nights (Stevenson), 165
New Caledonia, 115, 117
New Criticsm, tenets of, 15
New Guinea, 109, 117, 150
New Hebrides, 117
Ngugi, Wa Thiong'o, 104
Nigger of the "Narcissus," The (Conrad)
  fictional language, 18
  gothic tones, use of, 9
  preface to, 85–86, 225, 234, 236
  publisher, 2
  setting, 84

noise, importance of, 181
Nordau, Max, 93
Northcliffe, Lord, 224

Obeyesekere, Gananath, 114
O'Brien, Michael, 170
Oceana (Froude), 92
O'Donovan Rossa, Jeremiah, 161
"Olalla" (Stevenson), 65
Oliver Twist (Dickens), 196
"Only A Subaltern" (Kipling), 37
Oppenheim, Janet, 226
Orwell, George, 188
Osbourne, Fanny. *See* Stevenson, Fanny Vandergrift Osbourne
Osbourne, Lloyd, 134, 141, 152, 227
the Other, 11, 92–108
Outcast of the Islands, An (Conrad), 3, 61–62, 125–139
outcasts, degeneration of, 3
"Outpost of Progress, An" (Conrad), 94–95
Owen, Alex, 238
Owen, Robert, 237
Oxford Book of Sea Stories (Tanner), 126
Oxford Book of the Sea (Raban), 125, 126

Palladino, Eusapia, 235
"paper boats," 10, 19, 40, 43, 51n2
Papua, New Guinea, 117
paranormal, theories of, 228–229
Paris, France, 168
Parnellism and Crime (Anderson), 170
Pater, Walter, 17
"patrician view," 12
Pease, Captain, 149
Peck, John, 126
"Penny Plain, Twopence Coloured, A" (Stevenson), 239
People of the Abyss (London), 188
persona, use of term, 211
Personal Record, A, (Conrad), 26, 62, 233